S0-BOG-795

MER DE GLACE, MONT BLANC. *Frontispiece.*

Wonders of Nature

As Seen and Described by Famous Writers

EDITED AND TRANSLATED

BY ESTHER SINGLETON

AUTHOR OF "TURRETS, TOWERS AND TEMPLES," "GREAT PICTURES," "PARIS," AND "A GUIDE TO THE OPERA," AND TRANSLATOR OF THE MUSIC DRAMAS OF RICHARD WAGNER

With Numerous Illustrations

NEW YORK
DODD, MEAD & COMPANY
1900

Preface

IN my former collections of objects of interest to the tourist, I have confined myself to masterpieces of painting and architecture. The success of those books has encouraged me to carry the idea still further and make a compilation of pleasurable and striking impressions produced upon thoughtful travellers by a contemplation of the wonders of nature.

The range is somewhat limited, for I have confined myself to the description of the grand, the curious and the awe-inspiring in nature, leaving the beauties of landscape for future treatment. Those who miss the Lakes of Killarney or the vine-clad hills of the Rhine therefore will remember that in the following pages I have purposely neglected beautiful scenery.

The professional traveller, by which I mean the emissary of a scientific society, appears very seldom here, because it is the effect produced rather than the topographical or detailed description that I have sought. I hope this book will appeal to that large class of readers that takes pleasure in travelling by imagination, as well as to those who have actually seen the objects described and pictured here.

It is interesting to note the difference between the old and the modern travellers. The day of the Marco Polos has passed; the traveller of old seemed to feel himself under an obligation to record marvels and report trifling details, while the modern traveller is more concerned about describing or analyzing the effect produced upon himself. He feels it encumbent upon him to exhibit æsthetic appreciation. For this tendency we have to thank Gautier and his humble follower D'Amicis. Thackeray and Dickens write of their journeyings in a holiday spirit; Kipling is a stimulating combination of the flippant and the devout; Shelley is quite up to date; and Fromentin and Gautier always speak in terms of the palette. Thus we get an additional pleasure from the varied literary treatment of nature's wonders—apart from their intrinsic interest.

Though there is a great deal of information in the following pages, I have generally avoided what is simply instructive; my aim has been to suit all tastes.

For the kind permission to use *The Mammoth Cave*, *Fusi San* and *The Antarctic*, and *The Yellowstone*, my best thanks are due to Messrs. G. P. Putnam's Sons, Messrs. Longmans, Green and Co., and Mr. Rudyard Kipling.

E. S.

NEW YORK, *September*, 1900.

Contents

Illustrations

WONDERS OF NATURE

THE BLUE GROTTO OF CAPRI

ALEXANDRE DUMAS

WE were surrounded by five and twenty boatmen, each of whom exerted himself to get our custom: these were the *ciceroni* of the Blue Grotto. I chose one and Jadin another, for you must have a boat and a boatman to get there, the opening being so low and so narrow that one cannot enter unless in a very small boat.

The sea was calm, nevertheless, even in this beautiful weather it broke with such force against the belt of rocks surrounding the island that our barks bounded as if in a tempest, and we were obliged to lie down and cling to the sides to avoid being thrown into the sea. At last, after three-quarters of an hour of navigation, during which we skirted about one-sixth of the island's circumference, our boatmen informed us of our arrival. We looked about us, but we could not perceive the slightest suspicion of a grotto until we made out with difficulty a little black, circular point above the foaming waves: this was the orifice of the vault.

The first sight of this entrance was not reässuring: you could not understand how it was possible to clear it without breaking your head against the rocks. As the question seemed important enough for discussion, I put it to my boatman, who replied that we were perfectly right in remaining seated now, but presently we must lie down to avoid the danger. We had not come so far as this to flinch. It was my turn first; my boatman advanced, rowing with precaution and indicating that, accustomed as he was to the work, he could not regard it as exempt from danger. As for me, from the position that I occupied, I could see nothing but the sky; soon I felt myself rising upon a wave, the boat slid down it rapidly, and I saw nothing but a rock that seemed for a second to weigh upon my breast. Then, suddenly, I found myself in a grotto so marvellous that I gave a cry of astonishment, and I jumped up so quickly to look about me that I nearly capsized the boat.

In reality, before me, around me, above me, under me, and behind me were marvels of which no description can give an idea, and before which, the brush itself, the grand preserver of human memories, is powerless. You must imagine an immense cavern entirely of azure, just as if God had amused himself by making a pavilion with fragments of the firmament; water so limpid, so transparent, and so pure that you seemed floating upon dense air; from the ceiling stalactites hanging like inverted pyramids; in the background a golden sand mingled with submarine vegetation; along the walls which were bathed by the water there were trees of coral with irregular and dazzling branches; at

BLUE GROTTO, CAPRI.

the sea-entrance, a tiny point—a star—let in the half-light that illumines this fairy palace; finally, at the opposite end, a kind of stage arranged like the throne of a splendid goddess who has chosen one of the wonders of the world for her baths.

At this moment the entire grotto assumed a deeper hue, darkening as the earth does when a cloud passes across the sun at brightest noontide. It was caused by Jadin, who entered in his turn and whose boat closed the mouth of the cavern. Soon he was thrown near me by the force of the wave that had lifted him up; the grotto recovered its beautiful shade of azure; and his boat stopped tremblingly near mine, for this sea, so agitated and obstreperous outside, breathes here as serenely and gently as a lake.

In all probability the Blue Grotto was unknown to the ancients. No poet speaks of it, and certainly, with their marvellous imagination, the Greeks would not have neglected making of it the palace of some sea-goddess with a musical name and leaving some story to us. Suetonius, who describes for us with so much detail the Thermes and baths of Tiberius, would certainly have devoted a few words to this natural pool which the old emperor would doubtless have chosen as the theatre for some of his monstrous pleasures. No, the ocean must have been much higher at that epoch than it is at present, and this marvellous sea-cave was known only to Amphitrite and her court of Sirens, Naïads, and Tritons.

But sometimes Amphitrite is angered with the indiscreet travellers who follow her into this retreat, just as Diana was when surprised by Actæon. At such times the sea rises suddenly and closes the entrance so effectually that those who have entered cannot leave. In this case, they must wait until the wind, which has veered from east to west, changes to south or north; and it has even happened that visitors, who have come to spend twenty minutes in the Blue Grotto, have had to remain two, three, and, even four, days. Therefore, the boatmen always carry with them a certain portion of a kind of biscuit to nourish the prisoners in the event of such an accident. With regard to water, enough filters through two or three places in the grotto to prevent any fear of thirst. I bestowed a few reproaches upon my boatman for having waited so long to apprise me of so disquieting a fact; but he replied with a charming *naïveté*:

"*Dame! excellence!* If we told this to the visitors at first, only half would come, and that would make the boatmen angry."

I admit that after this accidental information, I was seized with a certain uneasiness, on account of which I found the Blue Grotto infinitely less delightful than it had appeared to me at first. Unfortunately, my boatman had told me these details just at the moment when I was undressing to bathe in this water, which is so beautiful and transparent that to attract the fisherman it would not need the song of Goethe's poetical Undine. We were unwilling to waste any time in preparations, and, wishing to enjoy ourselves as much as possible, we both dived.

It is only when you are five or six feet below the surface

of the water that you can appreciate its incredible purity. Notwithstanding the liquid that envelops the diver, no detail escapes him; he sees everything,—the tiniest shell at the base of the smallest stalactite of the arch, just as clearly as if through the air; only each object assumes a deeper hue.

At the end of a quarter of an hour, we clambered back into our boats and dressed ourselves without having apparently attracted one of the invisible nymphs of this watery palace, who would not have hesitated, if the contrary had been the case, to have kept us here twenty-four hours at least. The fact was humiliating; but neither of us pretended to be a Telemachus, and so we took our departure. We again crouched in the bottom of our respective canoes, and we went out of the Blue Grotto with the same precautions and the same good luck with which we had entered it: only it was six minutes before we could open our eyes; the ardent glare of the sun blinded us. We had not gone more than a hundred feet away from the spot we had visited before it seemed to have melted into a dream.

We landed again at the port of Capri. While we were settling our account with our boatmen, Pietro pointed out a man lying down in the sunshine with his face in the sand. This was the fisherman who nine or ten years ago discovered the Blue Grotto while looking for *frutti di mare* along the rocks. He went immediately to the authorities of the island to make his discovery known, and asked the privilege of being the only one allowed to conduct visitors to the new world he had found, and to have revenue from those visitors. The authorities, who saw in this discovery a means of attracting strangers to their island, agreed to the second proposition, and since that time this new Christopher Columbus has lived upon his income and does not trouble to conduct the visitors himself; this explains why he can sleep as we see him. He is the most envied individual in the island.

As we had seen all that Capri offered us in the way of wonders, we stepped into our launch and regained the *Speronare*, which, profiting by several puffs of the land breeze, set sail and gently glided off in the direction of Palermo.

Le Speronare: Impressions de Voyage (Paris, 1836).

MONT BLANC AND CHAMOUNI

PERCY BYSSHE SHELLEY

FROM Servoz three leagues remain to Chamouni—Mont Blanc was before us—the Alps, with their innumerable glaciers on high all around, closing in the complicated windings of the single vale—forests inexpressibly beautiful, but majestic in their beauty—intermingled beech and pine, and oak, overshadowed our road, or receded, whilst lawns of such verdure as I have never seen before occupied these openings, and gradually became darker in their recesses. Mont Blanc was before us, but it was covered with cloud; its base furrowed with dreadful gaps, was seen above. Pinnacles of snow intolerably bright, part of the chain connected with Mont Blanc, shone through the clouds at intervals on high. I never knew—I never imagined what mountains were before. The immensity of these aërial summits excited, when they suddenly burst upon the sight, a sentiment of extatic wonder, not unallied to madness. And remember this was all one scene, it all pressed home to our regard and our imagination. Though it embraced a vast extent of space, the snowy pyramids which shot into the bright blue sky seemed to overhang our path; the ravine, clothed with gigantic pines, and black with its depth below, so deep that the very roaring of the untameable Arve, which rolled through it could not be heard above—all was as much our own, as if we had been the creators of such impressions in the minds of others as now occupied our own. Nature was the poet, whose harmony held our spirits more breathless than that of the divinest.

As we entered the valley of Chamouni (which in fact may be considered as a continuation of those which we have followed from Bonneville and Cluses) clouds hung upon the mountains at the distance perhaps of 6,000 feet from the earth, but so as effectually to conceal not only Mont Blanc, but the other *aiguilles*, as they call them here, attached and subordinate to them. We were travelling along the valley, when suddenly we heard a sound as of the burst of smothered thunder rolling above; yet there was something earthly in the sound, that told us it could not be thunder. Our guide hastily pointed out to us a part of the mountain opposite, from whence the sound came. It was an avalanche. We saw the smoke of its path among the rocks, and continued to hear at intervals the bursting of its fall. It fell on the bed of a torrent, which it displaced, and presently we saw its tawny-coloured waters also spread themselves over the ravine, which was their couch.

We did not, as we intended, visit the *Glacier de Boisson* to-day, although it descends within a few minutes' walk of the road, wishing to survey it at least when unfatigued. We saw this glacier which comes close to the fertile plain, as we passed, its surface was broken into a thousand unac-

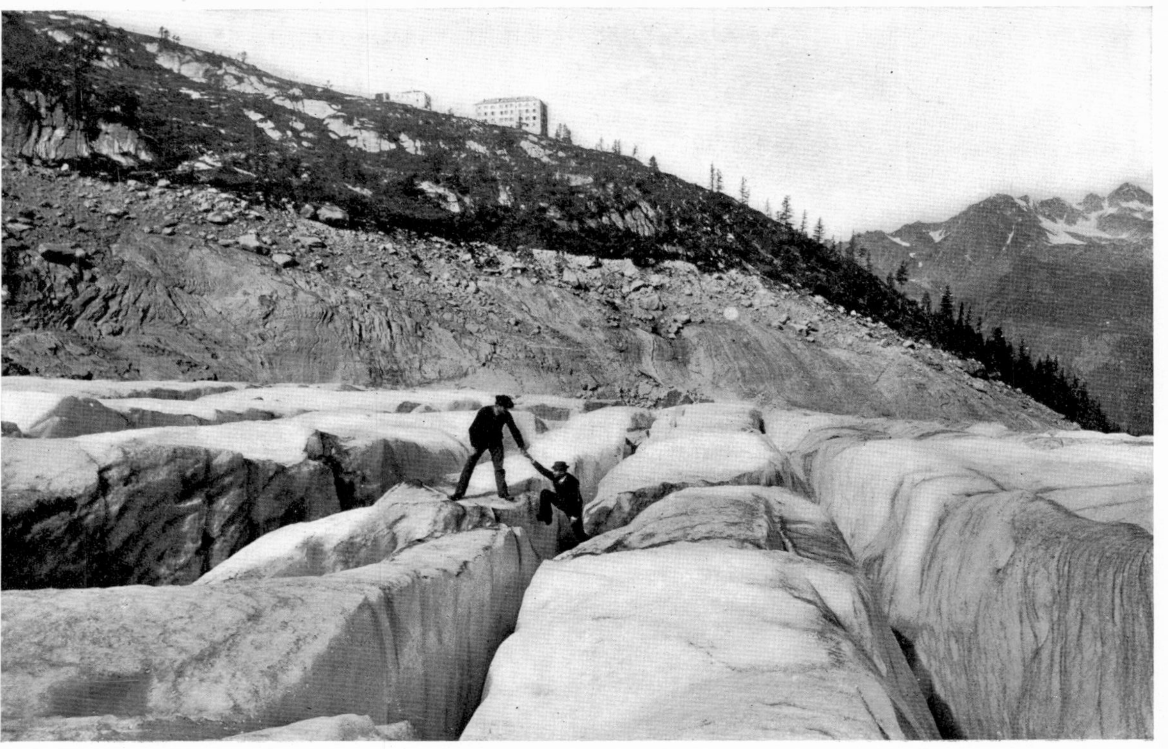

CHAMOUNI, MER DE GLACE,

countable figures: conical and pyramidical crystallizations, more than fifty feet in height, rise from its surface, and precipices of ice, of dazzling splendour, overhang the woods and meadows of the vale. This glacier winds upwards from the valley, until it joins the masses of frost from which it was produced above, winding through its own ravine like a bright belt flung over the black region of pines. There is more in all these scenes than mere magnitude of proportion: there is a majesty of outline; there is an awful grace in the very colours which invest these wonderful shapes—a charm which is peculiar to them, quite distinct even from the reality of their unutterable greatness.

Yesterday morning we went to the source of the Arveiron. It is about a league from this village; the river rolls forth impetuously from an arch of ice, and spreads itself in many streams over a vast space of the valley, ravaged and laid bare by its inundations. The glacier by which its waters are nourished, overhangs this cavern and the plain, and the forests of pine which surround it, with terrible precipices of solid ice. On the other side rises the immense glacier of Montanvert, fifty miles in extent, occupying a chasm among mountains of inconceivable height, and of forms so pointed and abrupt, that they seem to pierce the sky. From this glacier we saw as we sat on a rock, close to one of the streams of the Arveiron, masses of ice detach themselves from on high, and rush with a loud dull noise into the vale. The violence of their fall turned them into powder, which flowed over the rocks in imitation of waterfalls, whose ravines they usurped and filled.

In the evening I went with Ducrée, my guide, the only tolerable person I have seen in this country, to visit the glacier of Boisson. This glacier, like that of Montanvert, comes close to the vale, overhanging the green meadows and the dark woods with the dazzling whiteness of its precipices and pinnacles, which are like spires of radiant crystal covered with a network of frosted silver. These glaciers flow perpetually into the valley, ravaging in their slow but irresistible progress the pastures and the forests which surround them, performing a work of desolation in ages, which a river of lava might accomplish in an hour, but far more irretrievably; for where the ice has once descended, the hardiest plant refuses to grow; if even, as in some extraordinary instances, it should recede after its progress has once commenced. The glaciers perpetually move onward, at the rate of a foot each day, with a motion that commences at the spot where, on the boundaries of perpetual congelation, they are produced by the freezing of the waters which arise from the partial melting of the eternal snows. They drag with them from the regions whence they derive their origin, all the ruins of the mountain, enormous rocks, and immense accumulations of sand and stones. These are driven onwards by the irresistible stream of solid ice; and when they arrive at a declivity of the mountain, sufficiently rapid, roll down, scattering ruin. I saw one of these rocks which had descended in the spring (winter here is the season of silence and safety) which measured forty feet in every direction.

The verge of a glacier, like that of Boisson, presents the

most vivid image of desolation that it is possible to conceive. No one dares to approach it; for the enormous pinnacles of ice which perpetually fall, are perpetually reproduced. The pines of the forest, which bound it at one extremity, are overthrown and shattered to a wide extent at its base. There is something inexpressibly dreadful in the aspect of the few branchless trunks, which, nearest to the ice rifts, still stand in the uprooted soil. The meadows perish, overwhelmed with sand and stones. Within this last year, these glaciers have advanced three hundred feet into the valley. Saussure, the naturalist, says, that they have their periods of increase and decay: the people of the country hold an opinion entirely different; but as I judge, more probable. It is agreed by all, that the snow on the summit of Mont Blanc and the neighbouring mountains perpetually augments, and that ice, in the form of glaciers, subsists without melting in the valley of Chamouni during its transient and variable summer. If the snow which produces this glacier must augment, and the heat of the valley is no obstacle to the perpetual existence of such masses of ice as have already descended into it, the consequence is obvious; the glaciers must augment and will subsist, at least until they have overflowed this vale.

I will not pursue Buffon's sublime but gloomy theory—that this globe which we inhabit will at some future period be changed into a mass of frost by the encroachment of the polar ice, and of that produced on the most elevated points of the earth. Do you, who assert the supremacy of Ahriman, imagine him throned among these desolating snows, among these palaces of death and frost, so sculptured in this their terrible magnificence by the adamantine hand of necessity, and that he casts around him, as the first essays of his final usurpation, avalanches, torrents, rocks, and thunders, and above all these deadly glaciers, at once the proof and symbols of his reign;—add to this, the degradation of the human species—who in these regions are half-deformed or idiotic, and most of whom are deprived of anything that can excite interest or admiration. This is a part of the subject more mournful and less sublime; but such as neither the poet nor the philosopher should disdain to regard.

This morning we departed on the promise of a fine day, to visit the glacier of Montanvert. In that part where it fills a slanting valley, it is called the Sea of Ice. This valley is 950 toises, or 7,600 feet above the level of the sea. We had not proceeded far before the rain began to fall, but we persisted until we had accomplished more than half of our journey, when we returned, wet through.

CHAMOUNI, July 25th.

We have returned from visiting the glacier of Montanvert, or as it is called, the Sea of Ice, a scene in truth of dizzying wonder. The path that winds to it along the side of a mountain, now clothed with pines, now intersected with snowy hollows, is wide and steep. The cabin of Montanvert is three leagues from Chamouni, half of which distance is performed on mules, not so sure footed, but that on the first day the one I rode fell in what the guides call a *mauvais pas*, so that I narrowly escaped being precipitated down the mountain. We passed over a hollow covered with snow, down which vast stones are accustomed to roll. One had fallen the preceding day, a little time after we had returned: our guides desired us to pass quickly, for it is said that sometimes the least sound will accelerate their descent. We arrived at Montanvert, however, safe.

On all sides precipitous mountains, the abodes of unrelenting frost, surround this vale: their sides are banked up with ice and snow, broken, heaped high, and exhibiting terrific chasms. The summits are sharp and naked pinnacles, whose overhanging steepness will not even permit snow to rest upon them. Lines of dazzling ice occupy here and there their perpendicular rifts, and shine through the driving vapours with inexpressible brilliance: they pierce the clouds like things not belonging to this earth. The vale itself is filled with a mass of undulating ice, and has an ascent sufficiently gradual even to the remotest abysses of these horrible deserts. It is only half a league (about two miles) in breadth, and seems much less. It exhibits an appearance as if frost had suddenly bound up the waves and whirlpools of a mighty torrent. We walked some distance upon its surface. The waves are elevated about twelve or fifteen feet from the surface of the mass, which is intersected by long gaps of unfathomable depth, the ice of whose sides is more beautifully azure than the sky. In these regions everything changes, and is in motion. This vast mass of ice has one general progress, which ceases neither day nor night; it breaks and bursts forever: some undulations sink while others rise; it is never the same. The echo of rocks, or of the ice and snow which fall from their overhanging precipices, or roll from their aërial summits, scarcely ceases for one moment. One would think that Mont Blanc, like the god of the Stoics, was a vast animal, and that the frozen blood forever circulated through his stony veins.

Prose works (London, 1880).

THE DEAD SEA

PIERRE LOTI

A SOUND of church bells follows us for a long time in the lonely country as we ride away on horseback in the early morning towards Jericho, towards the Jordan and the Dead Sea. The Holy City speedily disappears from our eyes, hidden behind the Mount of Olives. There are fields of green barley here and there, but principally regions of stones and asphodels. Nowhere are there any trees. Red anemones and violet irises enamel the greyness of the rough country, all rock and desert. By a series of gorges, valleys, and precipices we follow a gradually descending route. Jerusalem is at an altitude of eight hundred metres and this Dead Sea to which we are going is four hundred metres below the level of other seas.

If it were not for this way for vehicles upon which our horses walk so easily, one would be tempted to call it every now and then Idumæa, or Arabia.

This road to Jericho is, moreover, full of people to-day: Bedouins upon camels; Arabian shepherds driving hundreds of black goats; bands of Cook's tourists on horseback, or in mule-chairs; Russian pilgrims, who are returning on foot from the Jordan, piously carrying gourds filled with water from the sacred river; numerous troops of Greek pilgrims from the island of Cyprus, upon asses; incongruous caravans and strange groups which we overtake or meet.

It is soon midday. The high mountains of the country of Moab which lie beyond the Dead Sea, and which we have seen ever since we reached Hebron like a diaphanous wall in the east seem to be as distant as ever, although for three hours we have been advancing towards them,—apparently fleeing before us like the visions of a mirage. But they have grown misty and gloomy; all that was trailing in the sky like light veils in the morning has gathered and condensed upon their peaks, while a purer and more magnificent blue now extends above our heads.

Half-way from Jericho, we make the great halt in a caravansary, where there are Bedouins, Syrians, and Greeks; then we again mount our horses beneath a burning sun.

Every now and then, in the yawning gulfs far below us the torrent of the Cedron is visible like a thread of foaming silver; its course here is not troubled as beneath the walls of Jerusalem, and it rushes along rapidly towards the Dead Sea, half-hidden in the deepest hollows of the abysses.

The mountain slopes continue to run down towards this strange and unique region, situated below the level of the sea, where sleep the waters which produce death. It seems that one is made conscious of something abnormal in this continuous descent by some unknown sense of oddity and even giddiness suggested by these slopes. Growing more and more grand and rugged, the country now presents almost the appearance of a true desert. But the

THE DEAD SEA.

impression of immeasurable solitude is not experienced here. And then there is always that road traced by human hands and these continual meetings with horsemen and various passengers.

The air is already dryer and warmer than at Jerusalem, and the light becomes more and more magnifying,—as is always the case when one approaches places devoid of vegetation.

The mountains are ever more and more denuded and more cracked by the dryness, opening everywhere with crevasses like great abysses. The heat increases in proportion as we descend to the shore of the Dead Sea which in summer is one of the hottest places in the world. A mournful sun darts its rays around us upon the rocks, masses of stone, and pale limestone where the lizards run about by the thousand; whilst over beyond us, serving as a background for everything, stands ever the chain of Moab, like a Dantesque wall. And to-day storm-clouds darken and deform it, hiding its peaks, or carrying them up too high into the sky and forming other imaginary peaks, thus producing the terror of chaos.

In a certain deep valley, through which our way lies for a moment, shut in without any view between vertical walls, some hundreds of camels are at pasture, hanging like great fantastic goats to the flanks of the mountains,—the highest perched one of all the troop silhouetted against the sky.

Then we issue from this defile and the mountains of Moab reäppear, higher then ever now and more obscured by clouds. Upon this sombre background the near prospective of this desolate country stands out very clearly ; the summits are whitish and all around us blocks, absolutely white, are delineated by the broiling sun with an extreme hardness of outline.

Towards three o'clock, from the elevated regions where we still are, we see before us the country that is lower than the sea, and, as if our eyes had preserved the remembrance of ordinary levels, this really seems not an ordinary plain, but something too low and a great depression of the earth, the bottom of a vast gulf into which the road is about to fall.

This sunken region has the features of the desert, with gleaming grey wastes like fields of lava, or beds of salt; in its midst an unexpectedly green patch, which is the oasis of Jericho,—and towards the south, a motionless expanse with the polish of a mirror and the sad hue of slate, which begins and loses itself in the distance with a limitless horizon: the Dead Sea, enwrapped in darkness to-day by all the clouds of the distance, by all that is heavy and opaque yonder weighing upon the border of Moab.

The few little white houses of Jericho are gradually outlined in the green of the oasis in proportion as we descend from our stony summits, inundated with the sun. One would hardly call it a village. It seems that there is not the least vestige of the three large and celebrated cities that formerly successively occupied this site and that in different ages were called Jericho. These utter destructions and annihilations of the cities of Canaan and Idumæa seem to be for the confounding of human reason. Truly a very powerful breath of malediction and death must have passed over it all.

When we are finally down in the plain, an insufferable heat surprises us; one would say that we had traversed an immense distance southward,—and yet, in reality, we have only descended a few hundred metres towards the bowels of the earth: it is to their depressed level that the environs of the Dead Sea owe their exceptional climate.

Jericho is composed to-day of a little Turkish citadel, three or four new houses built for pilgrims and tourists, half a hundred Arab habitations of mud with roofing of thorny branches and a few Bedouin tents. Round about them are gardens in which grow an occasional palm; a wood of green shrubs traversed by clear brooks; some paths overrun by grass, where horsemen in burnous caracole upon their horses with long manes and tails. And that is all. Immediately beyond the wood the uninhabitable desert begins; and the Dead Sea lies there very near, spreading its mysterious winding-sheet above the engulfed kingdoms of Sodom and Gomorrah. This Sea has a very individual aspect, and this evening it is very funereal; it truly gives the impression of death, with its heavy, leaden, and motionless waters between the deserts of its two shores where great confused mountains mingle with the storm-clouds hanging in the sky.

Sunday, April 8th.

From Jericho, where we passed the night, the Dead Sea seems very near; one would think in a few minutes it would be easy to reach its tranquil sheet,—which this morning is of a blue barely tinted with slate, under a sky rid of all of yesterday's clouds. Yet, to reach it, almost two hours on horseback are still required, under a heavy sun, across the little desert which, minus the immensity, resembles the large one in which we have just spent so many days; towards this Sea, which seems to flee in proportion as we approach, we descend by means of a series of exhausted strata and desolate plateaux, all glittering with sand and salt. Here we find a few of the odoriferous plants of Arabia Petræa, and even the semblance of a mirage, the uncertainty as to distances and the continual tremulousness of the horizon. We also find here a band of Bedouins resembling very closely our friends of the desert in their shirts with long pointed sleeves floating like wings, and their little brown veils tied to the forehead with black cords, the two ends of which stand up on the temples like the ears of an animal. Moreover, these shores of the Dead Sea, especially on the southern side, are frequented by pillagers almost as much as Idumæa.

We know that geologists trace the existence of the Dead Sea back to the first ages of the world; they do not contest, however, that at the period of the destruction of the accursed cities it must have suddenly overflowed, after some new eruption, to cover the site of the Moabite pentapolis. And it was at that time that was engulfed all this "Vale of Siddim," where were assembled, against Chedorlaomer, the kings of Sodom, of Gomorrah, of Admah, of Zeboiim, and of Zoar (*Genesis* xiv. 2, 3); all that "plain of Siddim" which "was well watered everywhere," like a garden of delight (*Genesis* xiii. 10). Since these remote times, this Sea has receded a little, without, however, its form being sensibly changed. And, beneath the shroud of its heavy waters, unfathomable to the diver by their very density, sleep strange ruins, *débris*, which, without doubt, will never be explored; Sodom and Gomorrah are there, buried in their dark depths.

At present, the Dead Sea, terminated at the north by the sands we cross, extends to a length of about eighty kilometres, between two ranges of parallel mountains: to the east, those of Moab, eternally oozing bitumen, which stand this morning in their sombre violet; to the west, those of Judea, of another nature, entirely of whitish limestone, at this moment dazzling with sunlight. On both shores the desolation is equally absolute; the same silence hovers over the same appearances of death. These are indeed the immutable and somewhat terrifying aspects of the desert,—and one can understand the very intense impression produced upon travellers who do not know the Arabia Magna; but, for us, there is here only a too greatly diminished image of the mournful phantasmagoria of that region. Besides, one does not lose altogether the view of the citadel of Jericho; from our horses we may still perceive it behind us, like a vague little white point, but still a protector. In the extreme distance of the desert sands, under the trembling network of mirage, appears also an ancient fortress, which is a monastery for Greek hermits. And, finally, another white blot, just perceptible above us, in a recess of the mountains of Judah, stands that mausoleum which passes for the tomb of Moses—for which a great Mohammedan pilgrimage is soon about to start.

However, upon the sinister strand where we arrive, death reveals itself, truly sovereign and imposing. First, like a line of defence which it is necessary to surmount, comes a belt of drift-wood, branches and trees stripped of all bark, almost petrified in the chemical bath, and whitened like bones,—one would call them an accumulation of great vertebræ. Then there are some rounded pebbles as on the shore of every sea; but not a single shell, not a piece of seaweed, not even a little greenish slime, nothing organic, not even of the lower order; and nowhere else has this ever been seen, a sea whose bed is as sterile as a crucible of alchemy; this is something abnormal and disconcerting. Some dead fish lie here and there, hardened like wood, mummified in the naptha and the salts: fish of the Jordan which the current brought here and which the accursed waters suffocated instantly.

And before us, this sea flees, between its banks of desert mountains, to the troubled horizon with an appearance of never ending. Its whitish, oily waters bear blots of bitumen, spread in large iridescent rings. Moreover, they burn, if you drink them, like a corrosive liquor; if you enter them up to your knees you have difficulty in walking, they are so heavy; you cannot dive in them nor even swim in the ordinary position, but you can float upon the surface like a cork buoy.

Once the Emperor Titus, as an experiment, had several

slaves bound together with iron chains and cast in, and they did not drown.

On the eastern shore, in the little sandy desert where we have just been marching for two hours, a line of a beautiful emerald serpentines; a few flocks and a few Arabian shepherds that are half bandits pass in the far distance.

Towards the middle of the day we reënter Jericho, whence we shall not depart until to-morrow morning, and there remain the tranquil hours of the evening for us to go over the still oasis.

When we are seated before the porch of the little inn of Jericho in the warm twilight, we see a wildly galloping horse, bringing a monk in a black robe with long hair floating in the wind. He is one of the hermits of the Mount of the Forty Days, who is trying to be the first to arrive and offer us some little objects in the wood of Jericho and shell rosaries from the Jordan.—At nightfall others come, dressed in the same black robe, and with the same thin hair around their bandit's countenance, and enter the inn to entice us with little carvings and similar chaplets.

The night is sultry here, and a little heavy, quite different to the cold nights of Jerusalem, and just as the stars begin to shine a concert of frogs begins simultaneously from every side, under the dark entanglement of the balms of Gilead,—so continuous and, moreover, so discreet is it, that it seems but another expression of the tranquil silence. You hear also the barking of the sheep-dogs, below, on the side of the Arabian encampments; then, very far away, the drum and the little Bedouin flute furnish the rhythm for some wild fête;—and, at intervals, but very distinctly, comes the lugubrious falsetto of a hyena or jackal.

Now, here is the unexpected refrain of the coffee-houses of Berlin, which suddenly bursts forth, in ironical dissonance, in the midst of these light and immutable sounds of ancient evenings in Judea: the German tourists who have been here since sunset, encamped under the tents of agencies; a band of "Cook's tourists" come to see and profane, as far as they can, this little desert.

It is after midnight, when everything is hushed and the silence belongs to the nightingales which fill the oasis with an exquisite and clear music of crystal.

Jérusalem (Paris, 1895).

MOUNT VESUVIUS

CHARLES DICKENS

A NOBLE mountain pass, with the ruins of a fort on a strong eminence, traditionally called the Fort of Fra Diavolo; the old town of Itrí, like a device in pastry, built up, almost perpendicularly, on a hill, and approached by long steep flights of steps; beautiful Mola di Gaëta, whose wines, like those of Albano, have degenerated since the days of Horace, or his taste for wine was bad: which is not likely of one who enjoyed it so much, and extolled it so well; another night upon the road at St. Agatha; a rest next day at Capua, which is picturesque, but hardly so seductive to a traveller now as the soldiers of Prætorian Rome were wont to find the ancient city of that name; a flat road among vines festooned and looped from tree to tree; and Mount Vesuvius close at hand at last!—its cone and summit whitened with snow; and its smoke hanging over it, in the heavy atmosphere of the day, like a dense cloud. So we go, rattling down-hill, into Naples.

Capri—once made odious by the deified beast Tiberius—Ischia, Procida, and the thousand distant beauties of the Bay, lie in the blue sea yonder, changing in the mist and sunshine twenty times a day: now close at hand, now far off, now unseen. The fairest country in the world is spread about us. Whether we turn towards the Miseno shore of the splendid watery amphitheatre, and go by the Grotto of Posilipo to the Grotto del Cane, and away to Baiæ: or take the other way, towards Vesuvius and Sorrento, it is one succession of delights. In the last-named direction, where, over doors and archways, there are countless little images of San Gennaro, with his Canute's hand stretched out to check the fury of the Burning Mountain, we are carried pleasantly, by a railroad on the beautiful Sea Beach, past the town of Torre del Greco, built upon the ashes of the former town, destroyed by an eruption of Vesuvius, within a hundred years, and past the flat-roofed houses, granaries, and macaroni manufactories; to Castel-a-Mare, with its ruined castle, now inhabited by fishermen, standing in the sea upon a heap of rocks. Here, the railroad terminates; but, hence we may ride on, by an unbroken succession of enchanting bays, and beautiful scenery, sloping from the highest summit of St. Angelo, the highest neighbouring mountain, down to the water's edge—among vineyards, olive-trees, gardens of oranges and lemons, orchards, heaped-up rocks, green gorges in the hills—and by the bases of snow-covered heights, and through small towns with handsome, dark-haired women at the doors—and pass delicious summer villas—to Sorrento, where the poet Tasso drew his inspiration from the beauty surrounding him. Returning, we may climb the heights above Castel-a-Mare, and, looking down among the boughs and leaves, see the crisp water glistening in the sun, and clusters of white houses in distant Naples, dwindling, in the great extent of

MOUNT VESUVIUS.

prospect, down to dice. The coming back to the city, by the beach again, at sunset: with the glowing sea on one side, and the darkening mountain, with its smoke and flame, upon the other, is a sublime conclusion to the glory of the day.

Stand at the bottom of the great market-place of Pompeii, and look up the silent streets, through the ruined temples of Jupiter and Isis, over the broken houses with their inmost sanctuaries open to the day, away to Mount Vesuvius, bright and snowy in the peaceful distance; and lose all count of time, and heed of other things, in the strange and melancholy sensation of seeing the Destroyed and the Destroyer making this quiet picture in the sun. Then, ramble on, and see, at every turn, the little familiar tokens of human habitation and every-day pursuits; the chafing of the bucket rope in the stone rim of the exhausted well; the track of carriage wheels in the pavement of the street; the marks of drinking vessels on the stone counter of the wine-shop; the amphoræ in private cellars, stored away so many hundred years ago, and undisturbed to this hour—all rendering the solitude and deadly lonesomeness of the place ten thousand times more solemn, than if the volcano, in its fury, had swept the city from the earth, and sunk it in the bottom of the sea.

After it was shaken by the earthquake which preceded the eruption, workmen were employed in shaping out, in stone, new ornaments for temples and other buildings that had suffered. Here lies their work, outside the city gate, as if they would return to-morrow.

In the cellar of Diomede's house, where certain skeletons were found huddled together, close to the door, the impression of their bodies on the ashes hardened with the ashes, and became stamped and fixed there, after they had shrunk, inside, to scanty bones. So, in the theatre of Herculaneum, a comic mask, floating on the stream when it was hot and liquid, stamped its mimic features in it as it hardened into stone, and now it turns upon the stranger the fantastic look it turned upon the audiences in that same theatre two thousand years ago.

Next to the wonder of going up and down the streets, and in and out of the houses, and traversing the secret chambers of the temples of a religion that has vanished from the earth, and finding so many fresh traces of remote antiquity: as if the course of Time had been stopped after this desolation, and there had been no nights and days, months, years, and centuries since: nothing is more impressive and terrible than the many evidences of the searching nature of the ashes as bespeaking their irresistible power, and the impossibility of escaping them. In the wine-cellars, they forced their way into the earthen vessels: displacing the wine, and choking them, to the brim, with dust. In the tombs, they forced the ashes of the dead from the funeral urns, and rained new ruin even into them. The mouths, and eyes, and skulls of all the skeletons were stuffed with this terrible hail. In Herculaneum, where the flood was of a different and a heavier kind, it rolled in, like a sea. Imagine a deluge of water turned to marble, at its height—and that is what is called "the lava" here.

Some workmen were digging the gloomy well on the brink of which we now stand, looking down, when they came on some of the stone benches of the theatre—those steps (for such they seem) at the bottom of the excavation—and found the buried city of Herculaneum. Presently going down, with lighted torches, we are perplexed by great walls of monstrous thickness, rising up between the benches, shutting out the stage, obtruding their shapeless forms in absurd places, confusing the whole plan, and making it a disordered dream. We cannot, at first, believe, or picture to ourselves, that THIS came rolling in, and drowned the city; and that all that is not here has been cut away, by the axe, like solid stone. But this perceived and understood, the horror and oppression of its presence are indescribable.

Many of the paintings on the walls in the roofless chambers of both cities, or carefully removed to the museum at Naples, are as fresh and plain as if they had been executed yesterday. Here are subjects of still life, as provisions, dead game, bottles, glasses, and the like; familiar classical stories, or mythological fables, always forcibly and plainly told; conceits of cupids, quarrelling, sporting, working at trades; theatrical rehearsals; poets reading their productions to their friends; inscriptions chalked upon the walls; political squibs, advertisements, rough drawings by schoolboys; everything to people and restore the ancient cities in the fancy of their wondering visitor. Furniture, too, you see, of every kind—lamps, tables, couches; vessels for eating, drinking, and cooking; workmen's tools, surgical instruments, tickets for the theatre, pieces of money, personal ornaments, bunches of keys found clinched in the grasp of skeletons, helmets of guards and warriors; little household bells, yet musical with their old domestic tones.

The least among these objects, lends its aid to swell the interests of Vesuvius, and invest it with a perfect fascination. The looking, from either ruined city, into the neighbouring grounds overgrown with beautiful vines and luxuriant trees; and remembering that house upon house, temple on temple, building after building, and street after street, are still lying underneath the roots of all the quiet cultivation, waiting to be turned up to the light of day; is something so wonderful, so full of mystery, so captivating to the imagination, that one would think it would be paramount, and yield to nothing else. To nothing but Vesuvius; but the mountain is the genius of the scene. From every indication of the ruin it has worked, we look, again, with an absorbing interest to where its smoke is rising up into the sky. It is beyond us, as we thread the ruined streets: above us, as we stand upon the ruined walls; we follow it through every vista of broken columns, as we wander through the empty court-yards of the houses; and through the garlandings and interlacings of every wanton vine. Turning away to Pæstum yonder, to see the awful structures built, the least aged of them hundreds of years before the birth of Christ, and standing yet, erect in lonely majesty, upon the wild malaria-blighted plain—we watch Vesuvius as it disappears from the prospect, and watch for it again, on our return, with the same thrill of interest: as the doom and destiny of all this beautiful country, biding its terrible time.

It is very warm in the sun, on this early spring day, when we return from Pæstum, but very cold in the shade: insomuch, that although we may lunch pleasantly, at noon, in the open air, by the gate of Pompeii, the neighbouring rivulet supplies thick ice for our wine. But, the sun is shining brightly; there is not a cloud or speck of vapour in the whole blue sky, looking down upon the Bay of Naples; and the moon will be at the full to-night. No matter that the snow and ice lie thick upon the summit of Vesuvius, or that we have been on foot all day at Pompeii, or that croakers maintain that strangers should not be on the mountain by night, in such an unusual season. Let us take advantage of the fine weather; make the best of our way to Resina, the little village at the foot of the mountain; prepare ourselves, as well as we can on so short a notice, at the guide's house; ascend at once, and have sunset half-way up, moonlight at the top, and midnight to come down in!

At four o'clock in the afternoon there is a terrible uproar in the little stable-yard of Signore Salvatore, the recognized head-guide, with the gold band around his cap; and thirty under-guides, who are all scuffling and screaming at once, are preparing half-a-dozen saddled ponies, three litters, and some stout staves for the journey. Every one of the thirty quarrels with the other twenty-nine, and frightens the six ponies; and as much of the village as can possibly squeeze itself into the little stable-yard participates in the tumult, and gets trodden on by the cattle.

After much violent skirmishing, and more noise than would suffice for the storming of Naples, the procession starts. The head-guide, who is liberally paid for all the attendants, rides a little in advance of the party; the other thirty guides proceed on foot. Eight go forward with the litters that are to be used by and by; and the remaining two-and-twenty beg.

We ascend, gradually, by stony lanes like rough broad flights of stairs, for some time. At length, we leave these, and the vineyards on either side of them, and emerge upon a bleak, bare region, where the lava lies confusedly in enormous rusty masses: as if the earth had been plowed up by burning thunder-bolts. And now we halt to see the sun set. The change that falls upon the dreary region, and on the whole mountain, as its red light fades, and the night comes on—and the unutterable solemnity and dreariness that reign around, who that has witnessed it can ever forget!

It is dark when, after winding for some time over the broken ground, we arrive at the foot of the cone: which is extremely steep, and seems to rise, almost perpendicularly, from the spot where we dismount. The only light is reflected from the snow, deep, hard, and white, with which the cone is covered. It is now intensely cold, and the air is piercing. The thirty-one have brought no torches, knowing that the moon will rise before we reach the top. Two of the litters are devoted to the two ladies; the third, to a rather heavy gentleman from Naples, whose hospitality and good nature have attached him to the expedition, and determined him to assist in doing the honours of the mountain. The rather heavy gentleman is carried by fifteen men; each of the ladies by half-a-dozen. We who walk make the best use of our staves; and so the whole party begin to labour upward over the snow—as if they were toiling to the summit of an antediluvian Twelfth-cake.

We are a long time toiling up; and the head-guide looks oddly about him when one of the company—not an Italian, though an habitué of the mountain for many years: whom we will call, for our present purpose, Mr. Pickle of Portici—suggests that, as it is freezing hard, and the usual footing of ashes is covered by the snow and ice, it will surely be difficult to descend. But the sight of the litters above, tilting up and down, and jerking from this side to that, as the bearers continually slip and tumble, diverts our attention; more especially as the whole length of the rather heavy gentleman is, at that moment, presented to us alarmingly foreshortened, with his head downward.

The rising of the moon soon afterward, revives the flagging spirits of the bearers. Stimulating each other with their usual watchword, "Courage, friend! It is to eat macaroni!" they press on, gallantly, for the summit.

From tingeing the top of the snow above us with a band of light, and pouring it in a stream through the valley below, while we have been ascending in the dark, the moon soon lights the whole white mountain-side, and the broad sea down below, and tiny Naples in the distance, and every village in the country round. The whole prospect is in this lovely state, when we come upon the platform on the mountain-top—the region of Fire—an exhausted crater formed of great masses of gigantic cinders, like blocks of stone from some tremendous waterfall, burned up; from every chink and crevice of which hot, sulphurous smoke is pouring out: while, from another conical-shaped hill, the present crater, rising abruptly from this platform at the end, great sheets of fire are streaming forth: reddening the night with flame, blackening it with smoke, and spotting it with red-hot stones and cinders, that fly up into the air like feathers, and fall down like lead. What words can paint the gloom and grandeur of this scene!

The broken ground; the smoke; the sense of suffocation from the sulphur; the fear of falling down through the crevices in the yawning ground; the stopping, every now and then, for somebody who is missing in the dark (for the dense smoke now obscures the moon); the intolerable noise of the thirty; and the hoarse roaring of the mountain; make it a scene of such confusion, at the same time, that we reel again. But, dragging the ladies through it, and across another exhausted crater to the foot of the present Volcano, we approach close to it on the windy side, and then sit down among the hot ashes at its foot, and look up in silence; faintly estimating the action that is going on within, from its being full a hundred feet higher, at this minute, than it was six weeks ago.

There is something in the fire and roar that generates an irresistible desire to get nearer to it. We cannot rest long, without starting off, two of us, on our hands and knees, accompanied by the head-guide, to climb to the brim of the flaming crater, and try to look in. Meanwhile, the thirty yell, as with one voice, that it is a dangerous proceeding, and call to us to come back; frightening the rest of the party out of their wits.

What with their noise, and what with the trembling of the thin crust of ground, that seems about to open underneath our feet, and plunge us into the burning gulf below (which is the real danger, if there be any); and what with the flashing of the fire in our faces, and the shower of red-hot ashes that is raining down, and the choking smoke and sulphur; we may well feel giddy and irrational, like drunken men. But, we contrive to climb up to the brim, and look down, for a moment, into the Hell of boiling fire below. Then, we all three come rolling down; blackened, and singed, and scorched, and hot, and giddy: and each with his dress alight in half-a-dozen places.

You have read, a thousand times, that the usual way of descending is by sliding down the ashes: which, forming a gradually increasing ledge below the feet, prevent too rapid a descent. But, when we have crossed the two exhausted craters on our way back, and are come to this precipitous place, there is (as Mr. Pickle has foretold) no vestige of ashes to be seen; the whole being a smooth sheet of ice.

In this dilemma, ten or a dozen of the guides cautiously join hands, and make a chain of men; of whom the foremost beat, as well as they can, a rough track with their sticks, down which we prepare to follow. The way being fearfully steep, and none of the party: even of the thirty:

being able to keep their feet for six paces together, the ladies are taken out of their litters, and placed, each between two careful persons; while others of the thirty hold by their skirts, to prevent their falling forward—a necessary precaution, tending to the immediate and hopeless dilapidation of their apparel. The rather heavy gentleman is adjured to leave his litter too, and be escorted in a similar manner; but he resolves to be brought down as he was brought up, on the principle that his fifteen bearers are not likely to tumble all at once, and that he is safer so than trusting to his own legs.

In this order, we begin the descent: sometimes on foot, sometimes shuffling on the ice: always proceeding much more quietly and slowly than on our upward way: and constantly alarmed by the falling among us of somebody from behind, who endangers the footing of the whole party, and clings pertinaciously to anybody's ankles. It is impossible for the litter to be in advance, too, as the track has to be made; and its appearance behind us, overhead—with some one or other of the bearers always down, and the rather heavy gentleman with his legs in the air—is very threatening and frightful. We have gone on thus; a very little way, painfully and anxiously, but quite merrily, and regarding it as a great success—and have all fallen several times, and have all been stopped, somehow or other, as we were sliding away—when Mr. Pickle, of Portici, in the act of remarking on these uncommon circumstances as quite beyond his experience, stumbles, falls, disengages himself with quick presence of mind, from those about him, plunges away head foremost, and rolls, over and over, down the whole surface of the cone!

Sickening as it is to look, and be so powerless to help him, I see him there, in the moonlight—I have had such a dream often—skimming over the white ice like a cannon-ball. Almost at the same moment, there is a cry from behind; and a man who has carried a light basket of spare cloaks on his head, comes rolling past at the same frightful speed, closely followed by a boy. At this climax of the chapter of accidents, the remaining eight-and-twenty vociferate to that degree, that a pack of wolves would be music to them!

Giddy and bloody, and a mere bundle of rags, is Pickle of Portici when we reach the place where we dismounted, and where the horses are waiting; but, thank God, sound in limb! And never are we likely to be more glad to see a man alive, and on his feet, than to see him now—making light of it too, though sorely bruised and in great pain. The boy is brought into the Hermitage on the Mountain, while we are at supper, with his head tied up; and the man is heard of some hours afterwards. He, too, is bruised and stunned, but has broken no bones; the snow having, fortunately, covered all the larger blocks of rock and stone, and rendered them harmless.

After a cheerful meal, and a good rest before a blazing fire, we again take horse, and continue our descent to Salvatore's house—very slowly, by reason of our bruised friend being hardly able to keep the saddle, or endure the pain of motion. Though it is so late at night, or early in the morning, all the people of the village are waiting about the little stable-yard when we arrive, and looking up the road by which we are expected. Our appearance is hailed with a great clamour of tongues, and a general sensation, for which, in our modesty, we are somewhat at a loss to account, until turning into the yard, we find that one of a party of French gentlemen, who were on the mountain at the same time, is lying on some straw in the stable with a broken limb; looking like Death and suffering great torture; and that we were confidently supposed to have encountered some worse accident.

So "well returned and Heaven be praised!" as the cheerful Vetturino, who has borne us company all the way from Pisa says with all his heart! And away with his ready horses into sleeping Naples!

It wakes again to Policinelli and pickpockets, buffo singers and beggars, rags, puppets, flowers, brightness, dirt, and universal degradation; airing its Harlequin suit in the sunshine, next day and every day; singing, starving, dancing, gaming on the seashore; and leaving all labour to the burning mountain, which is ever at its work.

Pictures from Italy (London, 1845).

THE FALLS OF THE RHINE

VICTOR HUGO

MY friend, what shall I say to you? I have just come from seeing that strange thing. I am only a few steps from it. I hear the noise of it. I am writing to you without knowing what falls from my thoughts. Ideas and images accumulate there pell-mell, hastening, jostling and bruising each other, and disappearing in vapour, in foam, in uproar, and in clouds.

Within me there is an immense ebullition. It seems to me that I have the Falls of the Rhine in my brain.

I write at random, just as it comes. You must understand if you can.

You arrive at Laufen. It is a castle of the Thirteenth Century, a very beautiful pile and of a very good style. At the door there are two gilded wyverns with open mouths. They are roaring. You would say that they are making the mysterious noise you hear.

You enter.

You are in the courtyard of a castle. It is no longer a castle, it is a farm. Hens, geese, turkeys, dirt; a cart in a corner; and a vat of lime. A door opens. The cascade appears.

Marvellous spectacle!

Frightful tumult! That is the first effect. Then you

look about you. The cataract cuts out the gulfs which it fills with large white sheets. As in a conflagration, there are some little peaceful spots in the midst of this object of terror; groves blended with foam; charming brooks in the mosses; fountains for the Arcadian Shepherds of Poussin, shadowed by little boughs gently agitated.—And then these details vanish, and the impression of the whole returns to you. Eternal tempest! Snow, vital and furious. The water is of a strange transparency. Some black rocks produce sinister aspects under the water. They appear to touch the surface and are ten feet down. Below the two principal leaps of the falls two great sheaves of foam spread themselves upon the river and disperse in green clouds. On the other side of the Rhine, I perceive a tranquil group of little houses, where the housekeepers come and go.

As I am observing, my guide tells me: "Lake Constance froze in the winter of 1829 and 1830. It had not frozen for a hundred and four years. People crossed it in carriages. Poor people were frozen to death in Schaffhausen."

I descended a little lower towards the abyss. The sky was grey and veiled. The cascade roared like a tiger. Frightful noise, terrible rapidity! Dust of water, smoke and rain at the same time. Through this mist you see the cataract in its full development. Five large rocks cut it into five sheets of water of diverse aspects and different sizes. You believe you see the five worn piers of a bridge of Titans. In the winter the ice forms blue arches upon these black abutments.

THE FALLS OF THE RHINE.

The nearest of these rocks is of a strange form; it seems as if the water issued full of rage from the hideous and impassive head of an Hindu idol with an elephant's head. Some trees and brambles, which intermingle at its summit, give it bristling and horrible hair.

At the most awe-inspiring point of the Falls, a great rock disappears and reäppears under the foam like the skull of an engulfed giant, beaten for six thousand years by this dreadful shower-bath.

The guide continues his monologue: "The Falls of the Rhine are one league from Schaffhausen. The whole mass of the river falls there at a height of seventy feet."—

The rugged path which descends from the castle of Laufen to the abyss crosses a garden. At the moment when I passed, deafened by the formidable cataract, a child, accustomed to living with this marvel of the world, was playing among the flowers.

This path has several barriers, where you pay a trifle from time to time. The poor cataract should not work for nothing. See the trouble it gives! It is very necessary that with all the foam that it throws upon the trees, the rocks, the river, and the clouds, that it should throw a few sous into the pocket of some one. That is the least it can do.

I came along this path until I reached a kind of balcony skilfully poised in reality right over the abyss.

There, everything moves you at once. You are dazzled, made dizzy, confused, terrified, and charmed. You lean on a wooden rail that trembles. Some yellow trees,—it is autumn,—and some red quick-trees surround a little pavilion in the style of the Café Turc, from which one observes the horror of the thing. The women cover themselves with an oil-skin (each one costs a franc). You are suddenly enveloped in a terrible, thundering and heavy shower.

Some pretty little yellow snails crawl voluptuously over this dew on the rail of the balcony. The rock that slopes beyond the balcony weeps drop by drop into the cascade. Upon this rock, which is in the centre of the cataract, a troubadour-knight of painted wood stands leaning upon a red shield with a white cross. Some man certainly risked his life to plant this doubtful ornament in the midst of Jehovah's grand and eternal poetry.

The two giants, who lift up their heads, I should say the two largest rocks, seem to speak. The thunder is their voice. Above an alarming mound of foam you see a peaceful little house with its little orchard. You would say that this terrible hydra is condemned to carry eternally upon his back that sweet and happy cabin.

I went to the extremity of the balcony; I leaned against the rock. The sight became still more terrible. It was a frightful descent of water. The hideous and splendid abyss angrily throws a shower of pearls in the face of those who dare to regard it so near. That is admirable. The four great heaps of the cataract fall, mount, and fall again without ceasing. You would believe that you were beholding the four lightning-wheels of the storm-chariot.

The wooden bridge was laid under water. The boards

were slippery. Some dead leaves quivered under my feet. In a cleft of the rock, I noticed a little tuft of dried grass. Dry under the cataract of Schaffhausen! in this deluge, it missed every drop of water! There are some hearts that may be likened to this tuft of grass. In the midst of a vortex of human prosperity, they wither of themselves. Alas! this drop of water which they have missed and which springs not forth from the earth but falls from heaven, is Love!

How long did I remain there, absorbed in that grand spectacle? I could not possibly tell you. During that contemplation the hours passed in my spirit like the waves in the abyss, without leaving a trace or memory.

However, some one came to inform me that the day was declining. I climbed up to the castle and from there I descended to the sandy shore whence you cross the Rhine to gain the right bank. This shore is below the Falls, and you cross the river at a few fathoms from the cataract. To accomplish this, you risk yourself in a little boat, charming, light, exquisite, adjusted like the canoe of a savage, constructed of wood as supple as the skin of a shark, solid, elastic, fibrous, grazing the rocks every instant and hardly escaping—being managed like all the small boats of the Rhine and the Meuse with a hook and an oar in the form of a shovel. Nothing is stranger than to feel in this little boat the deep and thunderous shocks of the water.

As the bark moved away from the bank, I looked above my head at the battlements covered with tiles and the sharp gable ends of the *château* that dominates the precipice.

Some fishermen's nets were drying up on the stones on the bank of the river. Do they fish in this vortex? Yes, without doubt. As the fish cannot leap over the cataract, many salmon are caught here. Moreover, where is the whirlpool in which man will not fish?

Now I will recapitulate my intense and almost poignant sensations. First impression: you do not know what to say, you are crushed as by all great poems. Then the whole unravels itself. The beauties disengage themselves from the cloud. Altogether it is grand, sombre, terrible, hideous, magnificent, unutterable.

On the other side of the Rhine, the Falls are made to turn mill-wheels.

Upon one bank, the castle; upon the other, the village, which is called Neuhausen.

It is a remarkable thing that each of the great Alpine rivers, on leaving the mountains, has the colour of the sea to which it flows. The Rhone, escaping from the Lake of Geneva, is blue like the Mediterranean; the Rhine, issuing from Lake Constance, is green like the ocean.

Unfortunately the sky was overcast. I cannot, therefore, say that I saw the Falls of Laufen in all their splendour. Nothing is richer nor more marvellous than that shower of pearls of which I have already told you. This should be, however, even more wonderful when the sun changes these pearls to diamonds and when the rainbow plunges its emerald neck into the foam like a divine bird that comes to drink in the abyss.

From the other side of the Rhine, whence I am now

writing, the cataract appears in its entirety, divided into five very distinct parts, each of which has its physiognomy quite apart from the others, and forming a kind of crescendo. The first is an overflowing from a mill; the second, almost symmetrically composed by the work of the wave and time, is a fountain of Versailles; the third, a cascade; the fourth, an avalanche; and the fifth, chaos.

A last word and I will close this letter. Several paces from the Falls, you explore a calcareous rock, which is very beautiful. In the midst of one of the quarries that are there a galley-slave, in stripes of grey and black, with pickaxe in his hand and a double chain on his feet, looked at the cataract. Chance seems to delight itself sometimes in placing in antitheses, sometimes sad and sometimes terrible, the work of nature and the work of society.

Le Rhin (Paris, 1846).

IN ARCTIC SEAS

LORD DUFFERIN

EVER since leaving England, as each four-and-twenty hours we climbed up nearer to the pole, the belt of dusk dividing day from day had been growing narrower and narrower, until having nearly reached the Arctic circle, this,—the last night we were to traverse,—had dwindled to a thread of shadow. Only another half-dozen leagues more, and we would stand on the threshold of a four months' day! For the few preceding hours, clouds had completely covered the heavens, except where a clear interval of sky, that lay along the northern horizon, promised a glowing stage for the sun's last obsequies. But like the heroes of old he had veiled his face to die, and it was not until he dropped down to the sea that the whole hemisphere overflowed with glory and the gilded pageant concerted for his funeral gathered in slow procession round his grave; reminding one of those tardy honours paid to some great prince of song, who—left during life to languish in a garret—is buried by nobles in Westminster Abbey. A few minutes more the last fiery segment had disappeared beneath the purple horizon, and all was over.

"The king is dead—the king is dead—the king is dead! Long live the king!" And up from the sea that had just entombed his sire, rose the young monarch of a new day; while the courtier clouds, in their ruby robes, turned faces still aglow with the favours of their dead lord, to borrow brighter blazonry from the smile of a new master.

A fairer or a stranger spectacle than the last Arctic sunset cannot be well conceived. Evening and morning—like kinsmen whose hearts some baseless feud has kept asunder—clasping hands across the shadow of the vanished night.

You must forgive me if sometimes I become a little magniloquent; for really, amid the grandeur of that fresh primæval world, it was almost impossible to prevent one's imagination from absorbing a dash of the local colouring. We seemed to have suddenly waked up among the colossal scenery of Keats's *Hyperion.* The pulses of young Titans beat within our veins. Time itself,—no longer frittered down into paltry divisions,—had assumed a more majestic aspect. We had the appetite of giants,—was it unnatural we should also adopt "the large utterance of the early gods"?

About 3 A. M. it cleared up a little. By breakfast-time the sun reäppeared, and we could see five or six miles ahead of the vessel. It was shortly after this, that as I was standing in the main rigging peering out over the smooth blue surface of the sea, a white twinkling point of light suddenly caught my eye about a couple of miles off on the port bow, which a telescope soon resolved into a solitary isle of ice, dancing and dipping in the sunlight. As you may suppose, the news brought everybody upon deck; and when almost immediately afterwards a string of other pieces —glittering like a diamond necklace—hove in sight, the excitement was extreme.

Here, at all events, was honest blue salt water frozen solid, and when—as we proceeded—the scattered fragments thickened, and passed like silver argosies on either hand, until at last we found ourselves enveloped in an innumerable fleet of bergs,—it seemed as if we could never be weary of admiring a sight so strange and beautiful. It was rather in form and colour than in size that these ice islets were remarkable; anything approaching to a real iceberg we neither saw, nor are we likely to see. In fact, the lofty ice mountains that wander like vagrant islands along the coast of America, seldom or never come to the eastward or northward of Cape Farewell. They consist of land ice, and are all generated among the bays and straits within Baffin's Bay, and first enter the Atlantic a good deal to the southward of Iceland; whereas the Polar ice, among which we have been knocking about, is field ice, and—except when packed one ledge above another, by great pressure—is comparatively flat. I do not think I saw any pieces that were piled up higher than thirty or thirty-five feet above the sea-level, although at a little distance through the mist they may have loomed much loftier.

In quaintness of form, and in brilliancy of colours, these wonderful masses surpassed everything I had imagined; and we found endless amusement in watching their fantastic procession.

At one time it was a knight on horseback, clad in sapphire mail, a white plume above his casque. Or a cathedral window with shafts of chrysophras, new powdered by a snowstorm. Or a smooth sheer cliff of lapis lazuli; or a Banyan tree, with roots descending from its branches, and a foliage as delicate as the efflorescence of molten metal; or a fairy dragon, that breasted the water in scales of emerald; or anything else that your fancy chose to conjure up. After a little time, the mist again descended on the scene, and dulled each glittering form to a shapeless mass of white; while in spite of all our endeavours to keep upon our northerly course, we were constantly compelled to turn and wind about in every direction—sometimes standing on for several hours at a stretch to the southward and eastward.

But why should I weary you with the detail of our various manœuvres during the ensuing days? they were too tedious and disheartening at the time for me to look back at them with any pleasure. Suffice it to say, that by dint of sailing north whenever the ice would permit us, and sailing west when we could not sail north,—we found ourselves on the 2d of August, in the latitude of the southern extremity of Spitzbergen, though divided from the land by about fifty miles of ice. All this while the weather had been pretty good, foggy and cold enough, but with a fine stiff breeze that rattled us along at a good rate whenever we did get a chance of making any Northing. But lately it had come on to blow very hard, the cold became quite piercing, and what was worse—in every direction round the whole circuit of the horizon, except along its southern segment,—a blaze of iceblink illuminated the sky. A more discouraging spectacle could not have met our eyes. The iceblink is a luminous appearance, reflected on the heavens from the fields of ice that still lie sunk beneath the horizon; it was therefore on this occasion an unmistakable indication of the encumbered state of the sea in front of us.

I had turned in for a few hours of rest, and release from the monotonous sense of disappointment, and was already lost in a dream of deep bewildering bays of ice, and gulfs whose shifting shores offered to the eye every possible combination of uncomfortable scenery, without possible issue, —when "a voice in my dreaming ear" shouted "*Land!*" and I awoke to its reality. I need not tell you in what double quick time I tumbled up the companion,—or with what greediness I feasted my eyes on that longed-for view,—the only sight—as I then thought—we were ever distined to enjoy of the mountains of Spitzbergen!

The whole heaven was overcast with a dark mantle of tempestuous clouds, that stretched down in umbrella-like points towards the horizon, leaving a clear space between their edge and the sea, illuminated by the sinister brilliancy of the iceblink. In an easterly direction, this belt of unclouded atmosphere was etherealized to an indescribable transparency, and up into it there gradually grew—above the dingy line of starboard ice—a forest of thin lilac peaks, so faint, so pale, that had it not been for the gem-like distinctness of their outline, one could have deemed them as unsubstantial as the spires of fairyland. The beautiful vision proved only too transient; in one short half hour mist and cloud had blotted it all out, while a fresh barrier of ice compelled us to turn our backs on the very land we were striving to reach.

It was one o'clock in the morning of the 6th of August, 1856, that after having been eleven days at sea, we came to an anchor in the silent haven of English Bay, Spitzbergen.

And now, how shall I give you an idea of the wonderful panorama in the midst of which we found ourselves? I think, perhaps, its most striking feature was the stillness—and deadness—and impossibility of this new world; ice, and rock, and water surrounded us; not a sound of any kind interrupted the silence; the sea did not break upon the shore; no bird or any living thing was visible; the midnight sun—by this time muffled in a transparent mist—shed an awful, mysterious lustre on glacier and mountain; no atom of vegetation gave token of the earth's vitality; an universal numbness and dumbness seemed to pervade the solitude. I suppose in scarcely any other part of the world is this appearance of deadness so strikingly exhibited.

On the stillest summer day in England, there is always perceptible an undertone of life thrilling through the atmosphere; and though no breeze should stir a single leaf, yet—in default of motion—there is always a sense of growth; but here not so much as a blade of grass was to be seen, on the sides of the bald, excoriated hills. Primeval rocks—and eternal ice—constitute the landscape.

Letters from High Latitudes (London, 1859).

IN ANTARCTIC SEAS

W. G. BURN MURDOCH

DAYS such as this are few in a lifetime, so full of interest has it been, and so fatiguing. Since early morning, rather since yesterday, for there was no night and no morning, we have been constantly marvelling at most astonishing and beautiful spectacles. We have been bathed in red blood, and for hours and hours we have rowed in the boats and plunged over miles of soft snow dragging seal-skins, and I have been drawing hard in the times between the boat excursions; but the air is exhilarating, and we feel equal to almost any amount of work. Sun and snow-showers alternate—fine hard snow it is, that makes our faces burn as if before a fire. It is very cold sketching, and incidents and effects follow each other so rapidly that there is time to make little more than mental notes.

Christmas Eve.

Those who have felt the peace of a summer night in Norway or Iceland, where the day sleeps with wide-open eyes, can fancy the quiet beauty of such a night among the white floes of the Antarctic.

To-day has passed, glistering in silky white, decked with sparkling jewels of blue and green, and we thought surely we had seen the last of Nature's white harmonies;

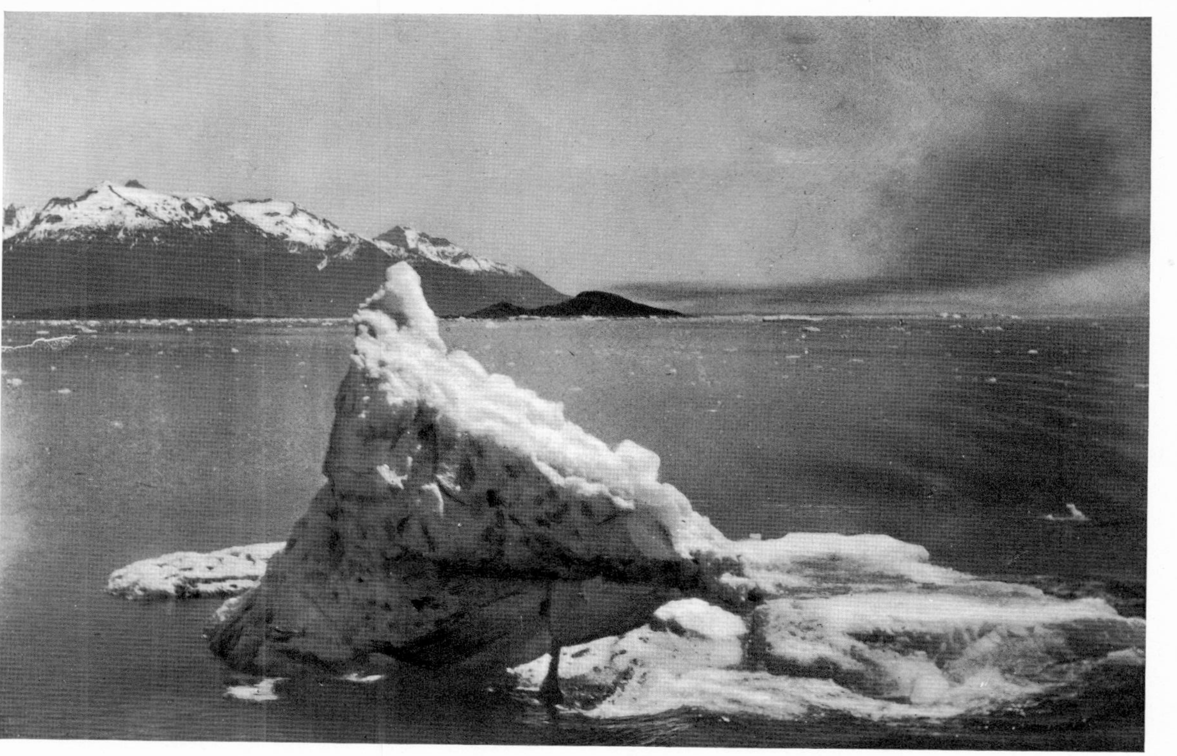

ICE FLOE, ANTARCTIC.

then evening came, pensive and soothing and grey, and all the white world changed into soft violet, pale yellow, and rose.

A dreamy stillness fills the air. To the south the sun has dipped behind a bank of pale grey cloud, and the sky above is touched with primrose light. Far to the north the dark, smooth sea is bounded by two low bergs, that stretch across the horizon. The nearest is cold violet white, and the sunlight strikes the furthest, making it shine like a wall of gold. The sky above them is of a leaden peacock blue, with rosy cloudlets hanging against it—such colouring as I have never before seen or heard described. To the westward, across the gulf, we can just distinguish the blue-black crags jutting from the snowy lomonds. Little clouds touched with gold and rose lie nestling in the black corries, and gather round the snowy peaks. To the south, in the centre of the floe, some bergs lie, cold and grey in the shadow of the bank of cloud. They look like Greek temples imprisoned forever in a field of snow. A faint cold air comes stealing to us over the floe; it ripples the yellow sky reflection at the ice-edge for a moment, and falls away. In the distance a seal is barking—a low muffled sound that travels far over the calm water, and occasionally a slight splash breaks the silence, as a piece of snow separates from the field and joins its companion pieces that are floating quietly past our stern to the north,—a mysterious, silent procession of soft, white spirits, each perfectly reflected in the lavender sea.

Nature sleeps—breathlessly—silent; perhaps she dreams

of the spirit-world, that seems to draw so close to her on such a night.

By midnight the tired crew were all below and sound asleep in their stuffy bunks. But the doctor and I found it impossible to leave the quiet decks and the mysterious daylight, so we prowled about and brewed coffee in the deserted galley. Then we watched the sun pass behind the grey bergs in the south for a few seconds, and appear again, refreshed, with a cool silvery light. A few flakes of snow floated in the clear, cold air, and two snowy petrels, white as the snow itself, flitted along the ice-edge.

A cold, dreamy, white Christmas morning,—beautiful beyond expression.

From Edinburgh to the Antarctic—An Artist's Notes and Sketches during the Dundee Antarctic Expedition of 1892-3 (London, 1894).

THE DESERT OF SAHARA

EUGENE FROMENTIN

THE Saharans adore their country,[1] and, for my part, I should come very near justifying a sentiment so impassioned, especially when it is mingled with the attachment to one's native soil. . . . It is a land without grace or softness, but it is severe, which is not an evil though its first effect is to make one serious—an effect that many people confound with weariness. A great land of hills expiring in a still greater flat land bathed in eternal light; empty and desolate enough, to give the idea of that surprising thing called the desert; with a sky almost always

[1] The word Sahara does not necessarily convey the idea of a desert immensity. Inhabited at certain points, it is called *Fiafi;* habitable at certain others, it takes the name of *Kifar*, a word whose signification is the same as that of the common word *Khela, abandoned;* habitable and inhabited at yet other points, it is called *Falat.*

These three words represent each of the characteristics of the Sahara.

Fiafi is the oasis where life retires, about the fountains and wells, under the palms and fruit trees, sheltered from the sun and *choub* (simoon).

Kifar is the sandy and void plain, which, however, when fertilized for a moment by the winter rains, is covered with grass (*a' cheb*) in the spring; and the nomadic tribes that ordinarily camp around the oases go thither to pasture their flocks.

Falat, finally, is the sterile and bare immensity, the sea of sand, whose eternal billows, to-day agitated by the *choub*, to-morrow will lie in motionless heaps;—the sea that is slowly ploughed by those fleets called caravans. —General Daumas, *Le Sahara Algérien.*

the same, silence, and on all sides a tranquil horizon. In the centre a kind of lost city, surrounded by solitude; then a little verdure, sandy islets, and, lastly, a few reefs of whitish calcareous stone or black schists on the margin of an expanse that resembles the sea;—in all this, but little variety, few accidents, few novelties, unless it be the sun that rises over the desert and sinks behind the hills, ever calm, rayless but devouring; or perhaps the banks of sand that have changed their place and form under the last wind from the South. Brief dawns, longer noons that are heavier than elsewhere, and scarcely any twilight; sometimes a sudden expansion of light and warmth with burning winds that momentarily give the landscape a menacing physiognomy and that may then produce crushing sensations; but more usually a radiant immobility, the somewhat mournful fixity of fine weather, in short, a kind of impassibility that seems to have fallen from the sky upon lifeless things and from them to have passed into human faces.

The first impression received from this ardent and inanimate picture, composed of sun, expanse, and solitude, is acute and cannot be compared with any other. However, little by little, the eye grows accustomed to the grandeur of the lines, the emptiness of the space, and the nakedness of the earth, and if one is still astonished at anything, it is at still remaining sensible to such slightly changing effects and at being so deeply stirred by what are in reality the most simple sights.

Here the sky is clear, arid, and unchanging; it comes in contact with fawn-coloured or white ground, and maintains

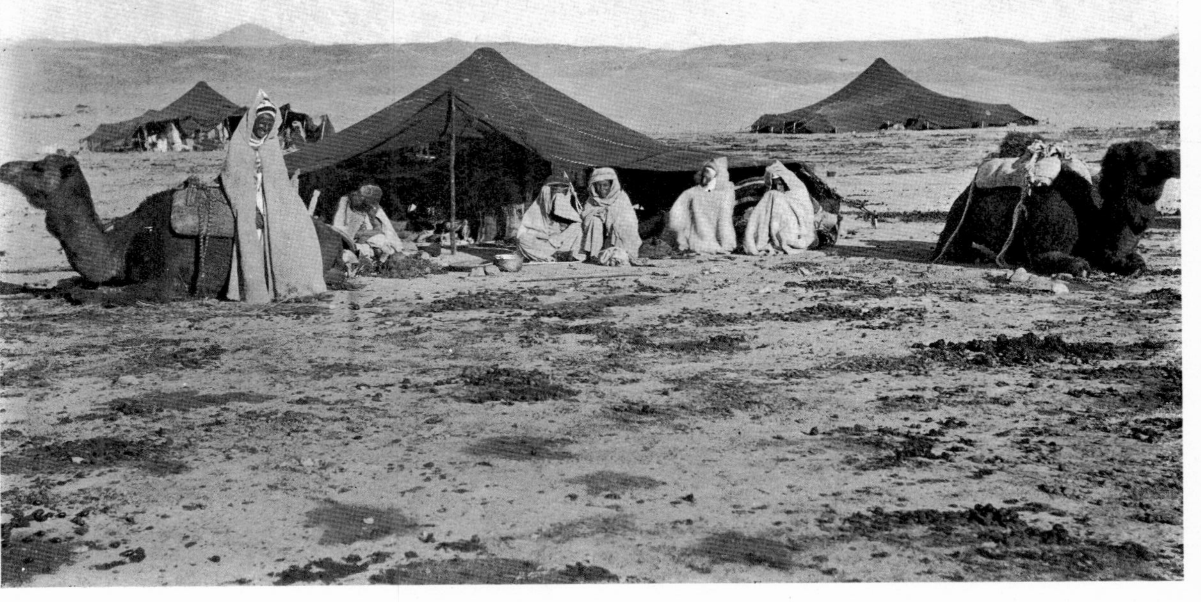

THE DESERT OF SAHARA.

a frank blue in its utmost extent; and when it puts on gold opposite the setting sun its base is violet and almost leaden-hued. I have not seen any beautiful mirages. Except during the sirocco, the horizon is always distinctly visible and detached from the sky; there is only a final streak of ash-blue which is vigorously defined in the morning, but in the middle of the day is somewhat confounded with the sky and seems to tremble in the fluidity of the atmosphere. Directly to the South, a great way off towards M'zab, an irregular line formed by groves of tamarinds is visible. A faint mirage, that is produced every day in this part of the desert, makes these groves appear nearer and larger; but the illusion is not very striking and one needs to be told in order to notice it.

Shortly after sunrise the whole country is rosy, a vivid rose, with depths of peach colour; the town is spotted with points of shadow, and some little white argils, scattered along the edge of the palms, gleam gaily enough in this mournful landscape which for a short moment of freshness seems to smile at the rising sun. In the air are vague sounds and a suggestion of singing that makes us understand that every country in the world has its joyous awakening.

Then, almost at the same moment every day, from the south we hear the approach of innumerable twitterings of birds. They are the *gangas* coming from the desert to drink at the springs. . . . It is then half-past six. One hour later and the same cries suddenly arise in the north; the same flocks pass over my head one by one, in the same numbers and order, and regain their desert plains. One might say that the morning is ended; and the sole smiling hour of the day has passed between the going and returning of the *gangas*. The landscape that was rose has already become dun; the town has far fewer little shadows; it greys as the sun gets higher; in proportion as it shines brighter the desert seems to darken; the hills alone remain rosy. If there was any wind it dies away; warm exhalations begin to spread in the air as if they were from the sands. Two hours later all movement ceases at once, and noontide commences.

The sun mounts and is finally directly over my head. I have only the narrow shelter of my parasol and there I gather myself together; my feet rest in the sand or on glittering stones; my pad curls up beside me under the sun; my box of colours crackles like burning wood. Not a sound is heard now. There are four hours of incredible calm and stupor. The town sleeps below me then dumb and looking like a mass of violet with its empty terraces upon which the sun illumines a multitude of screens full of little rose apricots, exposed there to dry;—here and there a black hole marks a window, or an interior door, and fine lines of dark violet show that there are only one or two strips of shadow in the whole town. A fillet of stronger light that edges the contour of the terraces helps us to distinguish these mud edifices from one another, piled as they are rather than built upon their three hills.

On all sides of the town extends the oasis, also dumb and slumbrous under the heavy heat of the day. It looks quite small and presses close against the two flanks of the town with an air of wanting to defend it at need rather than to entice it. I can see the whole of it: it resembles two squares of leaves enveloped by a long wall like a park, roughly drawn upon the sterile plain. Although divided by compartments into a multitude of little orchards, also all enclosed within walls, seen from this height it looks like a green tablecloth; no tree is distinguishable, two stages of forest only can be remarked: the first, round-headed clumps; the second, clusters of palms. At intervals some meagre patches of barley, only the stubble of which now remains, form shorn spaces of brilliant yellow amid the foliage; elsewhere in rare glades a dry, powdery, and ash-coloured ground shows. Finally, on the south side, a few mounds of sand, heaped by the wind, have passed over the surrounding wall; it is the desert trying to invade the gardens. The trees do not move; in the forest thickets we divine certain sombre gaps in which birds may be supposed to be hidden, sleeping until their second awakening in the evening.

This is also the hour when the desert is transformed into an obscure plain. The sun, suspended over its centre, inscribes upon it a circle of light the equal rays of which fall full upon it in all ways and everywhere at the same time. There is no longer any clearness or shadow; the perspective indicated by the fleeting colours almost ceases to measure distances; everything is covered with a brown tone, continuous without streaks or mixture; there are fifteen or twenty leagues of country as uniform and flat as a flooring.

It seems that the most minute salient object should be visible upon it, and yet the eye discerns nothing there; one could not even say now where there is sand, earth, or stony places, and the immobility of this solid sea then becomes more striking than ever. On seeing it start at our feet and then stretch away and sink towards the South, the East, and the West without any traced route or inflexion, we ask ourselves what may be this silent land clothed in a doubtful tone that seems the colour of the void; whence no one comes, whither no one goes, and which ends in so straight and clear a strip against the sky;—we do not know; we feel that it does not end there and that it is, so to speak, only the entrance to the high sea.

Then add to all these reveries the fame of the names we have seen upon the map, of places that we know to be there, in such or such direction, at five, ten, twenty, fifty days' march, some known, others only indicated and yet others more and more obscure. . . . Then the negro country, the edge of which we only know; two or three names of towns with a capital for a kingdom; lakes, forests, a great sea on the left, perhaps great rivers, extraordinary inclemencies under the equator, strange products, monstrous animals, hairy sheep, elephants, and what then? Nothing more distinct; unknown distances, an uncertainty, an enigma. Before me I have the beginning of this enigma and the spectacle is strange beneath this clear noonday sun. Here is where I should like to see the Egyptian Sphinx.

It is vain to gaze around, far or near; no moving thing can be distinguished. Sometimes by chance, a little convoy of laden camels appears, like a row of blackish points, slowly mounting the sandy slopes; we only perceive them when they reach the foot of the hills. They are travellers; who are they? whence come they? Without our perceiving them, they have crossed the whole horizon beneath our eyes. Or perhaps it is a spout of sand which suddenly detaches itself from the surface like a fine smoke, rises into a spiral, traverses a certain space bending under the wind and then evaporates after a few seconds.

The day passes slowly; it ends as it began with half rednesses, an amber sky, depths assuming colour, long oblique flames which will empurple the mountains, the sands and the eastern rocks in their turn; shadows take possession of that side of the land that has been fatigued by the heat during the first half of the day; everything seems to be somewhat comforted. The sparrows and turtle-doves begin to sing among the palms; there is a movement as of resurrection in the town; people show themselves on the terraces and come to shake the sieves; the voices of animals are heard in the squares, horses neighing as they are taken to water and camels bellowing; the desert looks like a plate of gold; the sun sinks over the violet mountains and the night makes ready to fall.

Un Été dans le Sahara (Paris, 1857).

FINGAL'S CAVE

SIR WALTER SCOTT

July 19, 1810.

YESTERDAY we visited Staffa and Iona: the former is one of the most extraordinary places I ever beheld. It exceeded, in my mind, every description I had heard of it; or rather, the appearance of the cavern, composed entirely of basaltic pillars as high as the roof of a cathedral,[1] and the running deep into the rock, eternally swept by a deep and swelling sea, and paved as it were with ruddy

[1] "——that wondrous dome,
Where, as to shame the temples deck'd
By skill of earthly architect,
Nature herself, it seem'd, would raise,
A minster to her Maker's praise!
Not for a meaner use ascend
Her columns, or her arches bend;
Nor of a theme less solemn tells
That mighty surge that ebbs and swells,
And still, beneath each awful pause
From the high vault an answer draws,
In varied tone prolonged and high
That mocks the organ's melody.
Nor doth its entrance front in vain
To old Iona's holy fane,
That Nature's voice might seem to say,
'Well hast thou done, frail Child of clay!
Thy humble powers that stately shrine
Task'd high and hard—but witness mine!'"

Lord of the Isles. Canto IV. St. 10.

FINGAL'S CAVE.

marble, baffles all description. You can walk along the broken pillars, with some difficulty, and in some places with a little danger, as far as the farthest extremity. Boats also can come in below when the sea is placid,—which is seldom the case. I had become a sort of favourite with the Hebridean boatmen, I suppose from my anxiety about their old customs, and they were much pleased to see me get over the obstacles which stopped some of the party. So they took the whim of solemnly christening a great stone at the mouth of the cavern, Clachan-an Bairdh, or the Poet's Stone. It was consecrated with a pibroch, which the echoes rendered tremendous, and a glass of whisky, not poured forth in the ancient mode of libation, but turned over the throats of the assistants. The head boatman, whose father had been himself a bard, made me a speech on the occasion; but as it was in Gaelic, I could only receive it as a silly beauty does a fine-spun compliment—bow, and say nothing.

When this fun was over (in which, strange as it may seem, the men were quite serious), we went to Iona, where there are some ancient and curious monuments. From this remote island the light of Christianity shone forth on Scotland and Ireland. The ruins are of a rude architecture, but curious to the antiquary. Our return was less comfortable; we had to row twenty miles against an Atlantic tide and some wind, besides the pleasure of seeing occasional squalls gathering to windward. The ladies were sick, especially poor Hannah Mackenzie, and none of the gentlemen escaped except Staffa and myself. The men, however, cheered by the pipes, and by their own interesting boat-songs, which were uncommonly wild and beautiful, one man leading and the others answering in chorus, kept pulling away without apparently the least sense of fatigue, and we reached Ulva at ten at night, tolerably wet, and well disposed for bed.

The haze and dullness of the atmosphere seem to render it dubious if we can proceed, as we intended, to Staffa to-day—for mist among these islands is rather unpleasant. Erskine reads prayers on deck to all hands, and introduces a very apt allusion to our being now in sight of the first Christian Church from which Revelation was diffused over Scotland and all its islands. There is a very good form of prayer for the Lighthouse Service composed by the Rev. Mr. Brunton. A pleasure vessel lies under our lee from Belfast, with an Irish party related to Macneil of Colonsay. The haze is fast degenerating into downright rain, and that right heavy—verifying the words of Collins —

> "And thither where beneath the *showery west*
> The mighty Kings of three fair realms are laid." [1]

After dinner, the weather being somewhat cleared, sailed for Staffa, and took boat. The surf running heavy up between the island and the adjacent rock, called Booshala, we landed at a creek near the Cormorant's cave. The mist now returned so thick as to hide all view of Iona, which was our landmark; and although Duff, Stevenson, and I, had been formerly on the isle, we could not agree upon the

[1] *Ode on the Superstitions of the Highlands.*

FINGAL'S CAVE

JOHN KEATS

I AM puzzled how to give you an Idea of Staffa. It can only be represented by a first-rate drawing. One may compare the surface of the Island to a roof—this roof is supported by grand pillars of basalt standing together as thick as honeycombs. The finest thing is Fingal's Cave—it is entirely a hollowing out of Basalt Pillars. Suppose now the Giants who rebelled against Jove had taken a whole Mass of black Columns and bound them together like bunches of matches—and then with immense axes had made a cavern in the body of these columns —— Of course the roof and floor must be composed of broken ends of the Columns—such is Fingal's Cave, except that the Sea has done the work of excavations, and is continually dashing there—so that we walk along the sides of the cave on the pillars which are left as if for convenient stairs. The roof is arched somewhat gothic-wise, and the length of some of the entire side-pillars is fifty feet. About the island you might seat an army of Men each on a pillar. The length of the cave is 120 feet, and from its extremity the view into the sea, through the large Arch at the entrance—the colour of the columns is a sort of black with a lurking gloom of purple therein. For solemnity and grandeur it terror—with which the scenes to which he is introduced fully correspond. On the other hand the dazzling whiteness of the incrustations in Macallister's Cave, the elegance of the entablature, the beauty of its limpid pool, and the graceful dignity of its arch, render its leading features those of severe and chastened beauty. Staffa, the third of these subterranean wonders, may challenge sublimity as its principal characteristic. Without the savage gloom of the Smowe cave, and investigated with more apparent ease, though, perhaps, with equal real danger, the stately regularity of its columns forms a contrast to the grotesque imagery of Macallister's Cave, combining at once the sentiments of grandeur and beauty. The former is, however, predominant, as it must necessarily be in any scene of the kind.

We had scarce left Staffa when the wind and rain returned.

Lockhart, *Life of Sir Walter Scott* (Edinburgh, 1878).

table. Here we were under the necessity of towing our Commodore, Hamilton, whose gallant heart never fails him, whatever the tenderness of his toes may do. He was successfully lowered by a rope down the precipice, and proceeding along the flat terrace or causeway already mentioned, we reached the celebrated cave. I am not sure whether I was not more affected by this second, than by the first view of it. The stupendous columnar side walls—the depth and strength of the ocean with which the cavern is filled—the variety of tints formed by stalactites dropping and petrifying between the pillars, and resembling a sort of chasing of yellow or cream-coloured marble filling the interstices of the roof—the corresponding variety below, where the ocean rolls over a red, and in some places a violet-coloured rock, the basis of the basaltic pillars—the dreadful noise of those august billows so well corresponding with the grandeur of the scene—are all circumstances elsewhere unparalleled. We have now seen in our voyage the three grandest caverns in Scotland,—Smowe, Macallister's Cave, and Staffa; so that, like the Troglodytes of yore, we may be supposed to know something of the matter. It is, however, impossible to compare scenes of natures so different, nor, were I compelled to assign a preference to any of the three, could I do it but with reference to their distinct characters, which might affect different individuals in different degrees. The characteristic of the Smowe cave may in this case be called the terrific, for the difficulties which oppose the stranger are of a nature so uncommonly wild, as, for the first time at least, to convey an impression of proper road to the cave. I engaged myself, with Duff and Erskine, in a clamber of great toil and danger, and which at length brought me to the *Cannon-ball*, as they call a round granite stone moved by the sea up and down in a groove of rock, which it has worn for itself, with a noise resembling thunder. Here I gave up my research, and returned to my companions, who had not been more fortunate. As night was now falling, we resolved to go aboard and postpone the adventure of the enchanted cavern until next day. The yacht came to an anchor with the purpose of remaining off the island all night, but the hardness of the ground, and the weather becoming squally, obliged us to return to our safer mooring at Y-Columb-Kill.

29th August, 1814.

Night squally and rainy—morning ditto—we weigh, however, and return towards Staffa, and, very happily, the day clears as we approach the isle. As we ascertained the situation of the cave, I shall only make this memorandum, that when the weather will serve, the best landing is to the lee of Booshala, a little conical islet or rock, composed of basaltic columns placed in an oblique or sloping position. In this way, you land at once on the flat causeway, formed by the heads of truncated pillars, which leads to the cave. But if the state of tide renders it impossible to land under Booshala, then take one of the adjacent creeks; in which case, keeping to the left hand along the top of the ledge of rocks which girdles in the isle, you find a dangerous and precipitous descent to the causeway aforesaid, from the far surpasses the finest Cathedral. At the extremity of the Cave there is a small perforation into another cave, at which the waters meeting and buffeting each other there is sometimes produced a report as of a cannon heard as far as Iona, which must be twelve Miles. As we approached in the boat, there was such a fine swell of the sea that the pillars appeared rising immediately out of the crystal. But it is impossible to describe it —

Not Aladdin magian
Ever such a work began.
Not the Wizard of the Dee
Ever such a dream could see,
Not St. John in Patmos Isle
In the passion of his toil
When he saw the churches seven
Golden-aisled built up in heaven
Gaz'd at such a rugged wonder.
As I stood its roofing under
Lo! I saw one sleeping there
On the marble cold and bare.
While the surges wash'd his feet
And his garments white did beat
Drench'd about the sombre rocks,
On his neck his well-grown locks
Lifted dry above the Main
Were upon the curl again —
"What is this? and what art thou?"
Whisper'd I, and touch'd his brow;
"What art thou? and what is this?"
Whisper'd I, and strove to kiss
The, Spirit's hand, to wake his eyes;
Up he started in a trice:
"I am Lycidas," said he
"Fam'd in funeral Minstrelsy —
This was architected thus
By the great Oceanus.

Here his mighty waters play
Hollow Organs all the day,
Here, by turns, his dolphins all,
Finny palmers great and small,
Come to pay devotion due —
Each a mouth of pearls must strew!
Many a mortal of these days
Dares to pass our sacred ways,
Dares to touch, audaciously
This Cathedral of the sea —
I have been the Pontiff-priest,
Where the Waters never rest,
Where a fledgy sea-bird choir
Soars for ever—holy fire
I have hid from Mortal Man.
Proteus is my Sacristan
But the stupid eye of Mortal
Hath pass'd beyond the Rocky portal,
So for ever will I leave
Such a taint and soon unweave
All the magic of the place —
'Tis now free to stupid face —
To cutters and to fashion boats,
To cravats and Petticoats.
The great Sea shall war it down,
For its fame shall not be blown
At every farthing quadrille dance."
So saying with a Spirit's glance
He dived —

I am sorry I am so indolent as to write such stuff as this. It can't be helped. The western coast of Scotland is a most strange place—it is composed of rocks, mountains, mountainous and rocky islands intersected by lochs—you can go but a short distance anywhere from salt water in the highlands.

Letters of John Keats (London and New York, 1891).

IN THE HIMALAYAS

G. W. STEEVENS

IN Calcutta they grumbled that the hot weather was beginning already. Mornings were steamy, days sticky, and the municipal impurities rose rankly. The carter squatted over his bullocks with his shining body stark naked but for a loin-cloth.

At Siliguri, the bottom of the ascent to Darjiling, the rough grass and the tea-gardens were sheeted at sunrise in a silver frost. What few natives appeared happed their heads in shawls as if they had toothache.

It takes you an afternoon and a night to get as far as Siliguri. What you principally notice on the way is the dullness of the flat, moist richness of Bengal, and the extraordinary fullness of the first-class carriages. Even at this winter season the residents of Calcutta snatch at the chance of being cold for twenty-four hours. When you get out of your carriage at the junction station, you see on the other side of the platform a dumpy little toy train—a train at the wrong end of a telescope with its wheels cut from beneath it. Engines and trucks and carriages seem to be crawling like snakes on their bellies. Six miniature easy-chairs, three facing three, on an open truck with an awning, make a first-class carriage.

This is the Darjiling-Himalaya Railway—two-foot gauge, climbing four feet to the hundred for fifty miles up the foothills of the greatest mountains in the world. It is extraordinary as the only line in India that has been built with Indian capital. But you will find that the least of its wonders. A flat-faced hillman bangs with a hammer twice three times on a spare bit of railway metal hung up by way of a gong, the whistle screams, and you pant away on surely the most entrancing railway journey in the world. Nothing very much to make your heart jump in the first seven miles. You bowl along the surface of a slightly ascending cart-load, and your view is mostly bamboo and tea. Graceful enough, and cool to the eye—the bamboos, hedges or clumps of slender stem with plumes of pale leaf swinging and nodding above them; the tea, trim ranks and files of short, well-furnished bushes with lustrous, dark-green leaves, not unlike evergreens or myrtle in a nursery at home,—but you soon feel that you have known bamboo and tea all your life. Then suddenly you begin to climb, and all at once you are in a new world—a world of plants.

A new world is easy to say, but this is new indeed and a very world—such a primeval vegetable world as you have read of in books and eked out with dreams. It has everything you know in your world, only everything expressed in vegetation. It is a world in its variety alone. Trees of every kind rise up round you at every angle—unfamiliar, most of them, and exaggerations of forms you know, as if they were seen through a microscope. You might come on such broad fleshy leaves by way of Jack's giant bean-

THE HIMALAYAS.

stalk. Other growths take the form of bushes as high as our trees; but beside them are skinny, stunted starvelings, such as the most niggardly country might show. Then there are grasses—tufted, ruddy bamboo grass, and huge yellow straws with giant bents leaning insolently over to flick your face as you go by. Smaller still grow the ferns, lurking shyly in the crevices of the banks. And over everything, most luxuriant of everything, crawl hundred-armed creepers, knitting and knotting the whole jungle into one mellay of struggling life.

The varieties—the trees and shrubs and grasses and ferns and creepers—you would see in any tropical garden; but you could not see them at home. You could not see them in their unpruned native intercourse one with the other. The rise and fall of the ground, the whims of light and air, coax them into shapes that answer to the most fantastic imagination. Now you are going through the solemn aisles of a great cathedral—grey trunks for columns, with arches and vaulted roofs of green, with dark, retreating chapels and altar-trappings of mingled flowers. Now it is a king's banqueting-hall, tapestried with white-flowering creeper and crimson and purple bougainvillea; overhead the scarlet-mahogany blossoms of a sparse-leaved tulip-tree might be butterflies frescoed on a ceiling.

Fancy can compel the wilderness into moments of order, but wild it remains. The growths are not generally buildings, but animate beings in a real world. You see no perfectly shaped tree, as in a park or garden; one is warped, another stunted, another bare below—each formed, like men, by the pressure of a thousand fellows. Here is a corpse spreading white, stark arms abroad. Here are half-a-dozen young creatures rolling over each other like puppies at play. And there is a creeper flinging tumultuous, enraptured arms round a stately tree; presently it is gripping it in thick bands like Laocöon's serpent, then choking it mercilessly to death, then dead itself, its bleached, bare streamers dangling limply in the wind. It is life, indeed, this forest—plants fighting, victorious and vanquished; loving and getting children; springing and waxing and decaying and dying—our own world of men translated into plants.

While I am spinning similitudes, the Darjiling-Himalaya Railway is panting always upwards, boring through the thick world of trees like a mole. Now it sways round a curve so short that you can almost look back into the next carriage, and you understand why the wheels are so low. Now it stops dead, and almost before it stops starts backwards up a zigzag, then forwards up another, and on again. In a moment it is skating on the brink of a slide of shale that trembles to come down and overwhelm it; next it is rumbling across a bridge above the point it passed ten minutes ago, and also that which it will reach ten minutes hence. Twisting, backing, circling, dodging, but always rising, it untreads the skein whose end is in the clouds and the snows.

Presently the little engine draws quite clear of the jungle. You skirt opener slopes, and the blue plain below is no longer a fleeting vista, but a broad prospect. You see how the forest spills itself on to the fields and spreads into a dark puddle over their lightness. You see a great river overlaying the dimness with a ribbon of steel. The ferns grow thicker about you; gigantic fronds bow at you from gullies overhead, and you see the tree-fern—a great crown of drooping green on a trunk of a man's height—standing superbly alone, knowing its supreme gracefulness. Next, as you rise and rise, the air gets sharp; through a gauzy veil of mist appear again huge forests, but dark and gloomy with brown moss dripping dankly from every branch. Rising, rising, and you have now come to Ghoom, the highest point. Amid the cold fog appears the witch of Ghoom—a hundred years old, with a pointed chin and mop of grizzled hair all witch-fashion, but beaming genially and requesting backsheesh.

Then round a corner—and here is Darjiling. A scattered settlement on a lofty ridge, facing a great cup enclosed by other ridges—mountains elsewhere, here hills. Long spurs run down into the hollow, half black with forest, half pale and veined with many paths. At the bottom is a little chequer of fresh green millet; the rim at the top seems to line the sky.

And the Himalayas and the eternal snows? The devil a Himalaya in sight. Thick vapours dip down and over the very rim of the cup; beyond Darjiling is a tumult of peaked creamy cloud. You need not be told it,—clouds that hide mountains always ape their shapes,—the majestic Himalayas are behind that screen, and you will not see them to-day, nor perhaps to-morrow, nor yet for a fortnight of to-morrows.

You must console yourself with Darjiling and the hillmen. And Darjiling is pleasant to the eye as you look down on it, a huddle of grey corrugated-iron roofs, one stepping over the other, hugging the hillside with one or two red ones to break the monotone. There is no continuous line of them: each stands by itself in a ring of deep green first. The place is cool and grateful after an Indian town—clean and roomy, a place of homes and not of pens.

In the middle of it is the bazaar, and my day, by luck, was market-day. Here, again, you could never fancy yourself in India. A few Hindus there are, but beside the dumpy hillmen their thin limbs, tiny features, and melting eyes seem hardly human. More like the men you know is the Tibetan, with a long profile and long, sharp nose, though his hat has the turned-up brim of the Chinese, though he wears a long bottle-green dressing-gown open to the girdle, and his pigtail knocks at the back of his knees. But the prevailing type, though as Mongolian, is far more genial than the Tibetan. Squat little men, for the most part, fill the bazaar, with broad faces that give room for the features, with button noses, and slits for eyes. They wear boots and putties, or gaiters made of many-coloured carpet-bagging; and their women are like them—with shawls over their heads, and broad sashes swathing them from bosom to below the waist, with babies slung behind their backs, not astride on the hip as are the spawn of India. Their eyes are black as sloes—puckered, too, but seeming puckered with laughter; and their clear yellow skins are actually rosy on the cheeks, like a ripe apricot. Square-faced, longpigtailed, plump, cheery, open of gaze, and easy of carriage, rolling cigarettes, and offering them to soothe babies—they might not be beautiful in Europe; here they are ravishing.

But you come to Darjiling to see the snows. So on a night of agonizing cold—feet and hands a block of ice the moment you cease to move them—must follow a rise before it is light. Maybe the clouds will be kinder this morning. No; the same stingy, clammy mist,—only there, breaking through it, high up in the sky—yes, there are a few faint streaks of white. Just a few marks of snow scored on the softer white of the cloud, chill with the utterly disconsolate cold of ice through a window of fog. Still, there are certainly Himalayas there.

Up and up I toiled; the sun was plainly rising behind the ridge of Darjiling. In the cup below the sunlight was drawing down the hillsides and peeling off the twilight. Then, at a sudden turn of the winding ascent, I saw the summit of Kinchinjunga. Just the summit, poised in the blue, shining and rejoicing in the sunrise. And as I climbed and climbed, other peaks rose into sight below and beside him, all dazzling white, mounting and mounting the higher I mounted, every instant more huge and towering and stately, boring into the sky.

Up—till I came to the summit, and the sun appeared—a golden ball swimming in a sea of silver. He was sending the clouds away curling before him; they drifted across the mountains, but he pursued and smote and dissolved them. And ever the mountains rose and rose, huger and huger; as they swelled up they heaved the clouds away in rolls off their shoulders. Now their waists were free, and all but their feet. Only a chasm of fog still hid their lower slopes. Fifty miles away, they looked as if I could toss a stone across to them; only you could never hope to hit their heads, they towered so gigantically. Now the clouds, clearing to right and left, laid bare a battlemented range of snow-white wall barring the whole horizon. Behind these appeared other peaks; it was not a range, but a country of mountains, not now a wall, but a four-square castle carved by giants out of eternal ice. It was the end of the world —a sheer rampart, which forbade the fancy of anything beyond.

And in the centre, by peak and col and precipice, the prodigy reared itself up to Kinchinjunga. Bare rock below, then blinding snow seamed with ridges of chimneys, and then, above, the mighty summit—a tremendous three-cornered slab of grey granite between two resplendent faces of snow. Other mountains tiptoe at the sky snatch at it with a peak like a needle. Kinchinjunga heaves himself up into it, broadly, massively, and makes his summit a diadem. He towers without effort, knowing his majesty. Sublime and inviolable, he lifts his grey nakedness and his mail of burnished snow, and turns his forehead serenely to sun and storm. Only their touch, of all things created, has perturbed his solitude since the birth of time.

In India (New York, 1899).

NIAGARA FALLS

ANTHONY TROLLOPE

IT has been said that it matters much from what point the Falls are first seen, but to this I demur. It matters, I think, very little, or not at all. Let the visitor first see it all, and learn the whereabouts of every point, so as to understand his own position and that of the waters; and then having done that in the way of business let him proceed to enjoyment. I doubt whether it be not the best to do this with all sight-seeing. I am quite sure that it is the way in which acquaintance may be best and most pleasantly made with a new picture. The Falls are, as I have said, made by a sudden breach in the level of the river. All cataracts are, I presume, made by such breaches; but generally the waters do not fall precipitously as they do at Niagara, and never elsewhere, as far as the world yet knows, has a breach so sudden been made in such a body of water. Up above the Falls, for more than a mile, the waters leap and burst over rapids, as though conscious of the destiny that awaits them. Here the river is very broad, and comparatively shallow, but from shore to shore it frets itself into little torrents, and begins to assume the majesty of its power. Looking at it even here, one feels sure that no strongest swimmer could have a chance of saving himself, if fate had cast him in even among those petty whirlpools. The waters, though so broken in their descent, are deliciously green. This colour as seen early in the morning, or just as the sun has set, is so bright as to give to the place of its chiefest charms.

This will be best seen from the further end of the island —Goat Island, as it is called, which, as the reader will understand, divides the river immediately above the Falls. Indeed the island is a part of that precipitously broken ledge over which the river tumbles; and no doubt in process of time will be worn away and covered with water. The time, however, will be very long. In the meanwhile it is perhaps a mile round, and is covered thickly with timber. At the upper end of the island the waters are divided, and coming down in two courses, each over its own rapids, form two separate falls. The bridge by which the island is entered is a hundred yards or more above the smaller fall. The waters here have been turned by the island, and make their leap into the body of the river below at a right angle with it,—about two hundred yards below the greater fall. Taken alone this smaller cataract would, I imagine, be the heaviest fall of water known, but taken in conjunction with the other it is terribly shorn of its majesty. The waters here are not green as they are at the larger cataract, and though the ledge has been hollowed and bowed by them so as to form a curve, that curve does not deepen itself into a vast abyss as it does at the horseshoe up above. This smaller fall is again divided, and the visitor passing down a flight of steps and over a frail wooden bridge finds himself on a smaller island in the midst of it.

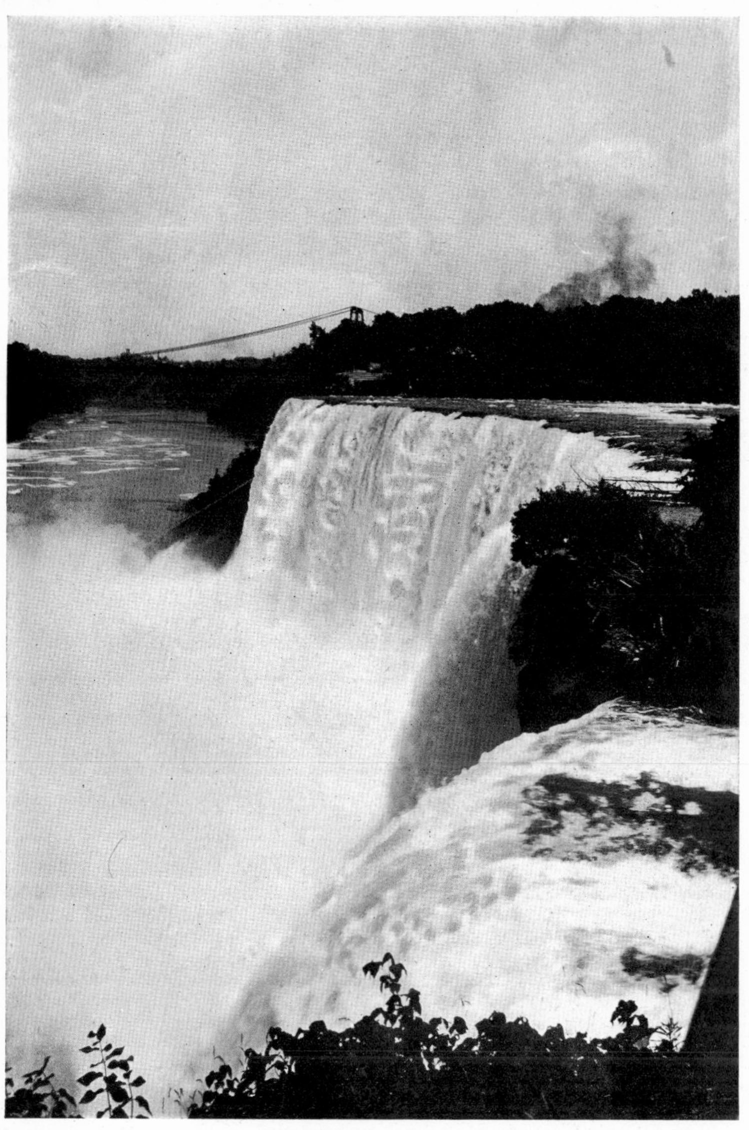

NIAGARA FALLS.

But we will go at once on to the glory, and the thunder, and the majesty, and the wrath of that upper hell of waters. We are still, let the reader remember, on Goat Island, still in the States, and on what is called the American side of the main body of the river. Advancing beyond the path leading down to the lesser fall, we come to that point of the island at which the waters of the main river begin to descend. From hence across to the Canadian side the cataract continues itself in one unabated line. But the line is very far from being direct or straight. After stretching for some little way from the shore, to a point in the river which is reached by a wooden bridge at the end of which stands a tower upon the rock,—after stretching to this, the line of the ledge bends inwards against the flood,—in, and in, and in, till one is led to think that the depth of that horseshoe is immeasurable. It has been cut with no stinting hand. A monstrous cantle has been worn back out of the centre of the rock, so that the fury of the waters converges, and the spectator as he gazes into the hollow with wishful eyes fancies that he can hardly trace out the centre of the abyss.

Go down to the end of that wooden bridge, seat yourself on the rail, and there sit till all the outer world is lost to you. There is no grander spot about Niagara than this. The waters are absolutely around you. If you have that power of eye-control, which is so necessary to the full enjoyment of scenery, you will certainly see nothing but the water. You will certainly hear nothing else; and the sound, I beg you to remember, is not an ear-cracking, agonizing crash and clang of noises; but is melodious and soft withal, though loud as thunder. It fills your ears, and as it were envelops them, but at the same time you can speak to your neighbour without an effort. But at this place, and in these moments, the less of speaking I should say the better. There is no grander spot than this. Here, seated on the rail of the bridge, you will not see the whole depth of the fall. In looking at the grandest works of nature, and of art too, I fancy, it is never well to see all. There should be something left to the imagination, and much should be half-concealed in mystery. The greatest charm of a mountain range is the wild feeling that there must be strange desolate worlds in those far-off valleys beyond. And so here, at Niagara, that converging rush of waters may fall down, down at once into a hell of rivers for what the eye can see. It is glorious to watch them in their first curve over the rocks. They come green as a bank of emeralds; but with a fitful flying colour, as though conscious that in one moment more they would be dashed into spray and rise into air, pale as driven snow. The vapour rises high into the air, and is gathered there, visible always as a permanent white cloud over the cataract; but the bulk of the spray which fills the lower hollow of that horseshoe is like a tumult of snow. This you will not fully see from your seat on the rail. The head of it rises ever and anon out of the caldron below, but the caldron itself will be invisible. It is ever so far down,—far as your own imagination can sink it. But your eyes will rest full upon the curve of the waters.

The shape you will be looking at is that of a horseshoe, but of a horseshoe miraculously deep from toe to heel;—and this depth becomes greater as you sit there. That which at first was only great and beautiful, becomes gigantic and sublime till the mind is at loss to find an epithet for its own use. To realize Niagara you must sit there till you see nothing else than that which you have come to see. You will hear nothing else, and think of nothing else. At length you will be at one with the tumbling river before you. You will find yourself among the waters as though you belonged to them. The cool liquid green will run through your veins, and the voice of the cataract will be the expression of your own heart. You will fall as the bright waters fall, rushing down into your new world with no hesitation and with no dismay; and you will rise again as the spray rises, bright, beautiful, and pure. Then you will flow away in your course to the uncompassed, distant, and eternal ocean.

And now we will cross the water, and with this object will return by the bridge out of Goat Island on the mainland of the American side. But as we do so let me say that one of the great charms of Niagara consists in this,—that over and above that one great object of wonder and beauty, there is so much little loveliness;—loveliness especially of water, I mean. There are little rivulets running here and there over little falls, with pendent boughs above them, and stones shining under their shallow depths. As the visitor stands and looks through the trees the rapids glitter before him, and then hide themselves behind islands. They glitter and sparkle in far distances under the bright foliage till the remembrance is lost, and one knows not which way they run.

Close to the cataract, exactly at the spot from whence in former days the Table Rock used to project from the land over the boiling caldron below, there is now a shaft down which you will descend to the level of the river, and pass between the rock and the torrent. This Table Rock broke away from the cliff and fell, as up the whole course of the river the seceding rocks have split and fallen from time to time through countless years, and will continue to do till the bed of the upper lake is reached. You will descend this shaft, taking to yourself or not taking to yourself a suit of oil-clothes as you may think best.

In the spot to which I allude the visitor stands on a broad safe path, made of shingles, between the rock over which the water rushes. He will go in so far that the spray rising back from the bed of the torrent does not incommode him. With this exception, the further he can go in the better; but circumstances will clearly show him the spot to which he should advance. Unless the water be driven in by a strong wind, five yards make the difference between a comparatively dry coat and an absolutely wet one. And then let him stand with his back to the entrance, thus hiding the last glimmer of the expiring day. So standing he will look up among the falling waters, or down into the deep misty pit, from which they reascend in almost as palpable a bulk. The rock will be at his right hand, high and hard, and dark and straight, like the wall of some huge cavern, such as children enter in their dreams. For the first five minutes he will be looking but at the waters of a cataract,—at the waters, indeed, of such a cataract as we know no other, and at their interior curves which elsewhere we cannot see. But by and by all this will change. He will no longer be on a shingly path beneath a waterfall; but that feeling of a cavern wall will grow upon him, of a cavern deep, below roaring seas, in which the waves are there, though they do not enter in upon him; or rather not the waves, but the very bowels of the ocean. He will feel as though the floods surrounded him, coming and going with their wild sounds, and he will hardly recognize that though among them he is not in them. And they, as they fall with a continual roar, not hurting the ear, but musical withal, will seem to move as the vast ocean waters may perhaps move in their internal currents. He will lose the sense of one continued descent, and think that they are passing round him in their appointed courses. The broken spray that rises from the depth below, rises so strongly, so palpably, so rapidly, that the motion in every direction will seem equal. And, as he looks on, strange colours will show themselves through the mist; the shades of grey will become green or blue, with ever and anon a flash of white; and then, when some gust of wind blows in with greater violence, the sea-girt cavern will become all dark and black. Oh, my friend, let there be no one there to speak to thee then; no, not even a brother. As you stand there speak only to the waters.

North America (London, 1862).

NIAGARA FALLS

CHARLES DICKENS

WE called at the town of Erie, at eight o'clock that night, and lay there an hour. Between five and six next morning, we arrived at Buffalo, where we breakfasted; and being too near the Great Falls to wait patiently anywhere else, we set off by the train, the same morning at nine o'clock, to Niagara.

It was a miserable day; chilly and raw; a damp mist falling; and the trees in that northern region quite bare and wintry. Whenever the train halted, I listened for the roar; and was constantly straining my eyes in the direction where I knew the Falls must be, from seeing the river rolling on towards them; every moment expecting to behold the spray. Within a few moments of our stopping, not before, I saw two great white clouds rising up slowly and majestically from the depths of the earth. That was all. At length we alighted; and then for the first time, I heard the mighty rush of water, and felt the ground tremble underneath my feet.

The bank is very steep, and was slippery with rain, and half-melted ice. I hardly know how I got down, but I was soon at the bottom, and climbing, with two English officers who were crossing and had joined me, over some broken

NIAGARA FALLS IN WINTER.

rocks, deafened by the noise, half-blinded by the spray, and wet to the skin. We were at the foot of the American Fall. I could see an immense torrent of water tearing headlong down from some great height, but had no idea of shape, or situation, or anything but vague immensity.

When we were seated in the little ferry-boat, and were crossing the swollen river immediately before both cataracts, I began to feel what it was—but I was in a manner stunned, and unable to comprehend the vastness of the scene. It was not until I came on Table Rock, and looked—Great Heaven, on what a fall of bright green water!—that it came upon me in its full might and majesty.

Then, when I felt how near to my Creator I was standing, the first effect, and the enduring one—instant and lasting—of the tremendous spectacle, was Peace. Peace of Mind, tranquillity, calm recollections of the Dead, great thoughts of Eternal Rest and Happiness: nothing of gloom or terror. Niagara was at once stamped upon my heart, an Image of Beauty; to remain there, changeless and indelible, until its pulses cease to beat, for ever.

Oh, how the strife and trouble of daily life receded from my view, and lessened in the distance, during the ten memorable days we passed on that Enchanted Ground! What voices spoke from out the thundering water; what faces, faded from the earth, looked out upon me from its gleaming depths; what Heavenly promise glistened in those angels' tears, the drops of many hues, that showered around, and twined themselves about the gorgeous arches which the changing rainbows made!

I never stirred in all that time from the Canadian side, whither I had gone at first. I never crossed the river again; for I knew there were people on the other shore, and in such a place it is natural to shun strange company. To wander to and fro all day, and see the cataracts from all points of view; to stand upon the edge of the great Horse-Shoe Fall, marking the hurried water gathering strength as it approached the verge, yet seeming too, to pause before it shot into the gulf below; to gaze from the river's level up at the torrent as it came streaming down; to climb the neighbouring heights and watch it through the trees, and see the wreathing water in the rapids hurrying on to take its fearful plunge; to linger in the shadow of the solemn rocks three miles below; watching the river as, stirred by no visible cause, it heaved and eddied and awoke the echoes, being troubled yet, far down beneath its surface, by its giant leap; to have Niagara before me, lighted by the sun and by the moon, red in the day's decline, and grey as evening slowly fell upon it; to look upon it every day, and wake up in the night and hear its ceaseless voice: this was enough.

I think in every quiet season now, still do those waters roll and leap, and roar and tumble, all day long; still are the rainbows spanning them, a hundred feet below. Still, when the sun is on them, do they shine and glow like molten gold. Still, when the day is gloomy, do they fall like snow, or seem to crumble away like the front of a great chalk cliff, or roll down the rock like dense white smoke. But always does the mighty stream appear to die as it comes down, and always from its unfathomable grave arises that tremendous ghost of spray and mist which is never laid: which has haunted this place with the same dread solemnity since Darkness brooded on the deep, and that first flood before the Deluge—Light—came rushing on Creation at the word of God.

American Notes for General Circulation (London, 1842).

FUJI-SAN

SIR EDWIN ARNOLD

I HAVE just made in the company of Captain John Ingles, R. N., Naval Adviser to the Imperial Government of this country, and a young Japanese gentleman—Mr. Asso—a very fortunate and delightful ascent of Fuji-San, the famous mountain—you would not wonder, residing here, that everybody in Japan talks about Fuji, and thinks about her; paints her on fans, and limns her with gold on lacquer; carves her on temple-gates and house-fronts, and draws her for curtains of shops and signboards of inns, rest-houses and public institutions. Living in Tokio or Yokohama, or anywhere along this Tokaidô—the Southern road of Japan—you would soon perceive how the great volcano dominates every landscape, asserts perpetually her sovereignty over all other hills and mountains, and becomes in reality as well as imagination, an indispensable element in the national scenery. Far away at sea, when approaching Japan, if the weather be clear, long before the faintest blue line of coast is discernible from the deck, there is seen hanging in the air a dim white symmetrical cone, too constant for a cloud, which is Fuji-San. After you have landed and taken up your residence in Yokohama, Tokio, or any point of the southeastern littoral, you will be always

FUJI SAN.

seeing Fuji-Yama from some garden-nook, some tea-house gallery, some grove of cryptomerias, or thicket of bamboo, or even from the railway-carriage window. In the spring and autumn, as frequently as not, she will, indeed, be shrouded in the dense masses of white or grey cumulus which her crest collects, and seems to create in the mists of the Pacific. But during summer, when the snows are all melted from the vast cone, and again in winter, when she is covered with snow half-way down her colossal sides, but the air is clear, the superb mountain stands forth, dawn after dawn, and evening after evening—like no other eminence in the world for beauty, majesty, and perfectness of outline. There are loftier peaks, of course, for Fuji-San is not much higher than Mont Blanc, but there is none—not even Etna—which rises so proudly alone, isolated, distinct, from the very brink of the sea—with nothing to hide or diminish the dignity of the splendid and immense curves sweeping up from where the broad foot rests, planted on the Suruga Gulf, to where the imperial head soars, lifted high above the clouds into the blue of the firmament. By many and many a picture or photograph you must know well those almost perfectly matched flanks, that massive base, the towering lines of that mighty cone, slightly truncated and dentated at the summit. But no picture gives, and no artist could ever reproduce, the variety and charm of the aspect which Fuji-San puts on from day to day and hour to hour under the differing influences of air and weather. Sometimes it is as a white cloud that you see her, among the white clouds, changeless among the changeful shapes from which she emerges. Sometimes there will break forth, high above all clouds, a patch of deep grey against the blue, the broad head of Fuji. Sometimes you will only know where she sits by the immense collection of cirrus and cirro-cumulus there alone gathered in the sky; and sometimes—principally at dawn and nightfall—she will suddenly manifest herself, from her foot, jewelled with rich harvests, to her brow, bare and lonely as a desert—all violet against the gold of the setting sun, or else all gold and green against the rose and silver of the daybreak. . . .

As late as the Fourteenth Century Fuji was constantly smoking, and fire is spoken of with the eruptions, the last of which took place in December, 1707, and continued for nearly forty days. The Ho-Yei-san, or hump in the south face, was probably then formed. In this, her final outbreak, Fuji covered Tokio itself, sixty miles away, with six inches of ash, and sent rivers of lava far and wide. Since then she has slept, and only one little spot underneath the Kwan-nom-Gatake, on the lip of the crater, where steam exhales, and the red pumice-cracks are hot, shows that the heart of this huge volcano yet glows, and that she is capable of destroying again her own beauty and the forests and rich regions of fertility which clothe her knees and feet.

It is a circuit of 120 miles to go all round the base of Fuji-San. If you could cut a tunnel through her from Yoshiwara to Kawaguchi, it would be forty miles long. Generally speaking, the lower portion of the mountain is cultivated to a height of 1,500 feet, and it is a whole province which thus climbs round her. From the border of the farms there begins a rough and wild, but flowery moorland, which stretches round the hill to an elevation of 4,000 feet, where there the thick forest-belt commences. This girdles the volcano up to 7,000 feet on the Subashiri side and 8,000 on the Murayama fall, but is lower to the eastward. Above the forest extends a narrow zone of thicket and bush, chiefly dwarfed larch, juniper and a *vaccinium;* after which comes the bare, burnt, and terribly majestic peak itself, where the only living thing is a little yellow lichen which grows in the fissures of the lava blocks, for no eagle or hawk ventures so high, and the boldest or most bewildered butterfly will not be seen above the bushes half-way down.

The best—indeed, the only—time for the ascent of the mountain is between July 15th and September 5th. During this brief season the snow will be melted from the cone, the huts upon the path will be opened for pilgrims, and there will be only the danger of getting caught by a typhoon, or reaching the summit to find it swathed day after day in clouds, and no view obtainable. Our party of three started for the ascent on August 25th, taking that one of the many roads by which Fuji is approached that goes by Subashiri. Such an expedition may be divided into a series of stages. You have first to approach the foot of the mountain by train or otherwise, then to ride through the long slope of cultivated region. Then, abandoning horses or vehicles, to traverse on foot the sharper slopes of the forest belt. At the confines of this you will reach the first station, called *Sho* or *Go;* for Japanese fancy has likened the mountain to a heap of dry rice and the stations are named by rice-measure. From the first station to the ninth, whatever road you take, all will be hard, hot, continuous climbing. You must go by narrow, bad paths, such as a goat might make, in loose volcanic dust, gritty pumice, or over the sharp edges of lava dykes, which cut boots and sandals to shreds. . . .

At daybreak the horses are brought, and the six coolies, two by two, bind upon their backs the *futons* and the food. We start, a long procession, through a broad avenue in the forest, riding for five miles, under a lovely dawn, the sun shining gloriously on the forehead of Fuji, who seems further off and more immensely lofty the nearer we approach. The woodland is full of wild strawberries and flowers; including tiger-lilies, clematis, Canterbury bells, and the blue *hotari-no hana*, or fire-fly blossom. At 6:30 A. M., we reach Uma-Gayeshi, or "turn-the-horses-back"; and hence to the mountain top there is nothing for it but to walk every step of the long, steep, and difficult path. Two of the men with the lightest loads led the way along the narrow path, in a wood so thick that we shall not see Fuji again till we have passed through it. It takes us every now and then through the gates and precincts of little Shinto temples, where the priests offer us tea or mountain water. In one of them, at Ko-mitake, we are invited to ring the brass gong in order that the Deity may make our limbs strong for the task before us. And this is solemnly done by all hands, the *ninsoku* slapping their brown thighs piously after sounding the bell. . . .

The shortest time in which the ascent has been made is six hours and a half. We, taking it more easily, made no attempt to beat the record, and stopped frequently to botanize, geologize, etc. The rarefaction of the air gave our Japanese companion, Takaji San, a slight headache, which soon passed as the circulation became accustomed to the atmosphere; but Captain Ingles and I, being I suppose, both in excellent health and strength, experienced no inconvenience worth mentioning.

At half-past four next morning, while I was dreaming under my thick coverings, a hand touched me and a voice said softly, "Danna Sama, hi no de!" "Master, here is the sun!" The *shoji* at my feet were thrown open. I looked out, almost as you might from the moon, over a prodigious abyss of space, beyond which the eastern rim of all the world seemed to be on fire with flaming light. A belt of splendid rose and gold illumined all the horizon, darting long spears of glory into the dark sky overhead, gilding the tops of a thousand hills, scattered over the purple plains below, and casting on the unbroken background of clouds beyond an enormous shadow of Fuji. The spectacle was of unparalleled splendour, recalling Lord Tennyson's line —

> "And, in the East,
> God made himself an awful Rose of Dawn."

Moment by moment it grew more wonderful in loveliness of colour and brilliant birth of day; and then, suddenly, just when the sun rolled into sight—an orb of gleaming gold, flooding the world beneath with almost insufferable radiance—a vast mass of dense white clouds swept before the north wind over the view, completely blotting out the sun, the belt of rose and gold, the lighted mountains and plains, and the lower regions of Fuji-San. It was day again, but misty, white, and doubtful; and when we started to climb the last two stages of the cone the flags of the stations were invisible, and we could not know whether we should find the summit clear, or wrapped in enveloping clouds.

All was to be fortunate, however, on this happy day; and after a hard clambering of the remaining 2,000 feet we planted our staffs victoriously on the level ground of the crater's lip and gazed north, south, east, and west through clear and cloudless atmosphere over a prodigious prospect, whose diameter could not be less than 300 miles. It was one of the few days when O-ana-mochi, the Lord of the Great Hole, was wholly propitious! Behind the long row of little black huts standing on the edge of the mountain, gaped that awful, deadly Cup of the Volcano—an immense pit half a mile wide and six or seven hundred feet deep, its sides black, yellow, red, white, and grey, with the varying hues of the lava and scoriæ. In one spot where a perpetual shadow lay, from the ridge-peaks of Ken-ga-mine and the Shaka-no-wari-ishi, or "Cleft Rock of Buddha," gleamed a large patch of unmelted snow, and there was dust-covered snow at the bottom of the crater. We skirted part of the crater, passed by the dangerous path which is styled "Oya-shirazu, Ko-shirazu," "The place where you must forget parents and children, to take care of yourself;" saw the issue of the Kim-mei-sai or "Golden famous water," and of the Gim-mei-sai, or "Silver famous water"; and came back to breakfast at our hut silent with the delight and glory, the beauty and terror of the scene. Enormous flocks of fleecy clouds and cloudlets wandered in the lower air, many thousand feet beneath, but nowhere concealed the lakes, peaks, rivers, towns, villages, valleys, seacoasts, islands, and distant provinces spreading out all round. Imagine the prospect obtainable at 13,000 feet of elevation through the silvery air of Japan on a summer's morning with not a cloud, except shifting, thin, and transitory ones, to veil the view! . . .

At the temple with the bell we were duly stamped—shirts, sticks, and clothing—with the sacred mark of the mountain, and having made the hearts of our faithful and patient *ninsoku* glad with extra pay, turned our backs on the great extinct volcano, whose crest, glowing again in the morning sunlight, had no longer any secrets for Captain Ingles, or Takaji San, or myself.

Seas and Lands (New York, 1891).

THE CEDARS OF LEBANON

ALPHONSE DE LAMARTINE

THE Sheik of Eden, the last inhabited village towards the summit of Lebanon, was the maternal uncle of M. Mazoyer, my interpreter. Informed by his nephew of our arrival in Tripoli, the venerable sheik descended the mountain with his eldest son and a portion of his retinue; he came to visit me at the convent of the Franciscans, and offered me hospitality at his home in Eden. From Eden to the Cedars of Solomon it is only a three hours' march; and if the snows that cover the mountains will permit us, we can visit these ancient trees that have spread their glory over all Lebanon and that are contemporaries of the great king; we accepted, and the start was arranged for the following day.

At five o'clock in the morning we were on horseback. The caravan, more numerous than usual, was preceded by the Sheik of Eden, an admirable old man whose elegance of manner, noble and easy politeness, and magnificent costume were far from suggesting an Arab chieftain; one would have called him a patriarch marching at the head of his tribe; he rode upon a mare of the desert whose golden-bay skin and floating mane would have made a worthy mount for a hero of Jerusalem; his son and his principal

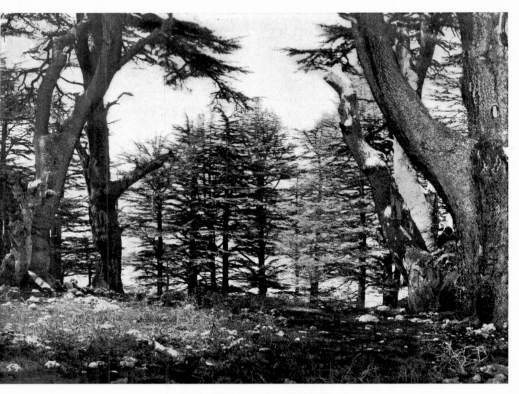

THE CEDARS OF LEBANON.

attendants caracoled upon magnificent stallions, a few paces before him; we came next, and then the long file of our *moukres* and our Saïs. . . .

The sheik has sent three Arabs over the route to the Cedars to learn if the snow will permit us to approach those trees; the Arabs returning say that access is impracticable; there are fourteen feet of snow in a narrow valley which must be crossed before reaching the trees;—wishing to get as near as possible, I entreat the sheik to give me his son and several horsemen; I leave my wife and my caravan at Eden; I mount the strongest of my horses, *Scham*, and we are *en route* at break of day;—a march of three hours over the crests of the mountains, or in the fields softened with melting snow. I arrive at the edge of the valley of the Saints, a deep gorge where the glance sweeps from the rocky height to a valley more confined, more sombre and more solemn even than that of Hamana; at the top of this valley, at the place where, after continually rising, it reaches the snows, a superb sheet of water falls, a hundred feet high and two or three *toises* wide; the entire valley resounds with this waterfall and the leaping torrents that it feeds; on every side the rocky flanks of the mountain stream with foam; we see almost beyond our vision, in the depths of the valley, two large villages the houses of which can scarcely be distinguished from the rocks rolled down by the torrent; the tops of the poplars and the mulberries from here look like tufts of reed or grass; we descend to the village of Beschieraï by paths cut in the rock, and so abrupt that one can hardly imagine that men will risk themselves upon them; people do perish sometimes; a stone thrown from the crest where we stand would fall upon the roofs of these villages where we shall arrive after an hour's descent; above the cascade and the snows, enormous fields of ice extend, undulating like vapours in tints greenish and blue by turns; in about a quarter of an hour towards the left in a half circular valley formed by the last mounts of Lebanon, we see a large, black blot upon the snow,—the famous group of cedars; they crown the brow of the mountain like a diadem; they mark the branching off of numerous and large valleys that descend from there; the sea and the sky are their horizon.

We put our horses to a gallop over the snow to get as near as possible to the forest; but on arriving five or six hundred steps from the trees, we plunge our horses up to their shoulders; we realize that the report of the Arabs is correct, and we must renounce the hope of touching these relics of the centuries and of nature; we alight and sit upon a rock to contemplate them.

These trees are the most celebrated natural monuments in the whole universe. Religion, poetry, and history have equally consecrated them. Holy Writ celebrates them in several places. They are one of the favourite images which the prophets employ. Solomon wished to consecrate them—doubtless on account of the renown of magnificence and sanctity that these prodigies of vegetation enjoyed at this epoch—to the ornamentation of the temple that he was the first to elevate to the one God. These were certainly the trees; for Ezekiel speaks of the cedars of Eden as the most beautiful of Lebanon. The Arabs of all sects have a traditional veneration for them. They attribute to these trees, not only a vegetative force that gives them eternal life, but even a soul that makes them give signs of wisdom, of foresight, similar to those of instinct in animals and intelligence in men. They know the seasons in advance; they move their enormous branches like human limbs, they spread or contract their boughs, they raise their branches towards the sky or incline them to the earth, according as the snow is preparing to fall or to melt. They are divine beings under the form of trees. They grow on this single spot of the mounts of Lebanon; they take root far beyond the region where all prolific vegetation dies. All this strikes the imagination of the Oriental people with astonishment, and I do not know that science is not even more astonished. Alas! however, Basan languishes and Carmel and the flower of Lebanon fade.—These trees diminish every century. Travellers formerly counted thirty or forty, later seventeen, and still later, about a dozen.—There are now only seven of those whose massive forms can presume to be contemporaneous with Biblical times. Around these old memorials of past ages, which know the history of the ground better than history herself, and which could tell us, if they could speak, of many empires, religions, and vanished human races, there remains still a little forest of cedars more yellow it appears to me than a group of four or five hundred trees or shrubs. Each year in the month of June the population of Beschieraï, Eden, and Kanobin, and all the villages of the neighbouring valleys, ascend to the cedars and celebrate mass at their feet. How many prayers have resounded beneath their branches! And what more beautiful temple, what nearer altar than the sky! What more majestic and holier daïs than the highest plateau of Lebanon, the trunks of the cedars and the sacred boughs that have shaded and that will still shade so many human generations pronouncing differently the name of God, but who recognize him everywhere in his works and adore him in his manifestations of nature! And I, I also prayed in the presence of those trees. The harmonious wind that resounded through their sonorous branches played in my hair and froze upon my eyelids those tears of sorrow and adoration.

Voyage en Orient (Paris, 1843).

THE GIANT'S CAUSEWAY

WILLIAM MAKEPEACE THACKERAY

THE road to the Causeway is bleak, wild, and hilly. The cabins along the road are scarcely better than those of Kerry, the inmates as ragged, and more fierce and dark-looking. I never was so pestered by juvenile beggars as in the dismal village of Ballintoy. A crowd of them rushed after the car, calling for money in a fierce manner, as if it was their right; dogs as fierce as the children came yelling after the vehicle; and the faces which scowled out of the black cabins were not a whit more good-humoured. We passed by one or two more clumps of cabins, with their turf and corn-stacks lying together at the foot of the hills; placed there for the convenience of the children, doubtless, who can thus accompany the car either way, and shriek out their "Bonny gantleman, gi'e us a ha'p'ny." A couple of churches, one with a pair of its pinnacles blown off, stood in the dismal open country, and a gentleman's house here and there: there were no trees about them, but a brown grass round about—hills rising and falling in front, and the sea beyond. The occasional view of the coast was noble; wild Bengore towering eastwards as we went along; Raghery Island before us, in the steep rocks and caves of which Bruce took shelter when driven from yonder Scottish coast, that one sees stretching blue in the northeast.

I think this wild gloomy tract through which one passes is a good prelude for what is to be the great sight of the day, and got my mind to a proper state of awe by the time we were near the journey's end. Turning away shorewards by the fine house of Sir Francis Macnaghten, I went towards a lone handsome inn, that stands close to the Causeway. The landlord at Ballycastle had lent me Hamilton's book to read on the road; but I had not time then to read more than half-a-dozen pages of it. They described how the author, a clergyman distinguished as a man of science, had been thrust out of a friend's house by the frightened servants one wild night, and butchered by some Whiteboys who were waiting outside and called for his blood. I had been told at Belfast that there was a corpse in the inn: was it there now? It had driven off, the car-boy said, "in a handsome hearse and four to Dublin the whole way." It was gone, but I thought the house looked as if the ghost was there. See, yonder are the black rocks stretching to Portrush: how leaden and grey the sea looks! how grey and leaden the sky! You hear the waters rushing evermore, as they have done since the beginning of the world. The car drives us with a dismal grinding noise of the wheels to the big lone house: there's no smoke in the chimneys; the doors are locked. Three savage-looking men rush after the car: are they the men who took out Mr. Hamilton—took him out and butchered him in the moonlight? Is everybody, I wonder, dead in that big house? Will they let us in before those men are up? Out comes a pretty smiling girl, with a curtsey, just as the savages are

THE GIANT'S LOOM, GIANT'S CAUSEWAY,

at the car, and you are ushered into a very comfortable room; and the men turn out to be guides. Well, thank Heaven it's no worse! I had fifteen pounds still left; and, when desperate, have no doubt should fight like a lion.

The traveller no sooner issues from the inn by a back door, which he is informed will lead him straight to the Causeway, than the guides pounce upon him, with a dozen rough boatmen who are likewise lying in wait; and a crew of shrill beggar-boys, with boxes of spars, ready to tear him and each other to pieces seemingly, yell and bawl incessantly round him. "I'm the guide Miss Henry recommends," shouts one. "I'm Mr. Macdonald's guide," pushes in another. "This way," roars a third, and drags his prey down a precipice; the rest of them clambering and quarrelling after. I had no friends; I was perfectly helpless. I wanted to walk down to the shore by myself, but they would not let me, and I had nothing for it but to yield myself into the hands of the guide who had seized me, who hurried me down the steep to a little wild bay, flanked on each side by rugged cliffs and rocks, against which the waters came tumbling, frothing, and roaring furiously. Upon some of these black rocks two or three boats were lying: four men seized a boat, pushed it shouting into the water, and ravished me into it. We had slid between two rocks, where the channel came gurgling in: we were up one swelling wave that came in a huge advancing body ten feet above us, and were plunging madly down another (the descent causes a sensation in the lower regions of the stomach which it is not at all necessary here to describe), before I had leisure to ask myself why the deuce I was in that boat, with four rowers hurrooing and bounding madly from one liquid mountain to another—four rowers whom I was bound to pay. I say, the query came qualmishly across me why the devil I was there, and why not walking calmly on the shore.

The guide began pouring his professional jargon into my ears. "Every one of them bays," says he, "has a name (take my place, and the spray won't come over you): that is Port Noffer, and the next, Port na Gange; them rocks is the Stookawns (for every rock has its name as well as every bay); and yonder—give way, my boys,—hurray, we're over it now: has it wet you much, sir?—that's a little cave: it goes five hundred feet under ground, and the boats goes into it easy of a calm day."

"Is it a fine day or a rough one now?" said I; the internal disturbance going on with more severity than ever.

"It's betwixt and between; or, I may say, neither one nor the other. Sit up, sir. Look at the entrance of the cave. Don't be afraid, sir; never has an accident happened in any one of these boats, and the most delicate ladies has rode in them on rougher days than this. Now, boys, pull to the big cave. That, sir, is six hundred and sixty yards in length, though some say it goes for miles inland, where the people sleeping in their houses hear the waters roaring under them."

The water was tossing and tumbling into the mouth of the little cave. I looked,—for the guide would not let me alone till I did,—and saw what might be expected: a black hole of some forty feet high, into which it was no more possible to see than into a millstone. "For Heaven's sake, sir," says I, "if you've no particular wish to see the mouth of the big cave, put about and let us see the Causeway and get ashore." This was done, the guide meanwhile telling some story of a ship of the Spanish Armada having fired her guns at two peaks of rock, then visible, which the crew mistook for chimney-pots—what benighted fools these Spanish Armadilloes must have been; it is easier to see a rock than a chimney-pot; it is easy to know that chimney-pots do not grow on rocks.—"But where, if you please, is the Causeway?"

"That's the Causeway before you," says the guide.

"Which?"

"That pier which you see jutting out into the bay right ahead."

"*Mon dieu!* and have I travelled a hundred and fifty miles to see *that?*"

I declare, upon my conscience, the barge moored at Hungerford Market is a more majestic object, and seems to occupy as much space. As for telling a man that the Causeway is merely a part of the sight; that he is there for the purpose of examining the surrounding scenery; that if he looks to the westward he will see Portrush and Donegal Head before him; that the cliffs immediately in his front are green in some places, black in others, interspersed with blotches of brown and streaks of vendure;—what is all this to a lonely individual lying sick in a boat, between two immense waves that only give him momentary glimpses of the land in question, to show that it is frightfully near, and yet you are an hour from it? They won't let you go away—that cursed guide *will* tell out his stock of legends and stories. The boatmen insist upon your looking at boxes of "specimens," which you must buy of them; they laugh as you grow paler and paler; they offer you more and more "specimens"; even the dirty lad who pulls number three, and is not allowed by his comrades to speak, puts in *his* oar, and hands you over a piece of Irish diamond (it looks like half-sucked alicompayne), and scorns you. "Hurry, lads, now for it, give way!" how the oars do hurtle in the rowlocks, as the boat goes up an aqueous mountain, and then down into one of those cursed maritime valleys where there is no rest as on shore!

At last, after they had pulled me enough about, and sold me all the boxes of specimens, I was permitted to land at the spot whence we set out, and whence, though we had been rowing for an hour, we had never been above five hundred yards distant. Let all cockneys take warning from this; let the solitary one caught issuing from the back door of the hotel, shout at once to the boatmen to be gone—that he will have none of them. Let him, at any rate, go first down to the water to determine whether it be smooth enough to allow him to take any decent pleasure by riding on its surface. For after all, it must be remembered that it *is* pleasure we come for—that we are not *obliged* to take those boats.—Well, well! I paid ten shillings for mine, and ten minutes after would cheerfully have paid five pounds to be allowed to quit it; it was no hard bargain after all.

THE KEYSTONE, GIANT'S CAUSEWAY.

As for the boxes of spar and specimens, I at once, being on terra firma, broke my promise, and said I would see them all—first. It is wrong to swear, I know; but sometimes it relieves one *so* much!

The first act on shore was to make a sacrifice to Sanctissima Tellus; offering up to her a neat and becoming Taglioni coat, bought for a guinea in Covent Garden only three months back. I sprawled on my back on the smoothest of rocks that is, and tore the elbows to pieces: the guide picked me up; the boatman did not stir, for they had their will of me; the guide alone picked me up, I say, and bade me follow him. We went across a boggy ground in one of the little bays, round which rise the green walls of the cliff, terminated on either side by a black crag, and the line of the shore washed by the poluphloisboiotic, nay the poluphloisboiotatotic sea. Two beggars stepped over the bog after us howling for money, and each holding up a cursed box of specimens. No oaths, threats, entreaties, would drive these vermin away; for some time the whole scene had been spoiled by the incessant and abominable jargon of them, the boatmen, and the guides. I was obliged to give them money to be left in quiet, and if, as no doubt will be the case, the Giant's Causeway shall be a still greater resort of travellers than ever, the county must put policemen on the rocks to keep the beggars away, or fling them in the water when they appear.

And now, by force of money, having got rid of the sea and land beggars, you are at liberty to examine at your leisure the wonders of the place. There is not the least need for a guide to attend the stranger, unless the latter have a mind to listen to a parcel of legends, which may be well from the mouth of a wild simple peasant who believes in his tales, but are odious from a dullard who narrates them at the rate of sixpence a lie. Fee him and the other beggars, and at last you are left tranquil to look at the strange scene with your own eyes, and enjoy your own thoughts at leisure.

That is, if the thoughts awakened by such a scene may be called enjoyment; but for me, I confess, they are too near akin to fear to be pleasant; and I don't know that I would desire to change that sensation of awe and terror which the hour's walk occasioned, for a greater familiarity with this wild, sad, lonely place. The solitude is awful. I can't understand how those chattering guides dare to lift up their voices here, and cry for money.

It looks like the beginning of the world, somehow: the sea looks older than in other places, the hills and rocks strange, and formed differently from other rocks and hills—as those vast dubious monsters were formed who possessed the earth before man. The hilltops are shattered into a thousand cragged fantastical shapes; the water comes swelling into scores of little strange creeks, or goes off with a leap, roaring into those mysterious caves yonder, which penetrate who knows how far into our common world. The savage rock-sides are painted of a hundred colours. Does the sun ever shine here? When the world was moulded and fashioned out of formless chaos, this must have been the *bit over*—a remnant of chaos! Think of that!—it is a tailor's simile. Well, I am a cockney: I wish I were in Pall Mall! Yonder is a kelp-burner: a lurid smoke from his burning kelp rises up to the leaden sky, and he looks as naked and fierce as Cain. Bubbling up out of the rocks at the very brim of the sea rises a little crystal spring: how comes it there? and there is an old grey hag beside, who has been there for hundreds and hundreds of years, and there sits and sells whisky at the extremity of creation! How do you dare to sell whisky there, old woman? Did you serve old Saturn with a glass when he lay along the Causeway here? In reply, she says, she has no change for a shilling: she never has; but her whisky is good.

This is not a description of the Giant's Causeway (as some clever critic will remark), but of a Londoner there, who is by no means so interesting an object as the natural curiosity in question. That single hint is sufficient; I have not a word more to say. "If," says he, "you cannot describe the scene lying before us—if you cannot state from your personal observation that the number of basaltic pillars composing the Causeway has been computed at about forty thousand, which vary in diameter, their surface presenting the appearance of a tesselated pavement of polygonal stones—that each pillar is formed of several distinct joints, the convex end of the one being accurately fitted in the concave of the next, and the length of the joints varying from five feet to four inches—that although the pillars are polygonal, there is but one of three sides in the whole forty thousand (think of that!), but three of nine sides, and that it may be safely computed that ninety-nine out of one hundred pillars have either five, six, or seven sides; if you cannot state something useful, you had much better, sir, retire and get your dinner."

Never was summons more gladly obeyed. The dinner must be ready by this time; so, remain you, and look on at the awful scene, and copy it down in words if you can. If at the end of the trial you are dissatisfied with your skill as a painter, and find that the biggest of your words cannot render the hues and vastness of that tremendous swelling sea—of those lean solitary crags standing rigid along the shore, where they have been watching the ocean ever since it was made—of those grey towers of Dunluce standing upon a leaden rock, and looking as if some old old princess, of old old fairy times, were dragon-guarded within—of yon flat stretches of sand where the Scotch and Irish mermaids hold conference—come away, too, and prate no more about the scene! There is that in nature, dear Jenkins, which passes even our powers. We can feel the beauty of a magnificent landscape, perhaps: but we can describe a leg of mutton and turnips better. Come, then, this scene is for our betters to depict. If Mr. Tennyson were to come hither for a month, and brood over the place, he might, in some of those lofty heroic lines which the author of the *Morte d'Arthur* knows how to pile up, convey to the reader a sense of this gigantic desolate scene. What! you, too, are a poet? Well, then Jenkins, stay! but believe me, you had best take my advice, and come off.

The Irish Sketch-Book (London, 1843).

THE GREAT GLACIER OF THE SELKIRKS

DOUGLAS SLADEN

IF Banff represents the Rocky Mountains made easy, the Glacier House represents the Selkirks made easy—a much more notable performance, for these mountains had long been regarded as impassable by engineering. The Glacier House is a few miles beyond Rogers' Pass, in the midst of the line's greatest marvels of nature and engineering. Just before comes the monarch of snow sheds; just above the monarch of glaciers; just below the monarch of viaducts. The Great Glacier of the Selkirks comes to a conclusion within a couple of miles above it. The moraines and splintered forests at its foot tell a frightful tale of destruction, and the glacier advances every year; but only a few inches, so the hotel is safe for the present.

The hotel is a pretty little châlet, mostly dining-room, with a trim, level lawn in front containing a fine fountain. Eighteen miles broad is the great Glacier of the Selkirks, one foot of which is planted so threateningly above the hotel and the railway station, that it looks as if it meant to stamp them out of existence with the stealth of a thief in the night.

A marvellous and delightful walk it is from the hotel to the Glacier—at first through dry woods of fir and spruce, and balsam and tamarack, carpeted, wherever the sun breaks through, with purple blueberries, wild raspberries, pigeon and salmon berries. Here you might meet a grizzly bear any minute. You pause, if you are only a man and a woman, on the lovers' seat under the thousand-ton boulder hurled down by the Glacier in the childhood of the earth. Then you pass the fierce glacial torrent of grey-green water, so cold or charged with impurities that fish refuse to live in it, swelling, as all snow-fed rivers do, as the heat of a summer's day waxes. Some of its pools are huge and deep; some of its falls and rapids as fierce as the cataract at Lorette, rounded boulders and splintered trunks everywhere attesting its fury. The path crosses and recrosses the river over bridges of tree-trunks, with smaller trunks loosely pinned across them, like the little straw mats in which cream cheeses are wrapped. As the path mounts, the scenery becomes more open, and you are greeted, according to the season, with Canada's gorgeous lily or Canada's prodigality of wild fruits; for you are in the track of the glacier and the avalanche, and in the death of the forest is the birth of blossoms and berries. All around you now is a scene of awful grandeur—boulders as big as settlers' huts, and giant tree trunks, many of them blackened with fire, tossed together like the rubbish on a dust-heap, and, brooding over all, the great Glacier like a dragon crouching for the spring. One can hardly believe it is the Glacier; the transitions are so abrupt. A turn of a path brings you almost in contact with a piece of ice larger than any lake in the British Islands. From under its skirts

THE GREAT GLACIER OF THE SELKIRKS.

trickle tiny rills; a few feet below, the rills league themselves into a river. Even a first-class glacier is a disappointing affair if you go too close. Its blueness disappears, also its luminosity, except in crevasses deep enough to show you the pure heart of the ice. The surface is a dirty-looking mixture of ice and snow. There were two lovely horizontal crevasses, one so spacious and shining that it is called the Fairy Cavern. The pleasure of standing in them is spoilt, because they look all the time as if they were going to close on you. At another foot of the Glacier there are immense moraines, looking like the earthworks of Dover Castle. I examined them one October day when I went with a guide to the top of the Glacier, eight thousand feet above sea-level, to see the splendid Glacier-girdled head of Mount Fox on the other side of the abyss.

I never intend to do any more mountain climbing through deep, fresh snow. For the last hour or two of the ascent the snow was as deep as one's thighs at every step, and though the guide was towing me by a rope tied round my waist, it was intolerably wearisome. To begin with, he had to sound with his staff at every step and see that we were on *terra firma*, and not on the *soufflet* of a crevasse; and though there had been such a snowfall the night before, the sun was as hot as summer overhead. The sight was worth doing once, with the miles and miles of the sea of ice all round one, and the long white slopes of virgin snow.

If it had not been for the aggressive visage of Mount Fox, it would have answered to the description of the interior of Greenland given me by Dr. Nansen, where the world consists of yourselves, the sun, and the snow. We started at eight o'clock in the morning, but in some way or other I was not quite as rapid as the guide had calculated, for a couple of hours before nightfall he began to get excited, if not alarmed. We were at the time clear of the deep snow, and muddling about in a mixture of drifts and moraines; but after dark he was not sure of his way until we struck the path at the foot of the Glacier. . . .

The Glacier House has not only its noble and easily accessible glacier; it is in the very heart of the finest mountain scenery in the Selkirks, which is so different to the scenery of the Rockies. The Canadian Rockies are blunt-topped *fisty* mountains, with knuckles of bare rock sticking out everywhere. The Selkirks are graceful pyramids and sharp sierras, up to their shoulders in magnificent forests of lofty pines. The trees on the Rockies are much smaller and poorer. Right above the hotel, to the left of the overhanging Glacier, is the bare steeple of Sir Donald, one of the monarchs of the range; Ross Peak and Cheops frown on the descent of the line to the Pacific; and the line of the Atlantic is guarded by the hundred pinnacles of the rifted mountain, formerly known as the Hermit, and now, with singular infelicity, re-christened, in an eponymous fit, Mount Tupper.

Sir Charles Tupper is one of Canada's greatest men, but his name is more suitable for a great man than a great mountain, especially since there is a very perfect effect of a hermit and his dog formed by boulders near the top of the mountain. The men in the railway camp have got over this difficulty with the doggerel:

> "That's Sir Charles Tupper
> Going home to his supper."

We made two long stays at the Glacier House, and I never enjoyed anything more in my life than the effect of the snug little châlet, with its velvety lawn, in the stronghold of the giant mountains, brought into touch with the great world twice a day by the trains east and west, which echoed their approach and departure miles on miles through the ranges.

On the Cars and Off (London, 1895).

MAUNA LOA

LADY BRASSEY

AT 6:30 A. M., we made the island of Hawaii, rather too much to leeward, as we had been carried by the strong current at least eighteen miles out of our course. We were therefore obliged to beat up to windward, in the course of which operation we passed a large bark running before the wind—the first ship we had seen since leaving Tahiti—and also a fine whale, blowing close to us. We could not see the high land in the centre of the island, owing to the mist in which it was enveloped, and there was great excitement and much speculation on board as to the principal points which were visible. At noon the observations taken proved that Tom was right in his opinion as to our exact position. The wind dropped as we approached the coast, where we could see the heavy surf dashing against the black lava cliffs, rushing up the little creeks, and throwing its spray in huge fountain-like jets high above the tall cocoanut-trees far inland.

We sailed along close to the shore, and by two o'clock were near the entrance to the Bay of Hilo. In answer to our signal for a pilot, a boat came off with a man who said he knew the entrance to the harbour, but informed us that the proper pilot had gone to Honolulu on a pleasure trip.

It was a clear afternoon. The mountains, Mauna Kea and Mauna Loa, could be plainly seen from top to bottom, their giant crests rising nearly 14,000 feet above our heads, their tree and fern clad slopes seamed with deep gulches or ravines, down each of which a fertilizing river ran into the sea. Inside the reef, the white coral shore, on which the waves seemed too lazy to break, is fringed with a belt of cocoanut palms, amongst which, as well as on the hill-sides, the little white houses are prettily dotted. All are surrounded by gardens, so full of flowers that the bright patches of colour were plainly visible even from the deck of the yacht. The harbour is large, and is exposed only to one bad wind, which is most prevalent during the winter months. . . .

It was half-past nine before we were all mounted and fairly off. The first part of our way lay along the flat ground, gay with bright scarlet Guernsey lilies, and shaded by cocoanut-trees, between the town and the sea. Then we struck off to the right, and soon left the town behind us, emerging into the open country. At a distance from the sea, Hilo looks as green as the Emerald Isle itself; but on a closer inspection the grass turns out to be coarse and dry, and many of the trees look scrubby and half dead. Except in the "gulches" and the deep holes, between the hills, the island is covered with lava, in many places of so recent a deposit that it has not yet had time to decompose, and there is consequently only a thin layer of soil on its surface. The soil being, however, very rich, vegetation flourishes luxuriantly for a time; but as soon as the roots have penetrated a certain depth, and have come into contact with the lava, the trees wither up and perish, like the seed that fell on stony ground.

The *ohia* trees form a handsome feature in the landscape, with their thick stems, glossy foliage, and light crimson flowers. The fruit is a small, pink, waxy-looking apple, slightly acid, pleasant to the taste when you are thirsty. The candle-nut trees attain to a large size, and their light green foliage and white flowers have a very graceful appearance. Most of the foliage, however, is spoiled by a deposit of a black dust, not unlike what one sees on the leaves of a London garden. I do not know whether this is caused by the fumes of the not far-distant volcano, or whether it is some kind of mold or fungus.

After riding about ten miles in the blazing sun we reached a forest, where the vegetation was quite tropical, though not so varied in its beauties as that of Brazil, or of the still more lovely South Sea Islands. There were ferns of various descriptions in the forest, and many fine trees, entwined, supported, or suffocated by numerous climbing plants, amongst which were blue and lilac convolvulus, and magnificent passion-flowers. The protection from the sun afforded by this dense mass of foliage was extremely grateful; but the air of the forest was close and stifling, and at the end of five miles we were glad to emerge once more into the open. The rest of the way lay over the hard lava, through a desert of scrubby vegetation, occasionally relieved by clumps of trees in hollows. More than once we had a fine view of the sea, stretching away into the far distance, though it was sometimes mistaken for the bright blue sky, until the surf could be seen breaking upon the black rocks, amid the encircling groves of cocoanut-trees.

The sun shone fiercely at intervals, and the rain came down several times in torrents. The pace was slow, the road was dull and dreary, and many were the inquiries made for the "Half-way House," long before we reached it.

Directly we had finished our meal—about three o'clock—the guide came and tried to persuade us that, as the baggage mules had not yet arrived, it would be too late for us to go on to-day, and that we had better spend the night where we were, and start early in the morning. We did not, however, approve of this arrangement, so the horses were saddled, and leaving word that the baggage-mules were to follow us on as soon as possible, we mounted, and set off for the "Volcano House." We had not gone far before we were again overtaken by a shower, which once more drenched us to the skin.

The scene was certainly one of extreme beauty. The moon was hidden by a cloud, and the prospect lighted only by the red glare of the volcano, which hovered before and above us like the Israelites' pillar of fire, giving us hope of a splendid spectacle when we should at last reach the long wished-for crater. Presently the moon shone forth again, and gleamed and glistened on the raindrops and silver grasses till they looked like fireflies and glowworms. When we emerged from the wood, we found ourselves at the very edge of the old crater, the bed of which, three or four hundred feet beneath us, was surrounded by steep and in many places overhanging sides. It looked like an enormous caldron, four or five miles in width, full of a mass of coloured pitch. In the centre was the still glowing stream of dark red lava, flowing slowly towards us, and in every direction were red-hot patches, and flames and smoke issuing from the ground. A bit of the "black country" at night, with all the coal-heaps on fire, would give you some idea of the scene. Yet the first sensation is rather one of disappointment, as one expects greater activity on the part of the volcano; but the new crater was still to be seen, containing the lake of fire, with steep walls rising up in the midst of the sea of lava. . . .

The grandeur of the view in the direction of the volcano increased as the evening wore on. The fiery cloud above the present crater augmented in size and depth of colour; the extinct crater glowed red in thirty or forty different places; and clouds of white vapour issued from every crack and crevice in the ground, adding to the sulphurous smell with which the atmosphere was laden. Our room faced the volcano: there were no blinds, and I drew back the curtains and lay watching the splendid scene until I fell asleep.

Sunday, December 24th (Christmas Eve).

I was up at four o'clock, to gaze once more on the wondrous spectacle that lay before me. The molten lava still flowed in many places, the red cloud over the fiery lake was bright as ever, and the stream was slowly ascending in every direction, over hill and valley, till, as the sun rose, it became difficult to distinguish clearly the sulphurous vapours from the morning mists. We walked down to the Sulphur Banks, about a quarter of a mile from the "Volcano House," and burned our gloves and boots in our endeavours to procure crystals, the beauty of which generally disappeared after a very short exposure to the air. We succeeded, however, in finding a few good specimens, and, by wrapping them at once in paper and cotton-wool and putting them into a bottle, hope to bring them home uninjured.

On our return we found a gentleman who had just arrived from Kan, and who proposed to join us in our expedition to the crater, and at three o'clock in the afternoon we set out, a party of eight, with two guides, and three porters to carry our wraps and provisions, and to bring back specimens. Before leaving the inn the landlord came to us and begged us in an earnest and confidential manner to be very careful to do exactly what our guides told us, and especially to follow in their footsteps exactly when returning in the dark. He added: "There never has been an accident happen to anybody from my house, and I should feel real mean if one did: but there have been a power of narrow escapes."

First of all we descended the precipice, 300 feet in depth, forming the wall of the old crater, but now thickly covered with vegetation. It is so steep in many places that flights of zigzag wooden steps have been inserted in the face of the cliff in some places, in order to render the descent practicable. At the bottom we stepped straight on to the surface of cold boiled lava, which we had seen from above last night. Even here, in every crevice where a few grains of soil had collected, delicate little ferns might be seen struggling for life, and thrusting out their green fronds towards the light. It was the most extraordinary walk imaginable over that vast plain of lava, twisted and distorted into every conceivable shape and form, according to the temperature it had originally attained, and the rapidity with which it had cooled, its surface, like half-molten glass, cracking and breaking beneath our feet. Sometimes we came to a patch that looked like the contents of a pot, suddenly petrified in the act of boiling; sometimes the black iridescent lava had assumed the form of waves, or more frequently of huge masses of rope, twisted and coiled together; sometimes it was piled up like a collection of organ-pipes, or had gathered into mounds and cones of various dimensions. As we proceeded the lava became hotter and hotter, and from every crack arose gaseous fumes, affecting our noses and throats in a painful manner; till at last, when we had to pass to leeward of the molten stream flowing from the lake, the vapours almost choked us, and it was with difficulty we continued to advance. The lava was more glassy and transparent-looking, as if it had been fused at a higher temperature than usual; and the crystals of sulphur, alum, and other minerals, with which it abounded, reflected the light in bright prismatic colours. In places it was quite transparent, and we could see beneath it the long streaks of a stringy kind of lava, like brown spun glass, called "Pélé's hair."

At last we reached the foot of the present crater, and commenced the ascent of the outer wall. Many times the thin crust gave way beneath our guide, and he had to retire quickly from the hot, blinding, choking fumes that immediately burst forth. But we succeeded in reaching the top; and then what a sight presented itself to our astonished eyes! I could neither speak nor move at first, but could only stand and gaze at the terrible grandeur of the scene.

We were standing on the extreme edge of the precipice, overhanging a lake of molten fire, a hundred feet below us, and nearly a mile across. Dashing against the cliffs on the opposite side, with a noise like the roar of a stormy ocean, waves of blood-red, fiery, liquid lava hurled their billows upon an iron-bound headland, and then rushed up the face of the cliffs to toss their gory spray high in the air. The restless, heaving lake boiled and bubbled, never remaining the same for two minutes together. Its normal colour seemed to be a dull, dark red, covered with a thin grey scum, which every moment and in every part swelled and cracked, and emitted fountains, cascades, and whirlpools of yellow and red fire, while sometimes one big golden river, sometimes four or five flowed across it. There was an island on one side of the lake, which the fiery waves seemed to attack unceasingly with relentless fury, as if bent on hurling it from its base. On the other side was a large cavern, into which the burning mass rushed with a loud roar, breaking down in its impetuous headlong career the gigantic stalactites that overhung the mouth of the cave, and flinging up the liquid material for the formation of fresh ones.

It was all terribly grand, magnificently sublime; but no words could adequately describe such a scene. The precipice on which we were standing overhung the crater so much that it was impossible to see what was going on immediately beneath; but from the columns of smoke and vapour that arose, the flames and sparks that constantly drove us back from the edge, it was easy to imagine that there must have been two or three grand fiery fountains below. As the sun set, and the darkness enveloped the scene, it became more awful than ever. We retired a little way from the brink, to breathe some fresh air, and to try and eat the food we had brought with us; but this was an impossibility. Every instant a fresh explosion or glare made us jump up to survey the stupendous scene. The violent struggles of the lava to escape from its fiery bed, and the loud and awful noises by which they were at times accompanied, suggested the idea that some imprisoned monsters were trying to release themselves from their bondage with shrieks and groans, and cries of agony and despair, at the futility of their efforts.

Sometimes there were at least seven spots on the borders of the lake where the molten lava dashed up furiously against the rocks—seven fire-fountains playing simultaneously. With the increasing darkness the colours emitted by the glowing mass became more and more wonderful, varying from the deepest jet-black to the palest grey, from darkest maroon through cherry and scarlet to the most delicate pink, violet, and blue; from the richest brown, through orange and yellow, to the lightest straw-colour. And there was yet another shade, only describable by the term "molten-lava colour." Even the smokes and vapours were rendered beautiful by their borrowed lights and tints, and the black peaks, pinnacles, and crags, which surrounded the amphitheatre, formed a splendid and appropriate background. Sometimes great pieces broke off and tumbled with a crash into the burning lake, only to be remelted and thrown up anew. I had for some time been feeling very hot and uncomfortable, and on looking round the cause was at once apparent. Not two inches beneath the surface, the grey lava on which we were standing and sitting was red-hot. A stick thrust through it caught fire, a piece of paper was immediately destroyed, and the gentlemen found the heat from the crevices so great that they could not approach near enough to light their pipes.

One more last look, and then we turned our faces away from the scene that had enthralled us for so many hours. The whole of the lava we had crossed, in the extinct crater, was now aglow in many patches, and in all directions flames were bursting forth, fresh lava was flowing, and smoke and steam were issuing from the surface. It was a toilsome journey back again, walking as we did in single file, and obeying the strict injunctions of our head guide to follow him closely, and to tread exactly in his footsteps. On the whole it was easier by night than by day to distinguish the route to be taken, as we could now see the dangers that before we could only feel; and many were the fiery crevices we stepped over or jumped across. Once I slipped, and my foot sank through the thin crust. Sparks issued from the ground, and the stick on which I leaned caught fire before I could fairly recover myself.

Monday, December 25th, (Christmas Day).

Turning in last night was the work of a very few minutes, and this morning I awoke perfectly refreshed and ready to appreciate anew the wonders of the prospect that met my eyes. The pillar of fire was still distinctly visible, when I looked out from my window, though it was not so bright as when I had last seen it: but even as I looked it began to fade, and gradually disappeared. At the same moment a river of glowing lava issued from the side of the bank which we had climbed with so much difficulty yesterday, and slowly but surely overflowed the ground we had walked over. I woke Tom, and you may imagine the feelings with which we gazed upon this startling phenomenon, which, had it occurred a few hours earlier, might have caused the destruction of the whole party.

A Voyage in the Sunbeam (London, 1878).

TROLLHÄTTA

HANS CHRISTIAN ANDERSEN

WHOM did we meet at Trollhätta? It is a strange story. We will relate it.

We landed at the first sluice and immediately stood in a kind of English garden; the broad pathways are covered with gravel and rise in low terraces between the green sun-lit greensward. It is charming and delightful here, but by no means imposing; if one desires to be excited in this manner, he must go a little higher up to the old sluices, that have burst, deep and narrow, through the hard rock. Nature is magnificent here, and the water roars and foams in its deep bed far below. Up here one looks over valley and river; the bank of the river on the other side rises in green undulating hills, with clusters of leafy trees and wooden houses painted red; rocks and pine forests hem in the land-scape. Through the sluices steamboats and sailing vessels are ascending; the water itself is the attendant spirit that must bear them up above the rock. And from the forest it issues, buzzing, roaring, and blustering. The din of the Trollhätta Falls mingles with the noise of the sawmills and the smithies.

"In three hours we shall be through the sluices," said the Captain, "and then you shall visit the Falls. We shall meet again at the inn above."

We went along the path that led through the forest and thickets; a whole flock of bare-headed boys surrounded us, all wishing to be our guides; each one outscreamed the other, and each gave contradictory explanations of how high was the water and how high it did not or could rise; and here was also a great difference of opinion among the learned. Soon we came to a halt on a large heather-covered rock, a dizzying eminence. Before us, but deep below, the foaming, roaring water—the Hell Fall, and over this, cascade after cascade, the rich, swelling, rushing river, the outlet of the largest lake in Sweden. What a sight, what a foaming above and below! It is like the waves of the sea, or like effervescing champagne, or like boiling milk; the water rushes around two rocky islands above so that the spray rises like mist from a meadow, while below, it is more compressed, and, hurrying away, returns in circles; then it rolls down in a long wave-like fall, the Hell Fall. What a roaring storm in the deep—what a spectacle! Man is dumb. And so were also the screaming little guides; they were silent, and when they renewed their explanations and stories, they did not get far before an old gentleman, whom none of us had noticed, although he was here among us, made himself heard above the noise with his peculiarly shrill voice; he spoke of the place and its former days as if they had been of yesterday.

"Here on the rocky isles," said he, "here in olden times the warriors, as they are called, decided their disputes. The warrior, Stärkodder, dwelt in this region, and took a fancy to the pretty maid Ogn; but she fancied

TROLLHÄTTA.

Hergrimer the more, and in consequence he was challenged by Stärkodder to a duel here by the Falls and met his death; but Ogn sprang towards them, and, seizing her lover's bloody sword, thrust it into her heart. Stärkodder did not get her. So a hundred years passed and another hundred; the forest became heavy and thick, wolves and bears prowled here summer and winter, and wicked robbers hid their booty here and no one could find them; yonder, by the Fall before Top Island, on the Norwegian side, was their cave; now it has fallen in—the cliff there overhangs it!"

"Yes, the Tailors' Cliff!" screamed all the boys. "It fell in the year 1755!"

"Fell!" cried the old man as if astonished that any one could know of it but himself. "Everything will fall: the tailor also fell. The robbers placed him upon the cliff and told him that if he would be liberated for his ransom he must sew a suit of clothes there; he tried to do it, but as he drew out his thread at the first stitch, he became dizzy and fell into the roaring water, and thus the rock got the name of The Tailors' Cliff. One day the robbers caught a young girl, and she betrayed them; she kindled a fire in the cavern, the smoke was seen, the cavern was discovered, and the robbers imprisoned and executed; that outside there is called The Thieves' Fall, and below, under the water, is another cave; the river rushes in there and issues out foaming; you can see it well up here and hear it too, but it can be heard better under the stony roof of the mountain sprite."

And we went on and on along the waterfall towards Top

Island, always on smooth paths covered with saw-dust to Polhelm's-Sluice; a cleft has been made in the rock for the first intended sluice-work, which was not finished, but on account of which has been shaped the most imposing of all the Trollhätta Falls; the hurrying water falls perpendicularly into the dark depth. The side of the rock here is connected with Top Island by means of a light iron bridge, which seems to be thrown over the abyss; we venture on this swaying bridge above the rushing, whirling water, and soon stand on the little rocky island between firs and pines that dart out of the crevices; before us rushes a sea of waves, broken as they rebound against the rock on which we stand, spraying us with their fine eternal mist; on each side the torrent flows as if shot from a gigantic cannon, waterfall upon waterfall; we look above them all and are lulled by the harmonic tone that has existed for thousands of years.

"No one can ever get to that island over there," said one of our party, pointing to the large island above the highest fall.

"I know one who got there!" exclaimed the old man, and nodded with a peculiar smile.

"Yes, my grandfather got there!" said one of the boys, "but for a hundred years scarcely any one else has reached it. The cross that stands there was set up by my grandfather. It had been a severe winter, the whole of Lake Venern was frozen, the ice dammed up the outlet, and for many hours the bottom was dry. Grandfather has told us about it: he and two others went over, set up the cross, and returned. Just then there was a thundering and cracking noise just like cannon, the ice broke up and the stream overflowed meadows and forest. It is true, every word I say!"

One of the travellers cited Tegner:

"Vildt Göta stortade fran Fjallen,
Hemsk Trollet fran sat Toppfall röt!
Men Snillet kom och sprängt stod Hallen,
Med Skeppen i sitt sköt!"

"Poor mountain sprite," he added, "thy power and glory are failing! Man flies beyond thee—Thou must learn of him!"

The garrulous old man made a grimace, and muttered something to himself—but we were now by the bridge before the inn, the steamboat glided through the open way, every one hurried on board and immediately it shot above the Fall just as if no Fall existed.

It was evening; I stood on the heights of Trollhätta's old sluices, and saw the ships with outspread sails glide away over the meadows like large white spectres. The sluice-gates opened with a heavy, crashing sound like that related of the copper gates of the *Vehmgericht;* the evening was so still; in the deep silence the tone of the Trollhätta Fall was like a chorus of a hundred water-mills, ever one and the same tone and sometimes the ringing of a deep and mighty note that seemed to pass through the very earth—and yet through all this the eternal silence of Nature was felt;—suddenly a great bird with heavily flapping wings flew out of the trees in the deep woods towards the waterfall. Was it the mountain sprite? We must believe so.

Pictures of Sweden (Leipzig, 1851).

THE GRAND CANYON OF THE COLORADO

C. F. GORDON-CUMMING

PROBABLY the greatest chasm in the known world is the grand canyon of the Colorado river (the Rio Colorado Grande), which is a gorge upward of two hundred miles in length, and of tremendous depth. Throughout this distance its vertical crags measure from *one* to upwards of *six thousand feet* in depth! Think of it! The highest mountain in Scotland measures 4,418 feet. The height of Niagara is 145 feet. And here is a narrow, tortuous pass where the river has eaten its way to a depth of 6,200 feet between vertical granite crags!

Throughout this canyon there is no cascade; and though the river descends 16,000 feet within a very short distance, forming rushing rapids, it is nevertheless possible to descend it by a raft—and this has actually been done, in defiance of the most appalling dangers and hardships. It is such a perilous adventure as to be deemed worthy of note even in this country, where every prospector carries his life in his hand, and to whom danger is the seasoning of daily life, which, without it, would appear positively monotonous.

I suppose no river in the world passes through scenery so extraordinary as does the Colorado river, in its journey of 2,000 miles from its birthplace in the Rocky mountains,

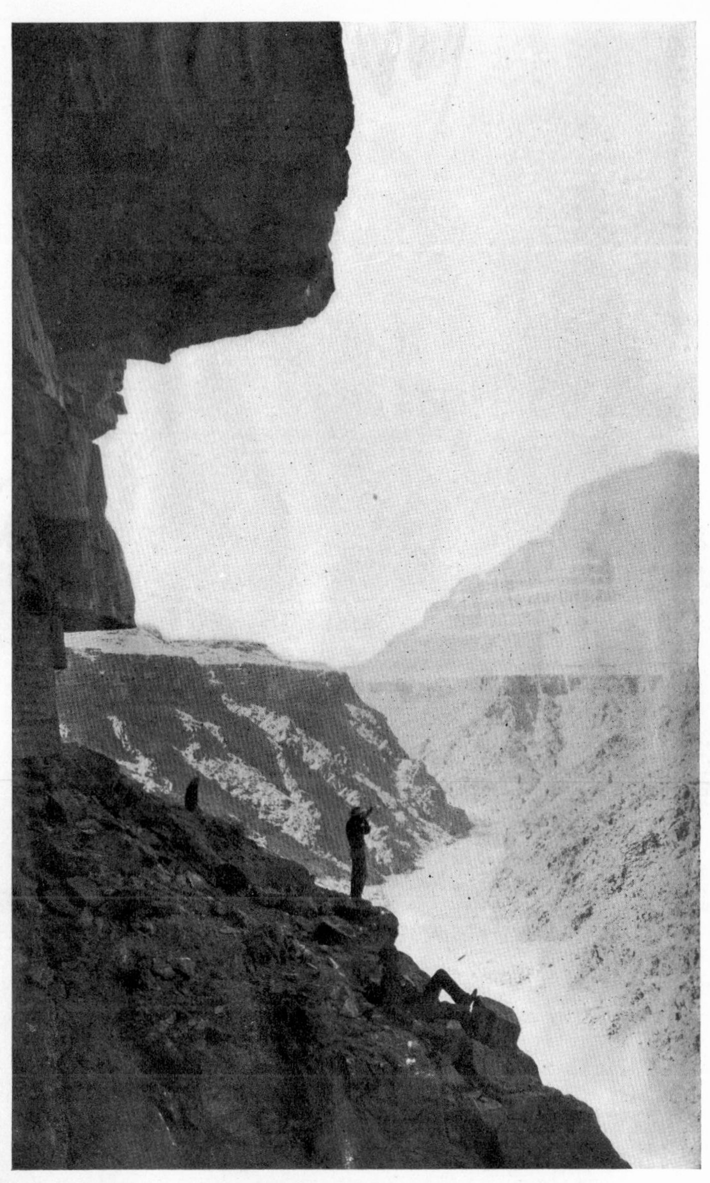

THE GRAND CAÑON OF THE COLORADO.

till, traversing the burning plains of New Mexico, it ends its course in the Gulf of California. Its early career is uneventful. In its youth it bears a maiden name, and, as the Green river, wends it way joyously through the upper forests. Then it reaches that ghastly country known as the *mauvaises terres* of Utah and Arizona—a vast region—extending also into Nevada and Wyoming, which, by the ceaseless action of water, has been carried into an intricate labyrinth of deep gloomy caverns.

For a distance of *one thousand miles* the river winds its tortuous course through these stupendous granite gorges, receiving the waters of many tributary streams, each rushing along similar deeply hewn channels.

In all the range of fiction no adventures can be devised more terrible than those which have actually befallen gold-seekers and hunters who, from any cause, have strayed into this dreary and awesome region. It was first discovered by two bold explorers, by name Strobe and White, who, being attacked by Indians, took refuge in the canyons. Preferring to face unknown dangers to certain death at the hands of the enemy, they managed to collect enough timber to construct a rude raft, and determined to attempt the descent.

Once embarked on that awful journey, there was no returning—they must endure to the bitter end.

On the fourth day the raft was upset. Strobe was drowned, and the little store of provisions and ammunition was lost. White contrived to right the raft, and for ten days the rushing waters bore him down the frightful chasm, seeing only the perpendicular cliffs on either side, and the strip of sky far overheard—never knowing, from hour to hour, but that at the next winding of the canyon the stream might overleap some mighty precipice, and so end his long anguish. During those awful ten days of famine, a few leaves and seed-pods, clutched from the bushes on the rocks, were his only food.

At length he reached a wretched settlement of half-bred Mexicans, who, deeming his escape miraculous, fed him; and eventually he reached the homes of white men, who looked on him (as well they might) as on one returned from the grave. The life thus wonderfully saved, was, however, sacrificed a few months later, when he fell into the hands of his old Indian foes.

The story of White's adventure was confirmed by various trappers and prospectors, who, from time to time, ventured some little way into this mysterious rock-labyrinth; and it was determined to attempt a government survey of the region. Accordingly, in 1869, a party, commanded by Major J. W. Powell, started on this most interesting but dangerous expedition. Warned by the fate of a party who attempted to explore the country in 1855, and who, with the exception of two men (Ashley and another), all perished miserably, the government party started with all possible precautions.

Four light Chicago-built boats were provisioned for six months, and, with infinite difficulty, were transported 1,500 miles across the desert. On reaching their starting-point, they were lowered into the awful ravines, from which it was, to say the least, problematic whether all would emerge alive. The dangers, great enough in reality, had been magnified by rumour. It was reported, with every semblance of probability, that the river formed terrible whirlpools—that it flowed underground for hundreds of miles, and emerged only to fall in mighty cataracts and appalling rapids. Even the friendly Indians entreated the explorers not to attempt so rash an enterprise, assuring them that none who embarked on that stream would escape alive.

But in the face of all such counsel, the expedition started, and for upwards of three months the party travelled, one may almost say in the bowels of the earth—at least in her deepest furrows—through canyons where the cliffs rise, sheer from the water, to a height of three-quarters of a mile!

They found, as was only natural, that imagination had exaggerated the horrors of the situation, and that it was possible to follow the rock-girt course of the Colorado through all its wanderings—not without danger, of course. In many places the boat had to be carried. One was totally wrecked and its cargo lost, and the others came to partial grief, entailing the loss of valuable instruments, and almost more precious lives. Though no subterranean passage was discovered, nor any actual waterfall, there were, nevertheless, such dangerous rapids as to necessitate frequent troublesome portage; and altogether, the expedition had its full share of adventure.

The ground was found to vary considerably. In some places the rock is so vivid in colour—red and orange—that the canyons were distinguished as the Red Canyon and the Flaming Gorge. Some are mere fissures of tremendous depth; while in other places, where the water has carved its way more freely, they are broad, here and there expanding into a fertile oasis, where green turf and lovely groves are enclosed by stupendous crags—miniature Yosemites—which to these travellers appeared to be indeed visions of Paradise.

Granite Crags (Edinburgh and London, 1884).

THE ROCK OF GIBRALTAR

AUGUSTUS J. C. HARE

IT was a lovely day, and a calm sea, which was a great subject of rejoicing, for even as it was the rickety Spanish vessel rolled disagreeably. Owing to the miserable slowness of everything, we were eleven hours on board. There was little interest till we reached the yellow headland of Trafalgar. Then the rugged outlines of the African coast rose before us, and we entered the straits, between Tarifa sleeping amid its orange groves on the Spanish coast, and the fine African peak above Ceuta. Soon, on the left, the great rock of Gibraltar rose from the sea like an island, though not the most precipitous side, which turns inwards towards the Mediterranean. But it was already gun-fire, and too late to join another steamer and land at the town, so we waited for a shoal of small boats which put out from Algeciras, and surrounded our steamer to carry us on shore.

Here we found in the Fonda Inglesa (kept by an English landlady), one of the most primitive but charming little hotels we ever entered. The view from our rooms alone decided us to stay there some days. Hence, framed by the balcony, Gibraltar rose before us in all the glory of its rugged sharp-edged cliffs, grey in the morning, pink in the evening light, with the town at its foot, whence, at night, thousands of lights were reflected on the still water. In the foreground were groups of fishing-boats at anchor, and, here and there, a lateen sail flitted, like a white albatross, across the bay. On the little pier beneath us was endless life and movement, knots of fishermen, in their blue shirts and scarlet caps and sashes, mingling with solemn-looking Moors in turbans, yellow slippers, and flowing burnouses, who were watching the arrival or embarcation of their wares; and an endless variety of travellers from all parts of Europe, waiting for different steamers, or come over to see the place. Here an invalid might stay, imbibing health from the fine air and sunshine, and never be weary of the ever changing diorama. In every direction delightful walks wind along the cliffs through groves of aloes and prickly-pear, or descend into little sandy coves full of beautiful shells. Behind the town, a fine old aqueduct strides across the valley, and beyond it the wild moors begin at once sweeping backwards to a rugged chain of mountains. Into the gorges of these mountains we rode one day, and most delightful they are, clothed in parts with magnificent old cork-trees, while in the depths of a ravine, overhung with oleander and rhododendron, is a beautiful waterfall.

It was with real regret that we left Algeciras and made the short voyage across the bay to Gibraltar, where we instantly found ourselves in a place as unlike Spain as it is possible to imagine. Upon the wharf you are assailed by a clamour of English-speaking porters and boatmen.

THE ROCK OF GIBRALTAR,

Passing the gates, you come upon a barrack-yard swarming with tall British soldiers, looking wonderfully bright and handsome, after the insignificant figures and soiled, shabby uniforms of the Spanish army. Hence the Waterport Street opens, the principal thoroughfare of the town, though from its insignificant shops, with English names, and its low public-houses, you have to look up at the strip of bright blue sky above, to be reminded that you are not in an English seaport.

Just outside the principal town, between it and the suburb of Europe, is the truly beautiful Alameda, an immense artificial garden, where endless gravel paths wind through labyrinths of geraniums and coronella and banks of flame-coloured ixia, which are all in their full blaze of beauty under the March sun, though the heat causes them to wither and droop before May. During our stay at Gibraltar, it has never ceased to surprise us that this Alameda, the shadiest and pleasantest place open to the public upon the Rock, should be almost deserted; but so it is. Even when the band playing affords an additional attraction, there are not a dozen persons to listen to it; whereas at Rome on such occasions, the Pincio, exceedingly inferior as a public garden, would be crowded to suffocation, and always presents a lively and animated scene.

One succession of gardens occupies the western base of the Rock, and most luxuriant and gigantic are the flowers that bloom in them. Castor-oil plants, daturas, and daphnes, here attain the dignity of timber, while geraniums and heliotropes many years old, so large as to destoy all the sense of floral proportions which has hitherto existed in your mind. It is a curious characteristic, and typical of Gibraltar, that the mouth of a cannon is frequently found protruding from a thicket of flowers.

The eastern side of the Rock, in great part a perpendicular precipice, is elsewhere left uncultivated, and is wild and striking in the highest degree. Here, beyond the quaint Jewish cemetery of closely set gravestones, bearing Hebrew inscriptions on the open hillside, a rugged path winds through rocks and tangled masses of flowers and palmists, to a curious stalactitic cavern called Martin's Cave. On this side of the cliff a remnant of the famous "apes of Tarshish" is suffered to remain wild and unmolested, though their numbers, always very small, have lately been reduced by the very ignorant folly of a young officer, who shot one and wounded nine others, for which he has been very properly impounded.

On the northern side of the Rock are the famous galleries tunnelled in the face of the precipice, with cannon pointing towards Spain from their embrasures. Through these, or, better, by delightful paths, fringed with palmettos and asphodel, you may reach El Hacho, the signal station, whence the view is truly magnificent over the sea, and the mountain chains of two continents, and down into the blue abysses beneath the tremendous precipice upon which it is placed.

The greatest drawback to the charms of Gibraltar has seemed to be the difficulty of leaving it. It is a beautiful

THE ROCK OF GIBRALTAR.

prison. We came fully intending to ride over the mountain passes by Ronda, but on arriving we heard that the whole of that district was in the hands of the brigands under the famous chief Don Diego, and the Governor positively refused to permit us to go that way. Our lamentations at this have since been cut short by the news of a double murder at the hands of the brigands on the way we wished to have taken, and at the very time we should have taken it. So we must go to Malaga by sea, and wait for the happy combination of a good steamer and calm weather falling on the same day.

Late in the afternoon of the 15th of March we embarked on board the *Lisbon* in the dockyard of Gibraltar. It had been a lovely day, and the grand Rock had looked its best, its every cleft filled with flowers and foliage. The sun set before we had rounded Europe Point, and the precipitous cliffs of the eastern bay rose utterly black against the yellow sky.

Wanderings in Spain (London, 1873).

THINGVALLA

LORD DUFFERIN

AT last I have seen the famous Geysers, of which every one has heard so much; but I have also seen Thingvalla, of which no one has heard anything. The Geysers are certainly wonderful marvels of nature, but more wonderful, more marvellous is Thingvalla; and if the one repay you for crossing the Spanish Sea, it would be worth while to go round the world to reach the other.

Of the boiling fountains I think I can give you a good idea, but whether I can contrive to draw for you anything like a comprehensible picture of the shape and nature of the Almanna Gja, the Hrafna Gja, and the lava vale, called Thingvalla, that lies between them, I am doubtful. Before coming to Iceland I had read every account that had been written of Thingvalla by any former traveller, and when I saw it, it appeared to me a place of which I had never heard; so I suppose I shall come to grief in as melancholy a manner as my predecessors, whose ineffectual pages whiten the entrance to the valley they have failed to describe.

After an hour's gradual ascent through a picturesque ravine, we emerged upon an immense desolate plateau of lava, that stretched away for miles and miles like a great

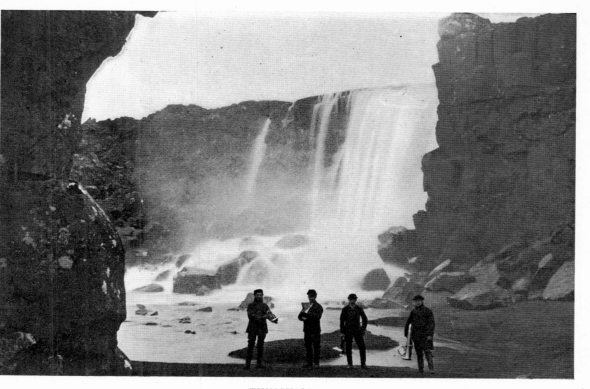

THINGVALLA.

stony sea. A more barren desert you cannot conceive. Innumerable boulders, relics of the glacial period, encumbered the track. We could only go at a foot-pace. Not a blade of grass, not a strip of green, enlivened the prospect, and the only sound we heard was the croak of the curlew and the wail of the plover. Hour after hour we plodded on, but the grey waste seemed interminable, boundless: and the only consolation Sigurdr would vouchsafe was that our journey's end lay on this side of some purple mountains that peeped like the tents of a demon leaguer above the stony horizon.

As it was already eight o'clock, and we had been told the entire distance from Reykjavik to Thingvalla was only five-and-thirty miles, I could not comprehend how so great a space should still separate us from our destination. Concluding more time had been lost in shooting, lunching, etc., by the way than we supposed, I put my pony into a canter, and determined to make short work of the dozen miles which seemed still to lie between us and the hills, on this side of which I understood from Sigurdr our encampment for the night was to be pitched.

Judge then of my astonishment when, a few minutes afterwards, I was arrested in full career by a tremendous precipice, or rather chasm, which suddenly gaped beneath my feet, and completely separated the barren plateau we had been so painfully traversing from a lovely, gay, sunlit flat, ten miles broad, that lay,—sunk at a level lower by a hundred feet,—between us and the opposite mountains. I was never so completely taken by surprise; Sigurdr's purposely vague description of our halting-place was accounted for.

We had reached the famous Almanna Gja. Like a black rampart in the distance, the corresponding chasm of the Hrafna Gja cut across the lower sloop of the distant hills, and between them now slept in sunshine and beauty the broad verdant plain[1] of Thingvalla.

Ages ago,—who shall say how long,—some vast commotion shook the foundations of the island, and bubbling up from sources far away amid the inland hills, a fiery deluge must have rushed down between their ridges, until, escaping from the narrow gorges, it found space to spread itself into one broad sheet of molten stone over an entire district of country, reducing its varied surface to one vast blackened level.

One of two things then occurred: either the vitrified mass contracting as it cooled,—the centre area of fifty square miles burst asunder at either side from the adjoining plateau, and sinking down to its present level, left the two paralleled Gjas, or chasms, which form its lateral boundaries, to mark the limits of the disruption; or else, while the pith or marrow of the lava was still in a fluid state, its upper surface became solid, and formed a roof beneath which the molten stream flowed on to lower levels, leaving a vast cavern into which the upper crust subsequently plumped down.

But to return where I left myself, on the edge of the

[1] The plain of Thingvalla is in a great measure clothed with birch brushwood.

cliff, gazing down with astonished eyes over a panorama of land and water imbedded at my feet. I could scarcely speak for pleasure and surprise; Fitz was equally taken aback, and as for Wilson, he looked as if he thought we had arrived at the end of the world. After having allowed us sufficient time to admire the prospect, Sigurdr turned to the left, along the edge of the precipice, until we reached a narrow pathway accidentally formed down a longitudinal niche in the splintered face of the cliff, which led across the bottom, and up the opposite side of the Gja, into the plain of Thingvalla.

Independently of its natural curiosities, Thingvalla was most interesting to me on account of the historical associations connected with it. Here, long ago, at a period when feudal despotism was the only government known throughout Europe, free parliaments used to sit in peace, and regulate the affairs of the young Republic; and to this hour the precincts of its Commons House of Parliament are as distinct and unchanged as on the day when the high-hearted fathers of the emigration first consecrated them to the service of a free nation. By a freak of nature, as the subsiding plain cracked and shivered into twenty thousand fissures, an irregular oval area, of about two hundred feet by fifty, was left almost entirely surrounded by a crevice so deep and broad as to be utterly impassable;—at one extremity alone a scanty causeway connected it with the adjoining level, and allowed of access to its interior. It is true, just at one point the encircling chasm grows so narrow as to be within the possibility of a jump; and an ancient worthy, named Flosi, pursued by his enemies, did actually take it at a fly: but as leaping an inch short would have entailed certain drowning in the bright green waters that sleep forty feet below, you can conceive there was never much danger of this entrance becoming a thoroughfare. I confess that for one moment, while contemplating the scene of Flosi's exploit, I felt, like a true Briton,—an idiotic desire to be able to say that I had done the same;—that I survive to write this letter is a proof of my having come subsequently to my senses.

This spot, then, erected by nature almost into a fortress, the founders of the Icelandic constitution chose for the meetings of their Thing, or Parliament; armed guards defended the entrance, while the grave bonders deliberated in security within: to this day, at the upper end of the place of meeting, may be seen the three hummocks, where sat in state the chiefs and judges of the land.

But those grand old times have long since passed away. Along the banks of the Oxeraa no longer glisten the tents and booths of the assembled lieges; no longer stalwart berserks guard the narrow entrance to the Althing; ravens alone sit on the sacred Logberg; and the floor of the old Icelandic House of Commons is ignominiously cropped by the sheep of the parson. For three hundred years did the gallant little Republic maintain its independence—three hundred years of unequalled literary and political vigour. At last its day of doom drew near. Like the Scotch nobles in the time of Elizabeth, their own chieftains intrigued against the liberties of the Icelandic people; and in 1261 the island became an appendage of the Norwegian crown.

Yet even then the deed embodying the concession of their independence was drawn up in such haughty terms as to resemble rather the offer of an equal alliance than the renunciation of imperial rights.

As I gazed around on the silent, deserted plain, and paced to and fro along the untrodden grass that now clothed the Althing, I could scarcely believe it had ever been the battle-field where such keen and energetic wits encountered,—that the fire-scathed rocks I saw before me were the very same that had once inspired one of the most successful rhetorical appeals ever hazarded in a public assembly.

From the Althing we strolled over to the Almanna Gja, visiting the Pool of Execution on our way. As I have already mentioned, a river from the plateau above leaps over the precipice into the bottom of the Gja, and flows for a certain distance between its walls. At the foot of the fall, the waters linger for a moment, in a dark, deep, brimming pool, hemmed in by a circle of ruined rocks; to this pool, in ancient times, all women convicted of capital crimes were immediately taken, and drowned. Witchcraft seems to have been the principal weakness of ladies in those days, throughout the Scandinavian countries. For a long period, no disgrace was attached to its profession. Odin himself, we are expressly told, was a great adept, and always found himself very much exhausted at the end of his performance; which leads me to think that, perhaps, he dabbled in electro-biology.

Turning aside from what, I dare say, was the scene of

many an unrecorded tragedy, we descended the gorge of the Almanna Gja, towards the lake; and I took advantage of the opportunity again to examine its marvellous construction. The perpendicular walls of rock rose on either hand from the flat greensward that carpeted its bottom, pretty much as the waters of the Red Sea must have risen on each side of the fugitive Israelites. A blaze of light smote the face of one cliff, while the other lay in the deepest shadow; and on the rugged surface of each might still be traced corresponding articulations, that once had dovetailed into each other, ere the igneous mass was rent asunder. So unchanged, so recent seemed the vestiges of this convulsion, that I felt as if I had been admitted to witness one of nature's grandest and most violent operations, almost in the very act of its execution. A walk of about twenty minutes brought us to the borders of the lake—a glorious expanse of water, fifteen miles long, by eight miles broad, occupying a basin formed by the same hills, which must also, I imagine, have arrested the further progress of the lava torrent. A lovelier scene I have seldom witnessed. In the foreground lay huge masses of rock and lava, tossed about like the ruins of a world, and washed by waters as bright and green as polished malachite. Beyond, a bevy of distant mountains, robed by the transparent atmosphere in tints unknown to Europe, peeped over each other's shoulders into the silver mirror at their feet, while here and there from among their purple ridges columns of white vapour rose like altar smoke towards the tranquil heaven.

The next morning we started for the Geysers; this time

dividing the baggage-train, and sending on the cook in light marching order, with the materials for dinner. The weather still remained unclouded, and each mile we advanced disclosed some new wonder in the unearthly landscape. A three hours' ride brought us to the Rabna Gja, the eastern boundary of Thingvalla, and, winding up its rugged face, we took our last look over the lovely plain beneath us, and then manfully set across the same kind of arid lava plateau as that which we had already traversed before arriving at the Almanna Gja.

Letters from High Latitude, being some account of a voyage in the schooner yacht Foam in 1856 (London, 1859).

LAND'S END AND LOGAN ROCK

JOHN AYRTON PARIS

"The sunbeams tremble, and the purple light
Illumes the dark Bolerium;—seat of storms,
High are his granite rocks; his frowning brow
Hangs o'er the smiling ocean. In his caves,
Where sleep the haggard spirits of the storm,
Wild dreary are the schistose rocks around,
Encircled by the waves, where to the breeze
The haggard cormorant shrieks; and far beyond
Are seen the cloud-like islands, grey in mists."

SIR H. DAVY.

IN an excursion to the *Land's End* the traveller will meet with several intermediate objects well worthy his attention, more worthy, perhaps, than the celebrated promontory itself, as being monuments of the highest antiquity in the kingdom. They consist of Druidical circles, cairns, or circular heaps of stones, cromlechs, crosses, military entrenchments, and the obsure remains of castles.

Having arrived at the celebrated promontory, we descend a rapid slope, which brings us to a bold group of rocks, composing the western extremity of our island. Some years ago a military officer who visited this spot, was rash enough to descend on horseback; the horse soon became unruly, plunged, reared, and, fearful to relate, fell backwards over the precipice, and rolling from rock to rock was

ROCKING STONES, LAND'S END, CORNWALL.

dashed to atoms before it reached the sea. The rider was for some time unable to disengage himself, but at length by a desperate effort he threw himself off, and was happily caught by some fragments of rock, at the very brink of the precipice, where he remained in a state of insensibility until assistance could be afforded him! The awful spot is marked by the figure of a horseshoe, traced on the turf with a deep incision, which is cleared out from time to time, in order to preserve it as a monument of rashness which could alone be equalled by the good fortune with which it was attended.

Why any promontory in an island should be exclusively denominated the Land's End, it is difficult to understand; yet so powerful is the charm of a name, that many persons have visited it on no other account; the intelligent tourist, however, will receive a much more substantial gratification from his visit; the great geological interest of the spot will afford him an ample source of entertainment and instruction, while the magnificence of its convulsed scenery, the ceaseless roar, and deep intonation of the ocean, and the wild shrieks of the cormorant, all combine to awaken the blended sensations of awe and admiration.

The cliff which bounds this extremity is rather abrupt than elevated, not being more than sixty feet above the level of the sea. It is composed entirely of granite, the forms of which present a very extraordinary appearance, assuming in some places the resemblance of *shafts* that had been regularly cut with the chisel; in others, regular equidistant fissures divide the rock into horizontal masses, and give it the character of basaltic columns; in other places, again, the impetuous waves of the ocean have opened, for their retreat, gigantic arches, through which the angry billows roll and bellow with tremendous fury.

Several of these rocks from their grotesque forms have acquired whimsical appellations, as that of the *Armed Knight*, the *Irish Lady*, etc. An inclining rock on the side of a craggy headland, south of the Land's End, has obtained the name of *Dr. Johnson's Head*, and visitors after having heard the appellation seldom fail to acknowledge that it bears some resemblance to the physiognomy of that extraordinary man.

On the north, this rocky scene is terminated by a promontory 229 feet above the level of the sea, called *Cape Cornwall*, between which and the Land's End, the coast retires, and forms *Whitesand Bay;* a name which it derives from the peculiar whiteness of the sand, and amongst which the naturalist will find several rare microscopic shells. There are, besides, some historical recollections which invest this spot with interest. It was in this bay that Stephen landed on his first arrival in England; as did King John, on his return from Ireland; and Perkin Warbeck, in the prosecution of those claims to the Crown to which some late writers have been disposed to consider that he was entitled, as the real son of Edward the Fourth. In the rocks near the southern termination of *Whitesand Bay* may be seen the junction of the granite and slate; large veins of the former may also be observed to traverse the latter in all directions.

We now return to the Land's End,—from which we should proceed to visit a promontory called "Castle Treryn," where is situated the celebrated "Logan Stone." If we pursue our route along the cliffs, it will be found to be several miles southeast of the Land's End, although by taking the direct and usual road across the country, it is not more than two miles distant; but the geologist must walk, or ride along the coast on horseback, and we can assure him that he will be amply recompensed for his trouble.

From the Cape on which the signal station is situated, the rock scenery is particularly magnificent, exhibiting an admirable specimen of the manner, and forms, into which granite disintegrates. About forty yards from this Cape is the promontory called Tol-Pedn-Penwith, which in the Cornish language signifies the *holed headland in Penwith*. The name is derived from a singular chasm, known by the appellation of the Funnel Rock; it is a vast perpendicular excavation in the granite, resembling in figure an inverted cone, and has been evidently produced by the gradual decomposition of one of those vertical veins with which this part of the coast is so frequently intersected. By a circuitous route you may descend to the bottom of the cavern, into which the sea flows at high water. Here the Cornish chough (*Corvus Graculus*) has built its nest for several years, a bird which is very common about the rocky parts of this coast, and may be distinguished by its red legs and bill, and the violaceous blackness of its feathers. This promontory forms the western extremity of the Mount's Bay. The antiquary will discover in this spot, the vestiges of one of the ancient "Cliff Castles," which were little else than stone walls, stretching across necks of land from cliff to cliff. The only geological phenomenon worthy of particular notice is a large and beautiful contemporaneous vein of *red* granite containing schorl; is one foot in width, and may be seen for about forty feet in length.

Continuing our route around the coast we at length arrive at Castle Treryn. Its name is derived from the supposition of its having been the site of an ancient British fortress, of which there are still some obscure traces, although the wild and rugged appearance of the rocks indicate nothing like art.

The foundation of the whole is a stupendous group of granite rocks, which rise in pyramidal clusters to a prodigious altitude, and overhang the sea. On one of those pyramids is situated the celebrated "Logan Stone," which is an immense block of granite weighing about sixty tons. The surface in contact with the under rock is of very small extent, and the whole mass is so nicely balanced, that, notwithstanding its magnitude, the strength of a single man applied to its under edge is sufficient to change its centre of gravity, and though at first in a degree scarcely perceptible, yet the repetition of such impulses, at each return of the stone, produces at length a very sensible oscillation! As soon as the astonishment which this phenomenon excites has in some measure subsided, the stranger anxiously inquires how, and whence the stone originated—was it elevated by human means, or was it produced by the agency of natural causes? Those who are in the habit of viewing mountain masses with geological eyes, will readily discover that the only chisel ever employed has been the tooth of time—the only artist engaged, the elements. Granite usually disintegrates into rhomboidal and tabular masses, which by the farther operation of air and moisture gradually lose their solid angles, and approach the spheroidal form. *De Luc* observed, in the giant mountains of Silesia, spheroids of this description so piled upon each other as to resemble Dutch cheeses; and appearances, no less illustrative of the phenomenon, may be seen from the signal station to which we have just alluded. The fact of the upper part of the cliff being more exposed to atmospheric agency, than the parts beneath, will sufficiently explain why these rounded masses so frequently rest on blocks which still preserve the tabular form; and since such spheroidal blocks must obviously rest in that position in which their lesser axes are perpendicular to the horizon, it is equally evident that whenever an adequate force is applied they must vibrate on their point of support.

Although we are thus led to deny the Druidical *origin* of this stone, for which so many zealous antiquaries have contended, still we by no means intend to deny that the Druids employed it as an engine of superstition; it is indeed very probable that, having observed so uncommon a property, they dexterously contrived to make it answer the purposes of an ordeal, and by regarding it as the *touchstone* of truth, acquitted or condemned the accused by its motions. Mason poetically alludes to this supposed property in the following lines:

"Behold yon huge
And unknown sphere of living adamant,
Which, pois'd by magic, rests its central weight
On yonder pointed rock: firm as it seems,
Such is its strange, and virtuous property,
It moves obsequious to the gentlest touch
Of him whose heart is pure, but to a traitor,
Tho' e'en a giant's prowess nerv'd his arm,
It stands as fix'd as—Snowdon."

The rocks are covered with a species of *Byssus* long and rough to the touch, forming a kind of hoary beard; in many places they are deeply furrowed, carrying with them a singular air of antiquity, which combines with the whole of the romantic scenery to awaken in the minds of the poet and enthusiast the recollection of the Druidical ages. The botanist will observe the common Thrift (*Statice Armeria*) imparting a glowing tinge to the scanty vegetation of the spot, and, by growing within the crevices of the rocks, affording a very picturesque contrast to their massive fabric. Here, too, the *Daucus Maritimus*, or wild carrot; *Sedum Telephium*, *Saxifraga Stellaris*, and *Asplenium Marinum*, may be found in abundance.

The granite in this spot is extremely beautiful on account of its porphyritic appearance; the crystals of feldspar are numerous and distinct; in some places the rock is traversed by veins of red feldspar, and of black tourmaline, or schorl, of which the crystalline forms of the prisms, on account of their close aggregation, are very indistinct. Here may also be observed a contemporaneous vein of *schorl rock* in the granite, nearly two feet wide, highly inclined and very short, and not having any distinct walls.

On the western side of the Logan Rock is a cavern, formed by the decomposition of a vein of granite, the feldspar of which assumes a brilliant flesh-red and lilac colour; and, where it is polished by the sea, exceeding even in beauty the *Serpentine caverns* at the Lizard.

A Guide to the Mount's Bay and the Land's End (London, 2d Ed., 1824).

MOUNT HEKLA[1]

SIR RICHARD F. BURTON

THE Hekla of our ingenuous childhood, when we believed in the "Seven Wonders of the World," was a mighty cone, a "pillar of heaven," upon whose dreadful summit white, black, and sanguine red lay in streaks and patches, with volumes of sooty smoke and lurid flames, and a pitchy sky. The whole was somewhat like the impossible illustrations of Vesuvian eruptions, in body-colours, plus the ice proper to Iceland. The Hekla of reality, No. 5 in the island scale, is a commonplace heap, half the height of Hermon, and a mere pigmy compared with the Andine peaks, rising detached from the plains, about three and a half miles in circumference, backed by the snows of Tindafjall and Torfajökull, and supporting a sky-line that varies greatly with the angle under which it is seen. Travellers usually make it a three-horned Parnassus, with the central knob highest—which is not really the case. From the south-west, it shows now four, then five, distinct

[1] Heklu-fjall derives from Hekla (akin to Hökull, a priest's cope), meaning a cowled or hooded frock, knitted of various colours, and applied to the "Vesuvius of the North" from its cap and body vest of snow. Icelanders usually translate it a chasuble, because its rounded black shoulders bear stripes of white, supposed to resemble the cross carried to Calvary.

points; the north-western lip of the northern crater, which hides the true apex; the south-western lip of the same; the north-eastern lip of the southern crater, which appears the culminating point, and the two eastern edges of the southern bowls. A pair of white patches represents the "eternal snows." On the right of the picture is the steep, but utterly unimportant Thríhyrningr, crowned with its bench-mark; to the left, the Skardsfjall, variegated green and black; and in the centre, the Bjólfell, a western buttress of the main building, which becomes alternately a saddleback, a dorsum, and an elephant's head, trunk, and shoulders.

We came upon the valley of the Western Rángá[1] at a rough point, a gash in the hard yellow turf-clad clay, dotted with rough lava blocks, and with masses of conglomerate, hollowed, turned, and polished by water: the shape was a succession of S, and the left side was the more tormented. Above the ford a dwarf cascade had been formed by the lava of '45, which caused the waters to boil, and below the ford jumped a second, where the stream forks. We then entered an Iceland "forest," at least four feet high; the "chapparal" was composed of red willow (*Salix purpurea*), of Grá-vidir, woolly-leaved willow (*Sulix lapponum*), the "tree under which the devil flayed the goats"—a diabolical difficulty, when the bush is a foot high—and the awful and venerable birch, "*la demoiselle des fôrets*," which has so often "blushed with patrician blood." About mid-

[1] Rángá ("wrong," or crooked stream) is a name that frequently occurs, and generally denotes either that the trend is opposed to the general water-shed, or that an angle has been formed in the bed by earthquakes or eruptions.

afternoon we reached Næfrholt (birch-bark hill), the "fashionable" place for the ascent, and we at once inquired for the guide. Upon the *carpe diem* principle, he had gone to Reykjavik with the view of drinking his late gains; but we had time to organize another, and even alpenstocks with rings and spikes are to be found at the farm-house. Everything was painfully tourist.

In the evening we scaled the stiff slope of earth and Palagonite which lies behind, or east of Næfrholt; this crupper of Bjólfell, the Elephant Mountain, gives perhaps harder work than any part of Hekla on the normal line of ascent. From the summit we looked down upon a dwarf basin, with a lakelet of fresh water, which had a slightly (carbonic) acid taste, and which must have contained lime, as we found two kinds of shells, both uncommonly thin and fragile. Three species of weeds floated off the clean sandstrips. Walking northward to a deserted byre, we found the drain gushing under ground from sand and rock, forming a distinct river-valley, and eventually feeding the Western Rángá. This "Vatn" is not in the map; though far from certain that it is not mentioned by Mackenzie, we named it the "Unknown Lake." Before night fell we received a message that three English girls and their party proposed to join us. This was a "scare," but happily the Miss Hopes proved plucky as they were young and pretty, and we rejoiced in offering this pleasant affront of the feminine foot to that grim old *solitaire*, Father Hekla.

Before the sleep necessary to prepare for the next day's work, I will offer a few words concerning the "Etna of the North," sparing the reader, however, the mortification of a regular history. It was apparently harmless, possibly dormant, till A. D. 1104, when Sæmund, the "Paris clerk," then forty-eight years old, threw in a casket, and awoke the sleeping lion. Since that time fourteen regular eruptions, without including partial outbreaks are recorded, giving an average of about two per century. The last was in 1845. The air at Reykjavik was flavoured, it is said, like a gun that wants washing; and the sounds of a distant battle were conducted by the lava and basaltic ground. The ashes extended to Scotland. When some writers tell us that on this occasion Hekla lost 500 feet in height, "so much of the summit having been blown away by the explosions," they forget or ignore the fact that the new crater opened laterally and low down.

Like Etna, Vesuvius, and especially Stromboli, Hekla became mythical in Middle-Age Europe, and gained wide repute as one of the gates of "Hel-viti." Witches' Sabbaths were held there. The spirits of the wicked, driven by those grotesque demons of Father Pinamonti which would make the fortune of a zoological society, were seen trooping into the infernal crater; and such facts as these do not readily slip off the mind of man. The Danes still say "Begone to Heckenfjæld!" the North Germans, "Go to Hackelberg!" and the Scotch consign you to "John Hacklebirnie's house." Even Goldsmith (Animated Nature, i. 48) had heard of the local creed, "The inhabitants of Iceland believe the bellowings of Hekla are nothing else but the cries of the damned, and that its eruptions are contrived to increase their tortures." Uno Van Troil (Letter I.) who in 1770, together with those "inclyti Brittannici," *Baron* Bank and Dr. Solander, "gained the pleasure of being the first who ever reached the summit of this celebrated volcano," attributes the mountain's virginity to the superstitions of the people. He writes soberly about its marvels; and he explains its high fame by its position, skirting the watery way to and from Greenland and North America. His companions show less modesty of imagination. We may concede that an unknown ascent "required great circumspection"; and that in a high wind ascensionists were obliged to lie down. But how explain the "dread of being blown into the most dreadful precipices," when the latter do not exist? Moreover, we learn that to "accomplish this undertaking" they had to travel from 300 to 360 miles over uninterrupted bursts of lava, which is more than the maximum length of the island, from northeast to southwest. As will be seen, modern travellers have followed suit passing well.

The next morning (July 13) broke fair and calm, reminding me

"*Del bel paese la dove il sì suona.*"

The Miss Hopes were punctual to a minute—an excellent thing in travelling womanhood. We rode up half-way somewhat surprised to find so few parasitic craters; the only signs of independent eruption on the western flank were the Raudkólar (red hills), as the people call their lava hornitos and spiracles, which are little bigger than the bottle-house cones of Leith.

At an impassable divide we left our poor nags to pass the dreary time, without water or forage, and we followed the improvised guide, who caused not a little amusement. His general port was that of a bear that has lost its ragged staff.—I took away his alpenstock for one of the girls—and he was plantigrade rather than cremnobatic; he had stripped to his underalls, which were very short, whilst his stockings were very long and the heraldic gloves converted his hands to paws. The two little snow fonds ("steep glassy slopes of hard snow"), were the easiest of walking. We had nerved ourselves to "Break neck or limbs, be maimed or boiled alive," but we looked in vain for the "concealed abysses," for the "crevasses to be crossed," and for places where a "slip would be to roll to destruction." We did not sight the "lava wall," a capital protection against giddiness. The snow was anything but slippery; the surface was scattered with dust, and it bristled with a forest of dwarf earth-pillars, where blown volcanic sand preserved the ice. After a slow hour and a half, we reached the crater of '45, which opened at 9 A. M. on September 2, and discharged lava till the end of November. It might be passed unobserved by the inexperienced man. The only remnant is the upper lip prolonged to the right; the dimensions may have been 120 by 150 yards, and the cleft shows a projecting ice-ledge ready to fall. The feature is well-marked by the new lava-field of which it is the source: the bristly "stone-river" is already degrading to superficial dust. A little beyond this bowl the ground smokes, discharging snow-steam made visible by the cold air. Hence doubtless those sententious travellers "experienced at one and the same time, a high degree of heat and cold."

Fifteen minutes more led us to the First or Southern Crater, whose Ol-bogi (elbow or rim) is one of the horns conspicuous from below. It is a regular formation about 100 yards at the bottom each way, with the right (east) side red and cindery, and the left yellow and sulphury; mosses and a few flowerets grow on the lips; in the sole rise jets of steam and a rock-rib bisects it diagonally from northeast to southwest. We thought it the highest point of the volcano, but the aneriod corrected our mistake.

From the First Crater we walked over the left or western dorsum, over which one could drive a coach, and we congratulated one another upon the exploit. Former travellers "balancing themselves like rope-dancers, succeeded in passing along the ridge of slags which was so narrow that there was scarcely room for their feet," the breadth being "not more than two feet, having a precipice on each side several hundred feet in depth." Charity suggests that the feature has altered, but there was no eruption between 1766 and 1845; moreover, the lip would have diminished, not increased. And one of the most modern visitors repeats the "very narrow ridge," with the classical but incorrect adjuncts of "Scylla here, Charybdis there." Scylla (say the crater slope) is disposed at an angle of 30°, and Mr. Chapman coolly walked down this "vast" little hollow. I descended Charybdis (the outer counterscarp) far enough to make sure that it is equally easy.

Passing the "carriage road" (our own name), we crossed

a *névé* without any necessity for digging foot-holes. It lies where sulphur is notably absent. The hot patches which account for the freedom from snow, even so high above the congelation-line, are scattered about the summit: in other parts the thermometer, placed in an eighteen-inch hole, made earth colder than air. After a short climb we reached the apex; the ruddy-walled northeastern lip of the Red Crater (No. 2): its lower or western rim forms two of the five summits seen from the prairie, and hides the highest point. We thus ascertained that Hekla is a linear volcano of two mouths, or three including that of '45, and that it wants a true apical crater. But how reconcile the accounts of travellers? Pliny Miles found one cone and three craters; Madam Ida Pfeiffer, like Metcalfe, three cones and no crater.

On the summit the guides sang a song of triumph, whilst we drank to the health of our charming companions and, despite the cold wind which eventually drove us down, carefully studied the extensive view. The glorious day was out of character with a scene *niente che Montagne*, as the unhappy Venetians described the Morea; rain and sleet and blinding snow would better have suited the picture, but happily they were conspicuous by their absence. Inland, beyond a steep snow-bed unpleasantly crevassed, lay a grim photograph all black and white; Lángjökull looking down upon us with a grand and freezing stare; the Hrafntinnu Valley marked by a dwarf cone, and beyond where streams head, the gloomy regions stretching to the Sprengisandur, dreary wastes of utter sterility, howling deserts of dark ashes, wholly lacking water and vegetable life, and wanting the gleam and the glow which light up the Arabian wild. Skaptár and Oræfa were hidden from sight. Seawards, ranging from west to south, the view, by contrast, was a picture of amenity and civilization. Beyond castellated Hljódfell and conical Skjaldbreid appeared the familiar forms of Esja, and the long lava projection of the Gold Breast country, melting into the western main. Nearer stretched the fair lowlands, once a broad deep bay, now traversed by the network of Ölfusá, Thjórsá, and the Markarfljót; while the sixfold bunch of the Westman Islands, mere stone lumps upon a blue ground, seemingly floating far below the raised horizon, lay crowned by summer sea.. Eastward we distinctly traced the Fiskivötn. Run the eye along the southern shore, and again the scene shifts. Below the red hornitos of the slope rises the classical Three-horned, not lofty, but remarkable for its trident top; Tindfjall (tooth-fell) with its two horns or pyramids of ice, casting blue shadows upon the untrodden snow; and the whole mighty mass known as the Eastern Jökull Eyjafjall (island-fell), so called from the black button of rock which crowns the long white dorsum; Kátlá (Költu-gjá), Merkrjökull, and Godalands, all connected by ridges, and apparently neither lofty nor impracticable.

Ultima Thule; or a Summer in Iceland (London and Edinburgh, 1875).

VICTORIA FALLS

DAVID LIVINGSTONE

WE proceeded next morning, 9th August, 1860, to see the Victoria Falls. Mosi-oa-tunya is the Makololo name, and means smoke sounding; Seongo or Chongwé, meaning the Rainbow, or the place of the Rainbow, was the more ancient term they bore. We embarked in canoes, belonging to Tuba Mokoro, "smasher of canoes," an ominous name; but he alone, it seems, knew the medicine which insures one against shipwreck in the rapids above the Falls. For some miles the river was smooth and tranquil, and we glided pleasantly over water clear as crystal, and past lovely islands densely covered with a tropical vegetation. Noticeable among the many trees were the lofty Hyphæne and Borassus palms; the graceful wild date-palm, with its fruit in golden clusters, and the umbrageous mokononga, of cypress form, with its dark-green leaves and scarlet fruit. Many flowers peeped out near the water's edge, some entirely new to us, and others, as the convolvulus, old acquaintances.

But our attention was quickly called from the charming islands to the dangerous rapids, down which Tuba might unintentionally shoot us. To confess the truth, the very ugly aspect of these roaring rapids could scarcely fail to cause some uneasiness in the minds of new-comers. It is only when the river is very low, as it was now, that any one durst venture to the island to which we were bound. If one went during the period of flood, and fortunately hit the island, he would be obliged to remain there till the water subsided again, if he lived so long. Both hippopotamus and elephants have been known to be swept over the Falls, and of course smashed to pulp.

Before entering the race of waters, we were requested not to speak, as our talking might diminish the virtue of the medicine; and no one with such boiling, eddying rapids before his eyes, would think of disobeying the orders of a "canoe-smasher." It soon became evident that there was sound sense in this request of Tuba's, although the reason assigned was not unlike that of the canoe-man from Sesheke, who begged one of our party not to whistle because whistling made the wind come. It was the duty of the man at the bow to look out ahead for the proper course, and when he saw a rock or snag to call out to the steersman. Tuba doubtless thought that talking on board might divert the attention of his steersman, at a time when the neglect of an order, or a slight mistake, would be sure to spill us all into the chafing river. There were places where the utmost exertions of both men had to be put forth in order to force the canoe to the only safe part of the rapid, and to prevent it from sweeping down broadside on, where in a twinkling we should have found ourselves floundering among the plotuses and cormorants, which were engaged in diving for their breakfast of small fish. At times it seemed as if

FALLS OF THE ZAMBESI.

nothing could save us from dashing in our headlong race against the rocks which, now that the river was low, jutted out of the water; but just at the very nick of time, Tuba passed the word to the steersman, and then with ready pole turned the canoe a little aside and we glided swiftly past the threatened danger. Never was canoe more admirably managed: once only did the medicine seem to have lost something of its efficacy. We were driving swiftly down, a black rock, over which the white foam flew, lay directly in our path, the pole was planted against it as readily as ever, but it slipped just as Tuba put forth his strength to turn the bow off. We struck hard, and were half-full of water in a moment; Tuba recovered himself as speedily, shoved off the bow, and shot the canoe into a still shallow place, to bale out the water. Here we were given to understand that it was not the medicine which was at fault; *that* had lost none of its virtue; the accident was owing entirely to Tuba having started without his breakfast. Need it be said we never left Tuba go without that meal again?

We landed at the head of Garden Island, which is situated near the middle of the river and on the lip of the Falls. On reaching that lip, and peering over the giddy height, the wondrous and unique character of the magnificent cascade at once burst upon us.

It is a rather hopeless task to endeavour to convey an idea of it in words, since, as was remarked on the spot, an accomplished painter, even by a number of views, could but impart a faint impression of the glorious scene. The probable mode of its formation may perhaps help to the conception of its peculiar shape. Niagara has been formed by a wearing back of the rock over which the river falls; but during the long course of ages, it has gradually receded, and left a broad, deep, and pretty straight trough in front. It goes on wearing back daily, and may yet discharge the lakes from which its river—the St. Lawrence—flows. But the Victoria Falls have been formed by a crack right across the river, in the hard, black, basaltic rock which there formed the bed of the Zambesi. The lips of the crack are still quite sharp, save about three feet of the edge over which the river rolls. The walls go sheer down from the lips without any projecting crag, or symptoms of stratification or dislocation. When the mighty rift occurred, no change of level took place in the two parts of the bed of the river thus rent asunder, consequently, in coming down the river to Garden Island, the water suddenly disappears, and we see the opposite side of the cleft, with grass and trees growing where once the river ran, on the same level as that part of its bed on which we sail. The first crack, is, in length, a few yards more than the breadth of the Zambesi, which by measurement we found to be a little over 1,860 yards, but this number we resolved to retain as indicating the year in which the Fall was for the first time carefully examined. The main stream here runs nearly north and south, and the cleft across it is nearly east and west. The depth of the rift was measured by lowering a line, to the end of which a few bullets and a foot of white cotton cloth were tied. One of us lay with his head over a projecting crag, and watched the descending calico, till, after his companions had paid out 310 feet, the weight rested on a sloping projection, probably fifty feet from the water below, the actual bottom being still further down. The white cloth now appeared the size of a crown-piece. On measuring the width of this deep cleft by sextant, it was found at Garden Island, its narrowest part, to be eighty yards, and at its broadest somewhat more. Into this chasm, of twice the depth of Niagara-fall, the river, a full mile wide, rolls with a deafening roar; and this is Mosi-oa-tunya, or the Victoria Falls.

Looking from Garden Island, down to the bottom of the abyss, nearly half a mile of water, which has fallen over that portion of the Falls to our right, or west of our point of view, is seen collected in a narrow channel twenty or thirty yards wide, and flowing at exactly right angles to its previous course, to our left; while the other half, or that which fell over the eastern portion of the Falls, is seen in the left of the narrow channel below, coming towards our right. Both waters unite midway, in a fearful boiling waterfall, and find an outlet by a crack situated at right angles to the fissure of the Falls. This outlet is about 1,170 yards from the western end of the chasm, and some 600 from its eastern end; the whirlpool is at its commencement. The Zambesi, now apparently not more than twenty or thirty yards wide, rushes and surges south, through the narrow escape-channel for 130 yards; then enters a second chasm somewhat deeper, and nearly parallel with the first. Abandoning the bottom of the eastern half of this second chasm to the growth of large trees, it turns sharply off to the west, and forms a promontory, with the escape-channel at its point, of 1,170 yards long, and 416 yards broad at the base. After reaching this base, the river runs abruptly round the head of another promontory, and flows away to the east, in a third chasm; then glides round a third promontory, much narrower than the rest, and away back to the west, in a fourth chasm; and we could see in the distance that it appeared to round still another promontory, and bend once more in another chasm toward the east. In this gigantic, zigzag, yet narrow trough, the rocks are all so sharply cut and angular, that the idea at once arises that the hard basaltic trap must have been riven into its present shape by a force acting from beneath, and that this probably took place when the ancient inland seas were cut off by similar fissures nearer the ocean.

The land beyond, or on the south of the Falls, retains, as already remarked, the same level as before the rent was made. It is as if the trough below Niagara were bent right and left, several times before it reached the railway bridge. The land in the supposed bends being of the same height as that above the Fall, would give standing-places, or points of view, of the same nature as that from the railway bridge, but the nearest would be only eighty yards, instead of two miles (the distance to the bridge) from the face of the cascade. The tops of the promontories are in general flat, smooth, and studded with trees. The first, with its base on the east, is at one place so narrow, that it would be dangerous to walk to its extremity. On the second, however, we found a broad rhinoceros path and a hut; but, unless the builder were a hermit, with a pet rhinoceros, we cannot conceive what beast or man ever went there for. On reaching the apex of this second eastern promontory we saw the great river, of a deep sea-green colour, now sorely compressed, gliding away, at least 400 feet below us.

Garden Island, when the river is low, commands the best view of the Great Fall chasm, as also of the promontory opposite, with its grove of large evergreen trees, and brilliant rainbows of three-quarters of a circle, two, three, and sometimes even four in number, resting on the face of the vast perpendicular rock, down which tiny streams are always running to be swept again back by the upward rushing vapour. But as, at Niagara, one has to go over to the Canadian shore to see the chief wonder—the Great Horse-shoe Fall—so here we have to cross over to Moselekatsé's side to the promontory of evergreens, for the best view of the principal Falls of Mosi-oa-tunya. Beginning, therefore, at the base of this promontory, and facing the Cataract, at the west end of the chasm, there is, first, a fall of thirty-six yards in breadth, and of course, as they all are, upwards of 310 feet in depth. Then Boaruka, a small island, intervenes, and next comes a great fall, with a breadth of 573 yards; a projecting rock separates this from a second grand fall of 325 yards broad; in all, upwards of 900 yards of perennial Falls. Further east stands Garden Island; then, as the river was at its lowest, came a good deal of the bare rock of its bed, with a score of narrow falls, which, at the time of flood, constitute one enormous cascade of nearly another half-mile. Near the east end of the chasm are two larger falls, but they are nothing at low water compared to those between the islands.

The whole body of water rolls clear over, quite unbroken; but, after a descent of ten or more feet, the entire mass suddenly becomes a huge sheet of driven snow. Pieces of water leap off it in the form of comets with tails streaming behind, till the whole snowy sheet becomes myriads of rushing, leaping, aqueous comets. This peculiarity was not observed by Charles Livingstone at Niagara, and here it happens, possibly from the dryness of the atmosphere, or whatever the cause may be which makes every drop of Zambesi water appear to possess a sort of individuality. It runs off the ends of the paddles, and glides in beads along the smooth surface, like drops of quicksilver on a table. Here we see them in a conglomeration, each with a train of pure white vapour, racing down till lost in clouds of spray. A stone dropped in became less and less to the eye, and at last disappeared in the dense mist below.

Charles Livingstone had seen Niagara, and gave Mosi-oa-tunya the palm, though now at the end of a drought, and the river at its very lowest. Many feel a disappointment on first seeing the great American Falls, but Mosi-oa-tunya is so strange, it must ever cause wonder. In the amount of water, Niagara probably excels, though not during the months when the Zambesi is in flood. The vast body of water, separating in the comet-like forms described, necessarily encloses in its descent a large volume of air, which, forced into the cleft, to an unknown depth, rebounds, and rushes up loaded with vapour to form the three or even six columns, as if of steam, visible at the Batoka village Moachemba, twenty-one miles distant. On attaining a height of 200, or at most 300 feet from the level of the river above the cascade, this vapour becomes condensed into a perpetual shower of fine rain. Much of the spray, rising to the west of Garden Island, falls on the grove of evergreen trees opposite; and from their leaves, heavy drops are for ever falling, to form sundry little rills, which, in running down the steep face of rock, are blown off and turned back, or licked off their perpendicular bed, up into the column from which they have just descended.

The morning sun gilds these columns of watery smoke with all the glowing colours of double or treble rainbows. The evening sun, from a hot yellow sky imparts a sulphureous hue, and gives one the impression that the yawning gulf might resemble the mouth of the bottomless pit. No bird sings and sings on the branches of the grove of perpetual showers, or ever builds his nest there. We saw hornbills and flocks of little black weavers flying across from the mainland to the islands, and from the islands to the points of the promontories and back again, but they uniformly shunned the region of perpetual rain, occupied by the evergreen grove. The sunshine, elsewhere in this land so overpowering, never penetrates the deep gloom of that shade. In the presence of the strange Mosi-oa-tunya, we can sympathize with those who, when the world was young, peopled earth, air, and river, with beings not of mortal form. Sacred to what deity would be this awful chasm and that dark grove, over which hovers an ever-abiding "pillar of cloud"?

The ancient Batoka chieftains used Kazeruka, now Garden Island, and Boaruka, the island further west, also on the lip of the Falls, as sacred spots for worshipping the Deity. It is no wonder that under the cloudy columns, and near the brilliant rainbows, with the ceaseless roar of the cataract, with the perpetual flow, as if pouring forth from the hand of the Almighty, their souls should be filled with reverential awe.

The Zambesi and its Tributaries 1858–1864 (London, 1865).

THE DRAGON-TREE OF OROTAVA[1]

ALEXANDER VON HUMBOLDT

OROTAVA, the ancient Taoro of the Guanches, is situated on a very steep declivity. The streets seem deserted; the houses are solidly built, and of gloomy appearance. We passed along a lofty aqueduct, lined with a great number of fine ferns; and visited several gardens, in which the fruit trees of the north of Europe are mingled with orange trees, pomegranates, and date trees. We were assured, that these last were as little productive here as on the coast of Cumana. Although we had been made acquainted, from the narratives of many travellers, with the dragon-tree in M. Franqui's garden, we were not the less struck with its enormous size. We were told, that the trunk of this tree, which is mentioned in several very ancient documents as marking the boundaries of a field, was as gigantic in the Fifteenth Century as it is in the present time. Its height appeared to us to be about fifty or sixty feet; its circumference near the roots is forty-five feet. We could not measure higher, but Sir George Staunton found that, ten feet from the ground, the diameter of the trunk is still twelve English feet; which corresponds perfectly with the statement of Borda, who found its mean circumference thirty-three feet, eight inches, French measure. The trunk

[1] This famous tree was blown down by a storm in 1868. Its age was estimated from five to six thousand years.—E. S.

is divided into a great number of branches, which rise in the form of a candelabrum, and are terminated by tufts of leaves, like the yucca which adorns the valley of Mexico. This division gives it a very different appearance from that of the palm-tree.

Among organic creations, this tree is undoubtedly, together with the Adansonia or baobab of Senegal, one of the oldest inhabitants of our globe. The baobabs are of still greater dimensions than the dragon-tree of Orotava. There are some which near the root measure thirty-four feet in diameter, though their total height is only from fifty to sixty feet. But we should observe, that the Adansonia, like the ochroma, and all the plants of the family of bombax, grow much more rapidly than the dracæna, the vegetation of which is very slow. That in M. Franqui's garden still bears every year both flowers and fruit. Its aspect forcibly exemplifies "that eternal youth of nature," which is an inexhaustible source of motion and of life.

The *dracæna*, which is seen only in cultivated spots in the Canary Islands, at Madeira, and Porto Santo, presents a curious phenomenon with respect to the emigration of plants. It has never been found in a wild state on the continent of Africa. The East Indies is its real country. How has this tree been transplanted to Teneriffe, where it is by no means common? Does its existence prove, that, at some very distant period, the Guanches had connexions with other nations originally from Asia?[1]

[1] The form of the dragon-tree is exhibited in several species of the genus Dracæna, at the Cape of Good Hope, in China, and in New Zea-

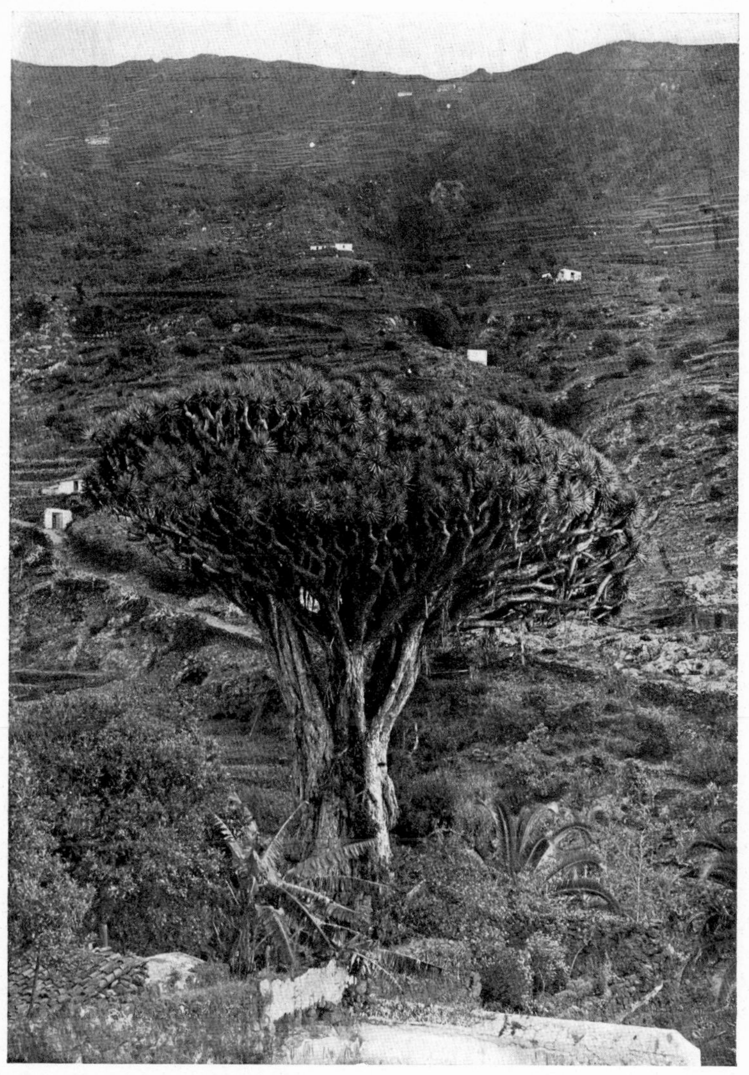

THE DRAGON TREE.

The age of trees is marked by their size, and the union of age with the manifestation of constantly renewed vigour is a charm peculiar to the vegetable kingdom. The gigantic Dragon-tree of Orotava (as sacred in the eyes of the inhabitants of the Canaries as the olive-tree in the Citadel of Athens, or the Elm of Ephesus), the diameter of which I found, when I visited those islands, to be more than sixteen feet, had the same colossal size when the French adventurers, the Béthencourts, conquered these gardens of the Hesperides in the beginning of the Fifteenth Century; yet it still flourishes, as if in perpetual youth, bearing flowers and fruit. A tropical forest of Hymenæas and Cæsalpinieæ may perhaps present to us a monument of more than a thousand years' standing.

This colossal dragon-tree, *Dracæna draco*, stands in one of the most delightful spots in the world. In June, 1799, when we ascended the Peak of Teneriffe, we measured the circumference of the tree and found it nearly forty-eight English feet. Our measurement was taken several feet above the root. Lower down, and nearer to the ground, Le Dru made it nearly seventy-nine English feet. The height of the tree is not much above sixty-nine English feet. According to tradition, this tree was venerated by

land. But in New Zealand it is superseded by the form of the yucca; for the *Dracæna borealis* of Aiton is a Convallaria, of which it has all the appearance. The astringent juice, known in commerce by the name of dragon's blood, is, according to the inquiries we made on the spot, the produce of several American plants. At Laguna, toothpicks steeped in the juice of the dragon-tree are made in the nunneries, and are much extolled as highly useful for keeping the gums in a healthy state.

the Guanches (as was the ash-tree of Ephesus by the Greeks, or as the Lydian plane-tree which Xerxes decked with ornaments, and the sacred Banyan-tree of Ceylon), and at the time of the first expedition of the Béthencourts in 1402, it was already as thick and as hollow as it now is. Remembering that the Dracæna grows extremely slowly, we are led to infer the high antiquity of the tree of Orotava. Bertholet in his description of Teneriffe, says: "*En comparant les jeunes Dragonniers, voisins de l'arbre gigantesque, les calcus qu'on fait sur l' âge de ce dernier effraient l' imagination.*" (Nova Acta Acad. Leop. Carol. Naturæ Curiosorum 1827, vol. xiii., p. 781.) The dragon-tree has been cultivated in the Canaries, and in Madeira and Porto Santo, from the earliest times; and an accurate observer, Leopold von Buch, has even found it wild in Teneriffe, near Igueste. . . .

The measurement of the dragon-tree of the Villa Franqui was made on Borda's first voyage with Pingré, in 1771; not in his second voyage, in 1776, with Varela. It is affirmed that in the earlier times of the Norman and Spanish conquests, in the Fifteenth Century, Mass was said at a small altar erected in the hollow trunk of the tree. Unfortunately, the dragon-tree of Orotava lost one side of its top in the storm of the 21st of July, 1819.

Personal Narrative of Travels to the Equinoctial Regions of America during the years 1799–1804 (London, 1825); and *Aspects of Nature* (Philadelphia, 1849).

MOUNT SHASTA

J. W. BODDAM-WHETHAM

MOUNT SHASTA is the most striking feature of Northern California. Its height is about 14,500 feet above the sea—very nearly the height of Mount Blanc. Mount Blanc is broken into a succession of peaks, but Shasta is one stupendous peak, set upon a broad base that sweeps out far and wide. From the base the volcanic cone rises up in one vast stretch of snow and lava. It is very precipitous to the north and south, but east and west there are two slopes right up to the crater. It is a matter of doubt whether Shasta is dead or only sleeping. Vesuvius slept calmly for centuries, and then spread death and desolation for miles around. The base of the mountain is magnificently watered and wooded, and forms a splendid hunting-ground. The woods are full of deer and bears; and now and then a mountain-goat, an animal very like the chamois of the Alps, is seen in the higher part of the mountains.

Well-provided with blankets and provisions, we started with a guide, and a man to look after the horses, at a very early hour, and rode through a beautiful forest of pines, silver firs, and cedars. Along the banks of the streams were aspens, willows, and the trees known by the name of the "Balm of Gilead," whose vivid green leaves were already changing to a rich orange or an apple-red—forming a beautiful contrast of colours with the glazed green of the cedars and the green-tinted white of the silver firs.

After an easy ascent to a height of about 8,000 feet, we reached the limits of vegetation. Thence our upward path lay over snow, ice, and lava—lonely, isolated barrenness on every side, relieved only by an occasional solitary dwarf-pine, struggling to retain life amidst fierce storms and heavy-weighing snow. Many of them were quite dead, but embalmed by frost and snow in a never-decaying death.

With a few loads of this fuel we soon made a splendid fire, the warmth of which was most welcome in the cold rarefied atmosphere. Scarcely had we finished a capital supper ere night descended, and great clouds and fitful fogs began to drift past. These in their turn broke, and the moon threw a weird light over the forest below; whilst above rose piles upon piles of pinkish lava and snow-fields, reaching far up into the sky, whose magnificent blue grew more sparkling and clear every moment.

Wrapping ourselves in our bundles of blankets, we crept as close as possible to the huge fire, and before long my companions were fast asleep and snoring. I could not sleep a wink, and mentally registered a vow never again to camp out without a pillow. No one can tell till he has tried it, the difference there is between going to sleep with a pillow under the head and a stone or a pair of boots or saddle as its resting-place.

The deep silence, unbroken save by a most unromantic

MOUNT SHASTA.

snore, was painfully oppressive, and I longed to hear even a growl from a bear or a deep whine from a California lion.[1] I listened intently, for it seemed as if the slightest sound, even a hundred miles away, ought to be heard, so still and frosty was the air.

But none fell on my ear, not even a murmur to soothe one to sleep, and I began to think bears and lions were snores and delusions, when, just as I was dozing off, I felt my arm violently pulled, and a voice called out that it was time for us to make a start. Hot coffee soon had a cheering effect, and long before daylight we left our warm camping-ground, and began the higher ascent on foot. Broken stone and slabs of lava afforded pretty good foothold, far preferable to the fields of frozen snow, which we carefully avoided. After a couple of hours' hard walking we seemed to be just as far from the summit as when we started; but the views gradually became grander. From a rocky promontory we looked back over a sea of glittering clouds, the only land visible being the peaks of the Coast range, near the Pacific; all else was cloud, to which the moonlight lent an almost dazzling whiteness:

> " Far clouds of feathery gold,
> Shaded with deepest purple, gleam
> Like islands on a dark blue sea."

When the sun rose and the mists cleared off, the scene was indescribably grand, and the gradual unfolding of the vast panorama unapproachable in its splendour.

[1] These so-called lions are a sort of panther, and abound in most parts of California and Oregon. They are very cowardly, and seldom attack a man, unless they can spring on him from a tree, and not often then.

After some hours of weary climbing over crumbling scoria and splintered rock, we reached the crater. In the ascent to the summit overlooking the crater, we had to cross an ice-field. It had that blue tinge found in the ice of which glaciers are composed, and its slipperiness made it almost impossible to walk over it, the ice lying often in ridges resembling the waves of the sea.

The main crater covers several acres. It is hemmed in by rims of rock, and is filled with volcanic *débris*, covered with snow and ice. Numbers of little boiling springs were bubbling up through the bed of sulphur, and were suggestive of the subterranean fires which once threw their molten lava over the surrounding country. The view from the summit was most extensive, and fortunately there was none of the usual smoke from the forest-fires, so prevalent in autumn in Northern California and Oregon, to impede the range of vision.

Looking northward, far over into Oregon, we could see her lakes, valleys, and mountains. Southward, we could trace the Sacramento and Pitt rivers. The great boundary-wall of the Sierra Nevada lay to the east, and farther onward, the deserts and sparkling lakes of Utah could be distinguished. To the west the sinuous outline of the Coast range was visible, and beyond, the broad Pacific shelved away to the horizon. Fertile valleys, rugged mountains, wood and water, all lent their aid to enhance the beauty of this unsurpassable scene.

The descent to our camping-ground was accomplished in a comparatively short time. On the way, we stopped to witness a most glorious sunset. Round the horizon ran a thin mist with a brilliant depth of colouring. To the east a blue gauze seemed to cover each valley as it sank into night, and the intervening ridges rose with increasing distinctness. The lower country was flooded with an exquisitely delicate light, and a few fleecy clouds tinted with gold, pale salmon, and sapphire, passed over the empurpled hills of the Coast range. The great shadow of Mount Shasta spread itself, cone-like, across the valley; the blue mists were quenched; the distant mountains glowed like fairy hills for a few moments; and the sun, poising itself like a great globe of fire in the darkening heavens, descended slowly below the golden ridge to illumine another hemisphere.

During our descent we passed through some patches of red snow, which leaves a crimson track behind those who cross over it. This curious phenomenon is always avoided by the Shasta Indians, when acting as guides or porters, as they say it brings death if you tread on it willingly and after due warning. We found a warm fire to welcome us on our arrival at the camp, and the exertions of the day made us very willing to turn in among the blankets where we slept soundly till long after daybreak. The following day, when we arrived at our original starting-point, my companions resumed their journey to San Francisco, and I went on to Sissons, a station on the stage-road, whence I was to start on a shooting expedition amongst the Castle Rocks.

Sissons, so-called after the name of the proprietor, is a

very delightful place to spend a few days at. The view of Mount Shasta, which is directly opposite the house, is magnificent; and Sisson himself is a capital sportsman guide, and succeeds in making his guests very comfortable. Looking at Mount Shasta is occupation enough for some time. The play of colour on the mountain is extraordinary. The lava, which is of a rosy hue, often penetrates through the snow, and when the sun shines upon it the effect is most beautiful. The pure white fields of snow are diversified by great blue glaciers, and when the sunbeams fall with refracted glory on the veins of ice they exhibit wonderful tints of opal, green, and pink. The effects produced by the mingling colours of lava, snow, and ice, and the contrasting shadows of a deep violet hue are so varied, and the radiation of colour at sunrise and sunset so vivid, that it is difficult to keep the eyes turned from the mountain—for nothing seems worthy of consideration in comparison with Shasta.

Western Wanderings: a Record of Travel in the Evening Land (London, 1874).

THE LAGOONS OF VENICE

JOHN RUSKIN

IN the olden days of travelling, now to return no more, in which distance could not be vanquished without toil, but in which that toil was rewarded, partly by the power of deliberate survey of the countries through which the journey lay, and partly by the happiness of the evening hours, when from the top of the last hill he had surmounted, the traveller beheld the quiet village where he was to rest, scattered among the meadows beside its valley stream; or, from the long hoped for turn in the dusty perspective of the causeway, saw, for the first time, the towers of some famed city, faint in the rays of sunset—hours of peaceful and thoughtful pleasure, for which the rush of the arrival in the railway station is perhaps not always, or to all men, an equivalent,—in those days, I say, when there was something more to be anticipated and remembered in the first aspect of each successive halting-place, than a new arrangement of glass roofing and iron girder, there were few moments of which the recollection was more fondly cherished by the travelled, than that which, as I endeavoured to describe in the close of the last chapter, brought him within sight of Venice as his gondola shot into the open lagoon from the canal of Mestre. Not but that the aspect of the city itself was generally the source of some slight disappointment, for seen in this direction, its buildings are far less characteristic than those of other great towns of Italy; but this inferiority was partly disguised by distance, and more than atoned for by the strange rising of its walls and towers out of the midst, as it seemed, of the deep sea, for it was impossible that the mind or the eye could at once comprehend the shallowness of the vast sheet of water which stretched away in leagues of rippling lustre to the north and south, or trace the narrow line of islets bounding it to the east. The salt breeze, the moaning sea-birds, the masses of black weed separating and disappearing gradually, in knots of heaving shoal, under the advance of the steady tide, all proclaimed it to be indeed the ocean on whose bosom the great city rested so calmly; not such blue, soft, lake-like ocean as bathes the Neapolitan promontories, or sleeps beneath the marble rocks of Genoa, but a sea with the bleak power of our own northern waves, yet subdued into a strange spacious rest, and changed from its angry pallor into a field of burnished gold, as the sun declined behind the belfry tower of the lonely island church, fitly named "St. George of the Seaweed." As the boat drew nearer to the city, the coast which the traveller had just left sank behind him into one long, low, sad-coloured line, tufted irregularly with brushwood and willows; but, at what seemed its northern extremity, the hills of Arqua rose in a dark cluster of purple pyramids, balanced on the bright mirage of the lagoon; two or three smooth surges of inferior hill extended themselves about

THE CITY OF THE LAGOONS.

their roots, and beyond these, beginning with the craggy peaks above Vicenza, the chain of the Alps girded the whole horizon to the north—a wall of jagged blue, here and there showing through its clefts a wilderness of misty precipices, fading far back into the recesses of Cadore, and itself rising and breaking away eastward, where the sun struck opposite upon its snow, into mighty fragments of peaked light, standing up behind the barred clouds of evening, one after another, countless, the crown of the Adrian Sea, until the eye turned back from pursuing them, to rest upon the nearer burning of the campaniles of Murano, and on the great city, where it magnified itself along the waves, as the quick, silent pacing of the gondola drew nearer and nearer. And at last, when its walls were reached, and the outmost of its untrodden streets was entered, not through towered gate or guarded rampart, but as a deep inlet between two rocks of coral in the Indian sea; when first upon the traveller's sight opened the long ranges of columned palaces,—each with its black boat moored at the portal,—each with its image cast down, beneath its feet, upon that green pavement which every breeze broke into new fantasies of rich tessellation; when first, at the extremity of the bright vista, the shadowy Rialto threw its colossal curve slowly forth from behind the palace of the Camerlenghi; that strange curve, so delicate, so adamantine, strong as a mountain cavern, graceful as a bow just bent; when first, before its moonlike circumference was all risen, the gondolier's cry, "Ah! Stalì," struck sharp upon the ear, and the prow turned aside under the mighty cornices that half met over the narrow canal, where the splash of the water followed close and loud, ringing along the marble by the boat's side; and when at last that boat darted forth upon the breadth of silver sea, across which the front of the Ducal palace, flushed with its sanguine veins, looks to the snowy dome of Our Lady of Salvation, it was no marvel that the mind should be so deeply entranced by the visionary charm of a scene so beautiful and so strange, as to forget the darker truths of its history and its being. Well might it seem that such a city had owed her existence rather to the rod of the enchanter, than the fear of the fugitive; that the waters which encircled her had been chosen for the mirror of her state, rather than the shelter of her nakedness; and that all which in nature was wild or merciless;—Time and Decay, as well as the waves and tempests,—had been won to adorn her instead of to destroy, and might still spare, for ages to come, that beauty which seemed to have fixed for its throne the sands of the hour-glass as well as of the sea.

From the mouths of the Adige to those of the Piave there stretches, at a variable distance of from three to five miles from the actual shore, a bank of sand, divided into long islands by narrow channels of sea. The space between this bank and the true shore consists of the sedimentary deposits from these and other rivers, a great plain of calcareous mud, covered, in the neighbourhood of Venice, by the sea at high water, to the depth in most places of a foot or a foot and a half, and nearly everywhere exposed at low tide, but divided by an intricate network of narrow and winding channels, from which the sea never retires. In some places, according to the run of the currents, the land has risen into marshy islets, consolidated, some by art, and some by time, into ground firm enough to be built upon, or fruitful enough to be cultivated; in others, on the contrary, it has not reached the sea level; so that, at the average low water, shallow lakelets glitter among its irregularly exposed fields of seaweed. In the midst of the largest of these, increased in importance by the confluence of several large river channels towards one of the openings in the sea bank, the city of Venice itself is built, on a crowded cluster of islands; the various plots of higher ground which appear to the north and south of this central cluster, have at different periods been also thickly inhabited, and now bear, according to their size, the remains of cities, villages, or isolated convents and churches, scattered among spaces of open ground, partly waste and encumbered by ruins, partly under cultivation for the supply of the metropolis.

The average rise and fall of the tide is about three feet (varying considerably with the season); but this fall, on so flat a shore, is enough to cause continual movement in the waters, and in the main canals to produce a reflux which frequently runs like a mill stream. At high water no land is visible for many miles to the north or south of Venice, except in the form of small islands crowned with towers or gleaming with villages; there is a channel, some three miles wide, between the city and the mainland, and some mile and a half wide between it and the sandy breakwater called the Lido, which divides the lagoon from the Adriatic, but which is so low as hardly to disturb the impression of the city's having been built in the midst of the ocean, although the secret of its true position is partly, yet not painfully, betrayed by the clusters of piles set to mark the deep water channels, which undulate far away in spotty chains like the studded backs of huge sea-snakes, and by the quick glittering of the crisped and crowded waves that flicker and dance before the strong winds upon the unlifted level of the shallow sea. But the scene is widely different at low tide. A fall of eighteen or twenty inches is enough to show ground over the greater part of the lagoon; and at the complete ebb, the city is seen standing in the midst of a dark plain of seaweed, of gloomy green, except only where the larger branches of the Brenta and its associated streams converge towards the port of the Lido. Through this salt and sombre plain the gondola and the fishing-boat advance by tortuous channels, seldom more than four or five feet deep, and often so choked with slime that the heavier keels furrow the bottom till their crossing tracks are seen through the clear sea water like the ruts upon a wintry road, and the oar leaves the gashes upon the ground at every stroke, or is entangled among the thick weed that fringes the banks with the weight of its sullen waves, leaning to and fro upon the uncertain sway of the exhausted tide. The scene is often profoundly oppressive, even at this day, when every plot of higher ground bears some fragment of fair building: but, in order to know what it was once, let the traveller follow in his boat at evening the windings of some unfrequented channel far into the midst of the melancholy plain; let him remove in his imagination, the brightness of the great city that still extends itself in the distance, and the walls and towers from the islands that are near; and so wait, until the bright investiture and sweet warmth of the sunset are withdrawn from the waters, and the black desert of their shore lies in its nakedness beneath the night, pathless, comfortless, infirm, lost in dark languor and fearful silence, except where the salt rivulets plash into the tideless pools, or the sea-birds flit from their margins with a questioning cry; and he will be enabled to enter in some sort into the horror of heart with which this solitude was anciently chosen by man for his habitation. They little thought, who first drove the stakes into the sand, and strewed the ocean reeds for their rest, that their children were to be the princes of the ocean, and their palaces its pride; and yet, in the great natural laws that rule that sorrowful wilderness, let it be remembered what strange preparation had been made for the things which no human imagination could have foretold, and how the whole existence and fortune of the Venetian nation were anticipated or compelled, by the setting of those bars and doors to the rivers and the sea. Had deeper currents divided their islands, hostile navies would again and again have reduced the rising city into servitude; had stronger surges beaten their shores, all the riches and refinement of the Venetian architecture must have been exchanged for the walls and bulwarks of an ordinary seaport. Had there been no tide, as in other parts of the Mediterranean, the narrow canals of the city would have become noisome, and the marsh in which it was built pestiferous. Had the tide been only a foot or eighteen inches higher in its rise, the water access to the doors of the palaces would have been impossible: even as it is, there is sometimes a little difficulty, at the ebb, in landing without setting foot upon the lower and slippery steps; and the highest tides sometimes enter the courtyards, and overflow the entrance halls. Eighteen inches more of difference between the level of the flood and ebb would have rendered the doorsteps of every palace, at low water, a treacherous mass of weeds and limpets, and the entire system of water-carriage for the higher classes, in their easy and daily intercourse, must have been done away with. The streets of the city would have been widened, its network of canals filled up, and all the peculiar character of the place and the people destroyed.

The reader may perhaps have felt some pain in the contrast between this faithful view of the site of the Venetian Throne, and the romantic conception of it which we ordinarily form; but this pain, if he have felt it, ought to be more than counterbalanced by the value of the instance thus afforded to us at once of the inscrutableness and the wisdom of the ways of God. If, two thousand years ago, we had been permitted to watch the slow setting of the shrine of those turbid rivers into the polluted sea, and the gaining upon its deep and fresh waters of the lifeless, impassable, unvoyageable plain, how little could we have understood the purpose with which those islands were shaped out of the void, and the torpid waters enclosed with their desolate walls of sand! How little could we have known, any more than of what now seems to us most distressful, dark, and objectless, the glorious aim which was then in the mind of Him in whose hands are all the corners of the earth! how little imagined that in the laws which were stretching forth the gloomy margins of those fruitless banks, and feeding the bitter grass among their shallows, there was indeed a preparation, and *the only preparation possible*, for the founding of a city which was to be set like a golden clasp on the girdle of the earth, to write her history on the white scrolls of the sea-surges, and to word it in their thunder, and to gather and give forth, in world-wide pulsation, the glory of the West and of the East, from the burning heart of her Fortitude and Splendour!

The Stones of Venice (Sunnyside, Orpington, Kent, 1886).

THE CATARACTS OF THE NILE

AMELIA B. EDWARDS

AT Assûan one bids good-bye to Egypt and enters Nubia through the gates of the Cataract—which is, in truth, no cataract, but a succession of rapids extending over two-thirds of the distance between Elephantine and Philæ. The Nile—diverted from its original course by some unrecorded catastrophe, the nature of which has given rise to much scientific conjecture—here spreads itself over a rocky basin bounded by sand slopes on the one side, and by granite cliffs on the other. Studded with numerous islets, divided into numberless channels, foaming over sunken rocks, eddying among water-worn boulders, now shallow, now deep, now loitering, now hurrying, here sleeping in the ribbed hollow of a tiny sand-drift, there circling above the vortex of a hidden whirlpool, the river, whether looked upon from the deck of the dahabeeyah, or the heights above the shore, is seen everywhere to be fighting its way through a labyrinth, the paths of which have never yet been mapped or sounded.

These paths are everywhere difficult and everywhere dangerous; and to that labyrinth the Shellalee, or Cataract Arab, alone possesses the key. At the time of the inundation, when all but the highest rocks are under water,

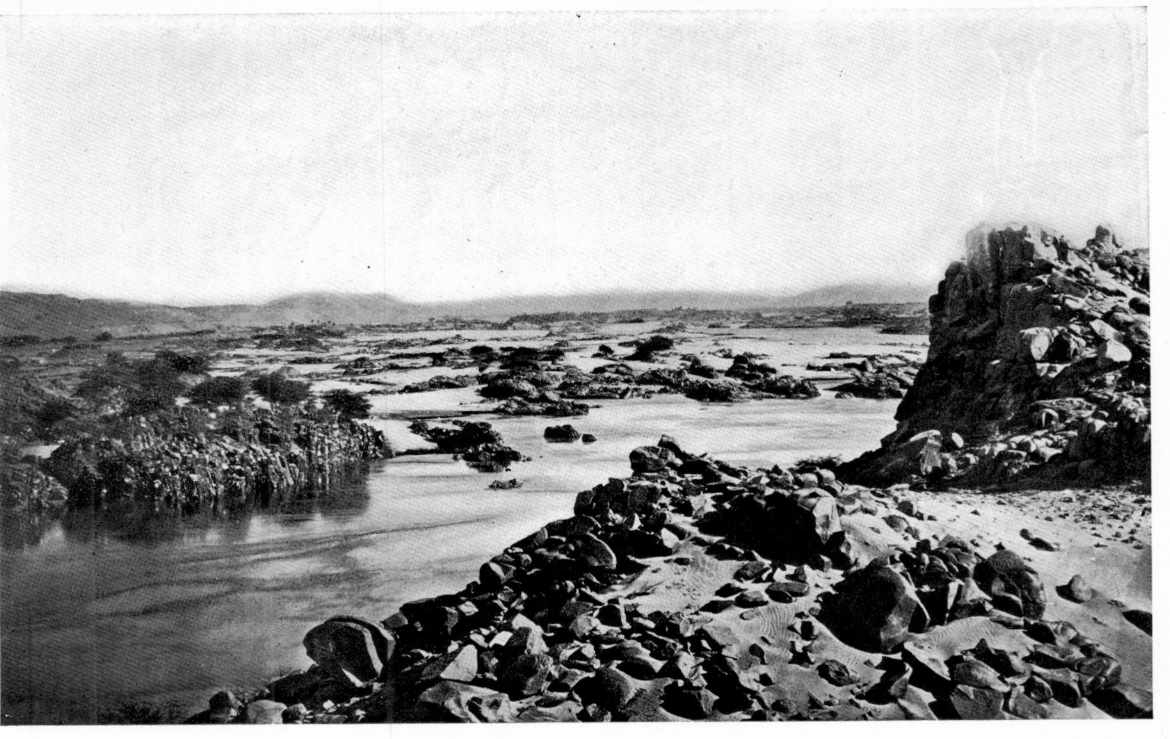

FIRST CATARACT OF THE NILE.

and navigation is as easy here as elsewhere, the Shellalee's occupation is gone. But as the floods subside and travellers begin to reappear, his work commences. To haul dahabeeyahs up those treacherous rapids by sheer stress of rope and muscle; to steer skillfully down again through channels bristling with rocks and boiling with foam, becomes now, for some five months of the year, his principal industry. It is hard work; but he gets well paid for it, and his profits are always on the increase. From forty to fifty dahabeeyahs are annually taken up between November and March; and every year brings a larger influx of travellers. Meanwhile, accidents rarely happen; prices tend continually upward; and the Cataract Arabs make a little fortune by their singular monopoly.

The scenery of the First Cataract is like nothing else in the world—except the scenery of the Second. It is altogether new and strange and beautiful. It is incomprehensible that travellers should have written of it in general with so little admiration. They seem to have been impressed by the wildness of the waters, by the quaint forms of the rocks, by the desolation and grandeur of the landscape as a whole; but scarcely at all by its beauty—which is paramount.

The Nile here widens to a lake. Of the islands, which it would hardly be an exaggeration to describe as some hundreds in number, no two are alike. Some are piled up like the rocks at the Land's End in Cornwall, block upon block, column upon column, tower upon tower, as if reared by the hand of man. Some are green with grass; some golden with slopes of drifted sand; some are planted with rows of blossoming lupins, purple and white. Others are again mere cairns of loose blocks, with here and there a perilously balanced top-boulder. On one, a singular upright monolith, like a menhir, stands conspicuous, as if placed there to commemorate a date, or to point the way to Philæ. Another mass rises out of the water squared and buttressed, in the likeness of a fort. A third, humped and shining like the wet body of some amphibious beast, lifts what seems to be a horned head above the surface of the rapids. All these blocks and boulders and fantastic rocks are granite; some red, some purple, some black. Their forms are rounded by the friction of ages. Those nearest the brink reflect the sky like mirrors of burnished steel. Royal ovals and hieroglyphed inscriptions, fresh as of yesterday's cutting, stand out here and there from those glittering surfaces with startling distinctness. A few of the larger islands are crowned with clumps of palms; and one, the loveliest of any, is completely embowered in gum-trees and acacias, dôm and date-palms, and feathery tamarisks, all festooned together under a hanging canopy of yellow-blossomed creepers.

On a brilliant Sunday morning, with a favourable wind, we entered on this fairy archipelago. Sailing steadily against the current, we glided away from Assûan, left Elephantine behind, and found ourselves at once in the midst of the islands. From this moment every turn of the tiller disclosed a fresh point of view, and we sat on deck, spectators of a moving panorama. The diversity of subjects was endless. The combinations of form and colour, of light and shadow, of foreground and distance, were continually changing. A boat or a few figures alone were wanting to complete the picturesqueness of the scene, but in all those channels and among all those islands, we saw no sign of any living creature.

The Second or Great Cataract, begins a little way above Wady Halfeh and extends over a distance of many miles. It consists, like the First Cataract, of a succession of rocks and rapids, and is skirted for the first five miles or so by the sand-cliff ridge, which, as I have said, forms a background to the ruins just opposite Wady Halfeh. This ridge terminates abruptly in the famous precipice known as the Rock of Abusîr. Only adventurous travellers bound for Dongola or Khartûm go beyond this point; and they, for the most part, take the shorter route across the desert from Korosko.

It is hard, now that we are actually here, to realize that this is the end of our journey. The Cataract—an immense multitude of black and shining islets, among which the river, divided into hundreds of separate channels, spreads far and wide for a distance, it is said of more than sixteen miles,—foams at our feet. Foams, and frets, and falls; gushing smooth and strong where its course is free; murmuring hoarsely where it is interrupted; now hurrying; now loitering; here eddying in oily circles; there lying in still pools unbroken by a ripple; everywhere full of life, full of voices; everywhere shining to the sun. Northwards, when it winds away towards Abou Simbel, we see all the fantastic mountains of yesterday on the horizon. To the east, still bounded by out-liers of the same disconnected chain, lies a rolling waste of dark and stony wilderness, trenched with innumerable valleys through which flow streams of sand. On the western side, the continuity of the view is interrupted by the ridge which ends with Abusîr. Southward the Libyan desert reaches away in one vast undulating plain; tawny, arid, monotonous; all sun; all sand; lit here and there with arrowy flashes of the Nile. Farthest of all, pale but distinct, on the outermost rim of the world, rise two mountain summits, one long, one domelike. Our Nubians tell us that they are the mountains of Dongola. Comparing our position with that of the Third Cataract as it appears upon the map, we come to the conclusion that these ghost-like silhouettes are the summits of Mount Fogo and Mount Arambo—two apparently parallel mountains situate on opposite sides of the river about ten miles below Hannek, and consequently about one hundred and forty-five miles, as the bird flies, from the spot on which we are standing.

In this extraordinary panorama, so wild, so weird, so desolate, there is nothing really beautiful, except the colour. But the colour is transcendent. Never, even in Egypt, have I seen anything so tender, so transparent, so harmonious. I shut my eyes, and it all comes before me. I see the amber of the sands; the pink and pearly mountains; the Cataract rocks all black and purple and polished; the dull grey palms that cluster here and there upon the larger islands; the vivid verdure of the tamarisks and pomegranates; the Nile, a greenish brown flecked with yeasty foam; over all, the blue and burning sky, permeated with light, and palpitating with sunshine.

I made no sketch. I felt that it would be ludicrous to attempt it. And I feel now that any endeavour to put the scene into words is a mere presumptuous effort to describe the indescribable. Words are useful instruments; but, like the etching needle and the burin, they stop short at form. They cannot translate colour.

If a traveller pressed for time asked me whether he should or should not go as far as the Second Cataract, I think I should recommend him to turn back from Abou Simbel. The trip must cost four days; and if the wind should happen to be unfavourable either way, it may cost six or seven. The forty miles of river that have to be twice traversed are the dullest on the Nile; the Cataract is but an enlarged and barren edition of the Cataract between Assûan and Philæ; and the great view, as I have said, has not that kind of beauty which attracts the general tourist.

It has an interest, however, beyond and apart from that of beauty. It rouses one's imagination to a sense of the greatness of the Nile. We look across a world of desert, and see the river still coming from afar. We have reached a point at which all that is habitable and familiar comes abruptly to an end. Not a village, not a bean-field, not a shâdûf, not a sakkieh, is to be seen in the plain below. There is no sail on these dangerous waters. There is no moving creature on these pathless sands. But for the telegraphic wires stalking ghost-like, across the desert, it would seem as if we had touched the limit of civilization, and were standing on the threshold of a land unexplored.

Yet for all this, we feel as if we were at only the beginning of the mighty river. We have journeyed well-nigh a thousand miles against the stream; but what is that to the distance which still lies between us and the Great Lakes? And how far beyond the Great Lakes must we seek for the source that is even yet undiscovered?

A Thousand Miles Up the Nile (London, 1890).

IN THE ALPS

THÉOPHILE GAUTIER

THE foot of the high mountains that form the chain of Mount Blanc, clothed with forests and pastures, revealed hues of delightful intensity and vigour. Imagine an immense piece of green velvet crumpled into large folds like the curtain of a theatre with the deep black of its hollows and the golden glitterings of its lights; this is a very faint image for the grandeur of the object, but I know of none that could better describe the effect.

Scheele's green, mineral green, all those greens that result from the combinations of Prussian blue and yellow ochre, or Naples yellow, the mixture of indigo and Indian yellow, Veronese green and *vert prasin* could not reproduce that quality of green that we might properly call mountain green and which passes from velvety black into the tenderest shades of green. In this play of shades, the firs form the shadows; the deciduous trees and the spaces of meadow or moss, the lights. The undulations and the cleft ravines of the mountain break these great masses of green, this vigorous foreground, this energetic *répoussoir*, rendering the light tones of the zones, (bare of verdue and crowned by the high lights of the snows,) more vaporous and throwing them back. In the various more open places, the grass grows green in the sun; and trees resembling little black patches sown upon this light ground give it the appearance of tufted material. But when we speak of trees and firs, woods and forests, do not picture to yourselves anything but vast blots of dark moss upon the slopes of the mountains: the highest trunks there assume the proportion of a blade of grass.

The road turns towards the left, and, gliding between stones and blocks that have fallen down or drifted into the valley by means of the winter torrents and avalanches, soon enters a forest of birch-trees, firs, and larches whose openings allow you to see on the other side the *Aiguilles Rouges* and *le Brevent*, which face Montanvert. The ascent was gentle enough and the mules climbed it with easy gait; in comparison with the road which we scaled the night before to go to the *Pierre pointue*, the route was a true alley of the Bois de Boulogne. The zigzags of the road turned at angles sufficiently long not to fatigue either the rider or his mount. The sunlight played in the foliage of the forest that we traversed and made a shadow shot through with rays float over us. Upon the rocks at the foot of the trees, mosses of emerald green gleamed and lovely little wild flowers brightly bloomed, while in the spaces through the branches a bluish mist betrayed the depth of the abyss, for the little caravan, going along single file and constantly ascending, had now reached the Caillet fountain, which is regarded as half-way up the mountain. This fountain, of excellent water, runs into a wooden trough. The mules halt there to drink. A cabin is built near the fountain and they offer you a glass of water made

MONT BLANC.

opalescent with a few drops of kirsch, cognac, beer, and other refreshments. We regaled our guides with a glass of brandy, which, notwithstanding their sobriety, they seemed to prefer to that diamond liquid that sprang from the rock.

From this point, the road began to grow steeper; the ascents multiplied without, however, offering any difficulties to mules or pedestrians. The air became more keen. The forest grew lighter, the trees stood at greater intervals from each other and stopped as if out of breath. They seemed to say to us, "Now, go up alone, we cannot go any further." The rounded plateau that we mount by keeping to the right is not desolate and denuded as one would believe; a grass, sturdy enough and enamelled with Alpine flowers, forms its carpet, and when you have gone beyond it, you perceive the *châlet* or inn of Montanvert below the *Aiguille de Charmoz*.

From this plateau you have a superb view, an astonishing, apocalyptic view, beyond all dreams. At your feet, between two banks of gigantic peaks, flows motionless, as if congealed during the tumult of a tempest, that broad river of crystal which is called the Mer de Glace, and which lower towards the plain is called the *Glacier des Bois*. The *Mer de Glace* comes from a high altitude; it receives many glaciers as a river its tributaries. We will speak of it presently, but for the moment let us occupy ourselves with the spectacle that unfolds beneath our eyes.

Opposite the inn of Montanvert, the glacier is half a league from one bank to the other, perhaps even more, for it is difficult to guage distance in the mountains with exactness; it is about the width of the Thames, the Neva or the Guadalquiver towards their mouth. But the slope is much more abrupt than was ever that of any river. It descends by large waves rounded at their tops, like billows that never break into foam and whose hollows take a bluish colour. When the ground that serves as a bed for this torrent of ice becomes too abrupt, the mass is dislocated and breaks up into slabs that rest one upon the other and which resemble those little columns of white marble in the Turkish cemeteries that are forced to lean to right or left by their own weight; crevasses more or less wide and deep manifest themselves, opening the immense block and revealing the virgin ice in all its purity. The walls of these crevasses assume magical colours, tints of an azure grotto. An ideal blue that is neither the blue of the sky nor the blue of the water, but the blue of ice, an unnamed tone that is never found on the artist's palette illumines these splendid clefts and turns sometimes to a green of aqua marine or mother of pearl by gradations of astonishing delicacy. On the other bank, clearly detached by its sharp escarpment like the spire of a gigantic cathedral, the high *Aiguille du Dru* rises with so proud, so elegant, and so bold a spring. Ascending the glacier, the *Aiguille Verte* stands out in front of it, being even higher though the perspective makes it appear lower. From the foot of the *Aiguille du Dru*, like a rivulet towards a river, descends the Mont Blanc glacier. A little further to the right, the *Aiguille du Moine* and that of *Léchaud* show themselves, obelisks of granite which the sunlight tints with reflections of rose and the snow makes gleam with several touches of silver. It is difficult to express in words the unexpected outlines, the strange flashes, the tops cut and indented in the form of saw-teeth, gable-ends and crosses that are affected by these inaccessible peaks with almost vertical walls,—often even sloping outwards and overhanging. Running your eye along the same bank of the glacier and descending towards the valley, you see the *Aiguille du Bochard*, *le Chapeau*, which is nothing more or less than a rounded mountain, grassy and enamelled with flowers, not so high as Montanvert, and the forests which have given to this portion of the *Mer de Glace* the name of *Glacier des Bois*, bordering it with a line of sombre verdure.

There are in the *Mer de Glace* two veins that divide it throughout its length like the currents of two rivers that never mingle: a black vein and a white vein. The black one flows by the side of the bank where the *Aiguille du Dru* rears itself, and the white one bathes the foot of Montanvert; but words when we speak of colour only half describe shades, and it must not be imagined that this demarcation is as clearly defined as we have indicated. It is, however, very sensible.

On looking towards the upper portion of the glacier, at the spot where it precipitates itself into the rock passage which conducts it to the valley like a furiously boiling cascade with wild spurts which some magic power has turned into ice at its strongest leap, you discover, arranged like an amphitheatre, the *Montagne des Périades*, the *Petites Jorasses*, the *Grandes Jorasses*, and the *Aiguille du Géant*, covered with eternal snow, the white diadem of the Alps which the suns of summer are powerless to melt and which scintillate with a pure and cold brilliancy in the clear blue of the sky.

At the foot of the Périades, the glacier, as may be seen from Montanvert, divides into two branches, one of which ascends towards the east and takes the name of the *Glacier de Léchaud*, while the other takes its course behind the *Aiguilles de Chamouni* towards *Mont Blanc du Tacul*, and is called the *Glacier du Géant*. A third branch, named the *Glacier du Talifre*, spreads out over the slopes of the *Aiguille Verte*.

It is in the middle of the *Talifre* where lies that oasis of the glaciers that is called the *Jardin*, a kind of basket of Alpine flowers, which find there a pinch of vegetable earth, a few rays of sunshine, and a girdle of stones that isolate them from the neighbouring ice; but to climb to the *Jardin* is a long, fatiguing and even dangerous excursion, necessitating a night's sleep at the *châlet* of Montanvert.

We resumed our journey not without having gathered several bunches of rhododendrons of the freshest green and brightest rose, that opened in the liberty and solitude of the mountains by means of the pure Alpine breeze. You descend by the same route more rapidly than you ascended.

The mules stepped gaily by the side of their leaders, who carried the sticks, canes and umbrellas, which had now become useless. We traversed the forest of pines pierced here and there by the torrents of stones of the avalanches; we gained the plain and were soon at Chamouni to go to

AIGUILLE DU DRU, ALPS,

the source of the Arveiron, which is found at the base of the *Glacier des Bois*, the name that is assumed by the *Mer de Glace* on arriving in the valley.

This is an excursion that you can make in a carriage. You follow the bottom of the valley, cross the Arve at the hamlet of Praz, and after having passed the *Hameau des Bois*, where you must alight, you arrive, winding among masses of rocks in disorder and pools of water across which logs are placed, at the wall of the glacier, which reveals itself by its slit and tortured edges, full of cavities and gashes where the blue-green hatchings colour the transparent whiteness of the mass.

The white teeth of the glacier stand out clearly against the sombre green of the forests of Bochard and Montanvert and are majestically dominated by the *Aiguille du Dru*, which shoots its granite obelisk three thousand nine hundred and six *mètres* into the depths of the sky, and the foreground is formed by the most prodigious confusion of stones, rocks and blocks that a painter could wish for giving value to those vapourous depths. The Arveiron foams and roars across this chaos and, after half an hour of frantic disordered course, loses itself in the Arve.

Les Vacances de Lundi (Paris, 1881).

THE VALE OF KASHMIR

ANDREW WILSON

ALMOST every one longs, and many hope, to see the beautiful Vale of Kashmir. Probably no region of the earth is so well known to the eye of imagination, or so readily suggests the idea of a terrestrial Paradise. So far from having been disappointed with the reality, or having experienced any cause for wishing that I had left Kashmir unvisited, I can most sincerely say that the beautiful reality excels the somewhat vague poetic vision which has been associated with the name. But Kashmir is rather a difficult country to get at, especially when you come down upon it from behind by way of Zanskar and Súrú. According to tradition, it was formerly the Garden of Eden; and one is very well disposed to accept that theory when trying to get into it from the north or northwest.

After months of the sterile, almost treeless Tibetan provinces, the contrast was very striking, and I could not but revel in the beauty and glory of the vegetation; but even to one who had come up upon it from below, the scene would have been very striking. There was a large and lively encampment at the foot of the pass, with tents prepared for the Yarkand envoy, and a number of Kashmir officers and soldiers; but I pushed on beyond that, and

THE VALE OF KASHMIR.

camped in solitude close to the Sind river, just beneath the Panjtarne valley, which leads up towards the caves of Ambernath, a celebrated place for Hindú pilgrimage. This place is called Báltal, but it has no human habitations. Smooth green meadows, carpet-like and embroidered with flowers, extended to the silvery stream, above which there was the most varied luxuriance of foliage, the lower mountains being most richly clothed with woods of many and beautiful colours. It was late autumn, and the trees were in their greatest variety of colour; but hardly a leaf seemed to have fallen. The dark green of the pines contrasted beautifully with the delicate orange of the birches, because there were intermingling tints of brown and saffron. Great masses of foliage were succeeded by solitary pines, which had found a footing high up the precipitous crags.

And all this was combined with peaks and slopes of pure white snow. *Aiguilles* of dark rock rose out of beds of snow, but their faces were powdered with the same element. Glaciers and long beds of snow ran down the valleys, and the upper vegetation had snow for its bed. The effect of sunset upon this scene was wonderful; for the colours it displayed were both heightened and more harmoniously blended. The golden light of eve brought out the warm tints of the forest; but the glow of the reddish-brown precipices, and the rosy light upon the snowy slopes and peaks, were too soon succeeded by the cold grey of evening. At first, however, the wondrous scene was still visible in a quarter-moon's silvery light, in which the Panjtarne valley was in truth —

> "A wild romantic chasm that slanted
> Down the sweet hill athwart a cedarn cover—
> A savage place, as holy and enchanted
> As e'er beneath the waning moon was haunted
> By woman wailing for her demon lover."

The demon lovers to be met with in that wild valley are bears, which are in abundance, and a more delightful place for a hunter to spend a month in could hardly be invented; but he would have to depend on his rifle for supplies, or have them sent up from many miles down the Sind valley.

The remainder of my journey down the latter valley to the great valley or small plain of Kashmir was delightful. A good deal of rain fell, but that made one appreciate the great trees all the more, for the rain was not continuous, and was mingled with sunshine. At times, during the season when I saw it, this "inland depth" is "roaring like the sea;"

> "While trees, dim-seen in frenzied numbers tear
> The lingering remnant of their yellow hair;"

but soon after it is bathed in perfect peace and mellow sunlight. The air was soft and balmy; but, at this transfer from September to October, it was agreeably cool even to a traveller from the abodes and sources of snow. As we descended, the pine-forests were confined to the mountain-slopes; but the lofty deodar began to appear in the valley, as afterwards the sycamore, the elm, and the horse-chestnut. Round the picturesque villages, and even forming considerable woods, there were fruit-trees—as the walnut, the chestnut, the peach, the apricot, the apple, and the pear. Large quantities of timber (said to be cut recklessly) was in course of being floated down the river; and where the path led across it there were curious wooden bridges for which it was not necessary to dismount. This Sind valley is about sixty miles long, and varies in breadth from a few hundred yards to about a mile, except at its base, where it opens out considerably. It is considered to afford the best idea of the mingled beauty and grandeur of Kashmir scenery; and when I passed through its appearance was greatly enhanced by the snow, which not only covered the mountain-tops, but also came down into the forests which clothed the mountain-sides. The path through it, being part of the great road from Kashmir to Central Asia, is kept in tolerable repair, and it is very rarely that the rider requires to dismount. Anything beyond a walking-pace, however, is for the most part out of the question. Montgomerie divides the journey from Srinagar to Báltal (where I camped below the Zoji La) into six marches, making in all sixty-seven miles; and though two of these marches may be done in one day, yet if you are to travel easily and enjoy the scenery, one a day is sufficient. The easiest double march is from Sonamarg to Gond, and I did it in a day with apparent ease on a very poor pony; but the consequence is that I beat my brains in order to recall what sort of a place Gond was, no distinct recollection of it having been left on my mind, except of a grove of large trees and a roaring fire in front of my tent at night. Sonamarg struck me as a very pleasant place; and I had there, in the person of a youthful captain from Abbotabad, the pleasure of meeting the first European I had seen since leaving Lahaul. We dined together, and I found he had come up from Srinagar to see Sonamarg, and he spoke with great enthusiasm of a view he had had, from another part of Kashmir, of the 26,000 feet mountain Nanga Parbat. *Marg* means " meadow," and seems to be applied especially to elevated meadows; *sona* stands for "golden": and this place is a favourite resort in the hot malarious months of July and August, both for Europeans in Kashmir and for natives of rank.

At Ganderbahl I was fairly in the great valley of Kashmir, and encamped under some enormous *chúnár* or sycamore trees; the girth of one was so great that its trunk kept my little mountain-tent quite sheltered from the furious blasts. Truly —

> "There was a roaring in the wind all night,
> The rain fell heavily, and fell in floods,

but that gigantic *chúnár* kept off both wind and rain wonderfully. Next day a small but convenient and quaint Kashmir boat took me up to Srinagar; and it was delightful to glide up the backwaters of the Jhelam, which afforded a highway to the capital. It was the commencement and the promise of repose, which I very sadly needed, and in a beautiful land.

I afterwards went up to Islamabad, Martand, Achibal, Vernag, the Rozlú valley, and finally went out of Kashmir by way of the Manas and Wúlar Lakes, and the lower valley of the Jhelam, so that I saw the most interesting places in the country, and all the varieties of scenery which it affords. That country has been so often visited and described, that, with one or two exceptions, I shall only touch generally upon its characteristics. It doubtless owes some of its charm to the character of the regions in its neighbourhood. As compared with the burning plains of India, the sterile steppes of Tibet, and the savage mountains of the Himalaya and of Afghanistan, it presents an astonishing and beautiful contrast. After such scenes even a much more commonplace country might have afforded a good deal of the enthusiasm which Kashmir has excited in Eastern poetry, and even in common rumour; but beyond that it has characteristics which give it a distinct place among the most pleasing regions of the earth. I said to the Maharajah, or ruling Prince of Kashmir, that the most beautiful countries I had seen were England, Italy, Japan, and Kashmir; and though he did not seem to like the remark much, probably from a fear that the beauty of the land he governed might make it too much an object of desire, yet there was no exaggeration in it. Here, at a height of nearly 6,000 feet, in a temperate climate, with abundance of moisture, and yet protected by lofty mountains from the fierce continuous rains of the Indian southwest monsoon, we have the most splendid amphitheatre in the world. A flat oval valley about sixty miles long, and from forty in breadth, is surrounded by magnificent mountains, which, during the greater part of the year, are covered more than half-way down with snow, and present vast upland beds of pure white snow. This valley has fine lakes, is intersected with water-courses, and its land is covered with brilliant vegetation, including gigantic trees of the richest foliage. And out of this great central valley there rise innumerable, long, picturesque mountain-valleys, such as that of the Sind river, which I have just described; while above these there are great pine-forests, green slopes of grass, glaciers, and snow. Nothing could express the general effect better than Moore's famous lines on sainted Lebanon —

> "Whose head in wintry grandeur towers,
> And whitens with eternal sleet;
> While Summer, in a vale of flowers,
> Is sleeping rosy at his feet."

The great encircling walls of rock and snow contrast grandly with the soft beauty of the scene beneath. The snows have a wonderful effect as we look up to them through the leafy branches of the immense *chúnár*, elm, and poplar trees. They flash gloriously in the morning sunlight above the pink mist of the valley-plain; they have a rosy glow in the evening sunlight; and when the sunlight has departed, but ere darkness shrouds them, they gleam, afar off, with a cold and spectral light, as if they belonged to a region where man had never trod. The deep black gorges in the mountains have a mysterious look. The sun lights up some softer grassy ravine or green slope, and then displays splintered rocks rising in the wildest confusion. Often long lines of white clouds lie along the line of mountain-summits, while at other times every white peak and precipice-wall is distinctly marked against the deep-blue sky. The valley-plain is especially striking in clear mornings and evenings, where it lies partly in golden sunlight, partly in the shadow of its great hills.

The green mosaic of the level land is intersected by many streams, canals or lakes, or beautiful reaches of river which look like small lakes. The lakes have floating islands composed of vegetation. Besides the immense *chúnárs* and elms, and the long lines of stately poplars, great part of the plain is a garden filled with fruits and flowers, and there is almost constant verdure.

> "There eternal summer dwells,
> And west winds, with musky wing,
> About the cedar'd alleys fling
> Nard and cassia's balmy smells."

Travel, Adventure and Sport from Blackwood's Magazine (Edinburgh and London), Vol. vi.

THE LAKE OF PITCH

CHARLES KINGSLEY

THIS Pitch Lake should be counted among the wonders of the world; for it is, certainly, tolerably big. It covers ninety-nine acres, and contains millions of tons of so-called pitch.

Its first discoverers were not bound to see that a pitch lake of ninety-nine acres was no more wonderful than any of the little pitch wells—"spues" or "galls," as we should call them in Hampshire—a yard across; or any one of the tiny veins and lumps of pitch which abound in the surrounding forests; and no less wonderful than if it had covered ninety-nine thousand acres instead of ninety-nine.

As we neared the shore, we perceived that the beach was black with pitch; and the breeze being off the land, the asphalt smell (not unpleasant) came off to welcome us. We rowed in, and saw in front of a little row of wooden houses, a tall mulatto, in blue policeman's dress, gesticulating and shouting to us. He was the ward policeman, and I found him (as I did all the coloured police) able and courteous, shrewd and trusty. These police are excellent specimens of what can be made of the Negro, or Half-Negro, if he be but first drilled, and then given a responsibility which calls out his self-respect. He was warning our crew not to run aground on one or other of the pitch reefs, which here take the place of rocks. A large one, a hundred yards off on the left, has been almost all dug away, and carried to New York or to Paris to make asphalt pavement.

The boat was run ashore, under his directions, on a spit of sand between the pitch; and when she ceased bumping up and down in the muddy surf, we scrambled out into a world exactly the hue of its inhabitants—of every shade, from jet-black to copper-brown. The pebbles on the shore were pitch. A tide-pool close by was enclosed in pitch: a four-eyes was swimming about in it, staring up at us; and when we hunted him, tried to escape, not by diving, but by jumping on shore on the pitch, and scrambling off between our legs. While the policeman, after profoundest courtesies, was gone to get a mule-cart to take us up to the lake, and planks to bridge its water-channels, we took a look round at this oddest of the corners of the earth.

In front of us was the unit of civilization—the police-station, wooden on wooden stilts (as all well-built houses are here), to ensure a draught of air beneath them. We were, of course, asked to come and sit down, but preferred looking around, under our umbrellas; for the heat was intense. The soil is half pitch, half brown earth, among which the pitch sweals in and out, as tallow sweals from a candle. It is always in slow motion under the heat of the tropic sun: and no wonder if some of the cottages have sunk right and left in such a treacherous foundation. A stone or brick house could not stand here: but wood and palm-thatch are both light and tough enough to be safe, let the ground give way as it will.

The soil, however, is very rich. The pitch certainly does not injure vegetation, though plants will not grow actually in it. The first plants which caught our eyes were pine-apples; for which La Brea is famous. The heat of the soil, as well as of the air, brings them to special perfection. They grow about anywhere, unprotected by hedge or fence; for the Negroes here seem honest enough, at least towards each other. And at the corner of the house was a bush worth looking at, for we had heard of it for many a year. It bore prickly, heart-shaped pods an inch long, filled with seeds coated with a rich waxy pulp.

This was a famous plant—Bixa, Orellana, Roucou; and that pulp was the well-known Arnotta dye of commerce. In England and Holland, it is used merely, I believe, to colour cheeses; but in the Spanish Main, to colour human beings. As we went onward up the gentle slope (the rise is one hundred and thirty-eight feet in rather more than a mile), the ground became more and more full of pitch, and the vegetation poorer and more rushy, till it resembled on the whole, that of an English fen. An Ipomœa or two, and a scarlet-flowered dwarf Heliconia kept up the tropic type as does a stiff brittle fern about two feet high.

The plateau of pitch now widened out, and the whole ground looked like an asphalt pavement, half overgrown with marsh-loving weeds, whose roots feed in the sloppy water which overlies the pitch. But, as yet, there was no sign of the lake. The incline, though gentle, shuts off the view of what is beyond. This last lip of the lake has surely overflowed, and is overflowing still, though very slowly. Its furrows all curve downward; and, it is, in fact, as one of our party said, "a black glacier." The pitch, expanding under the burning sun of day, must needs expand most towards the line of least resistance, that is, down hill; and when it contracts again under the coolness of night, it contracts surely from the same cause, more downhill than it does uphill; so that each particle never returns to the spot whence it started, but rather drags the particles above it downward towards itself. At least, so it seemed to us.

At last we surmounted the last rise, and before us lay the famous lake—not at the bottom of a depression, as we expected, but at the top of a rise, whence the ground slopes away from it on two sides, and rises from it very slightly on the two others. The black pool glared and glittered in the sun. A group of islands, some twenty yards wide, were scattered about the middle of it. Beyond it rose a noble forest of Moriche fan-palms; and to the right of them high wood with giant Mombins and undergrowth of Cocorite—a paradise on the other side of the Stygian pool.

We walked, with some misgivings, on to the asphalt, and found it perfectly hard. In a few yards we were stopped by a channel of clear water, with tiny fish and water-beetles in it; and, looking round, saw that the whole lake was intersected with channels, so unlike anything which can be seen elsewhere, that it is not easy to describe them.

Conceive a crowd of mushrooms, of all shapes from ten to fifty feet across, close together side by side, their tops being kept at exactly the same level, their rounded rims squeezed tight against each other; then conceive water poured on them so as to fill the parting seams, and in the wet season, during which we visited it, to overflow the tops somewhat. Thus would each mushroom represent, tolerably well, one of the innumerable flat asphalt bosses, which seem to have sprung up each from a separate centre.

In five minutes we had seen, handled, and smelt enough to satisfy us with this very odd and very nasty vagary of tropic nature; and as we did not wish to become faint or ill, between the sulphuretted hydrogen and the blaze of the sun reflected off the hot black pitch, we hurried on over the water-furrows, and through the sedge-beds to the further shore—to find ourselves in a single step out of an Inferno into a Paradise.

We looked back at the foul place, and agreed that it is well for the human mind that the Pitch Lake was still unknown when Dante wrote that hideous poem of his—the opprobrium (as I hold) of the Middle Age. For if such were the dreams of its noblest and purest genius, what must have been the dreams of the ignoble and impure multitude? But had he seen this lake, how easy, how tempting too, it would have been to him to embody in imagery the surmise of a certain "Father," and heighten the torments of the lost being, sinking slowly into that black Bolge beneath the baking rays of the tropic sun, by the sight of the saved, walking where we walked, beneath cool fragrant shade, among the pillars of a temple to which the Parthenon is mean and small.

Sixty feet and more aloft, the short, smooth columns of the Moriches towered around us, till, as we looked through the "pillared shade," the eye was lost in the green abysses of the forest. Overhead, their great fan-leaves form a grooved roof, compared with which that of St. Mary Radcliff, or even of King's College, is as clumsy as all man's works are beside the works of God; and beyond the Moriche wood, ostrich plumes packed close round madder-brown stems, formed a wall to our temple, which bore such tracery, carving, and painting, as would have stricken dumb with awe and delight him who ornamented the Loggie of the Vatican.

What might not have been made, with something of justice and mercy, common sense and humanity, of these gentle Arawaks and Guaraons. What was made of them, almost ere Columbus was dead, may be judged from this one story, taken from Las Casas.

"There was a certain man named Juan Bono, who was employed by the members of the Andencia of St. Domingo to go and obtain Indians. He and his men to the number of fifty or sixty, landed on the Island of Trinidad. Now the Indians of Trinidad were a mild, loving, credulous race, the enemies of the Caribs, who ate human flesh. On Juan Bono's landing, the Indians armed with bows and arrows, went to meet the Spaniards, and to ask them who they were, and what they wanted. Juan Bono replied that his men were good and peaceful people, who had come to live with the Indians; upon which, as the commencement of good fellowship, the natives offered to build houses for the Spaniards. The Spanish captain expressed a wish to have one large house built. The accommodating Indians set about building it. It was to be in the form of a bell and to be large enough for a hundred persons to live in. On any great occasion it would hold many more. . . . Upon a certain day Juan Bono collected the Indians together—men, women, and children—in the building 'to see,' as he told them, 'what was to be done.' . . . A horrible massacre ensued. . . ."

Such was the fate of the poor gentle folk who for unknown ages had swung their hammocks to the stems of these Moriches, spinning the skin of the young leaves into twine, and making sago from the pith, and then wine from the sap and fruit, while they warned their children not to touch the nests of the humming-birds, which even till lately swarmed around the lake. For—so the Indian story ran—once on a time a tribe of Chaymas built their palm-leaf ajoupas upon the very spot, where the lake now lies, and lived a merry life. The sea swarmed with shell-fish and turtle, and the land with pine-apples; the springs were haunted by countless flocks of flamingoes and horned screamers, pajuis and blue ramiers; and, above all, by humming-birds. But the foolish Chaymas were blind to the mystery and beauty of the humming-birds, and would not understand how they were no other than the souls of dead Indians, translated into living jewels; and so they killed them in wantonness, and angered "The Good

Spirit." But one morning, when the Guaraons came by, the Chayma village had sunk deep into the earth, and in its place had risen this Lake of Pitch. So runs the tale, told forty years since to Mr. Joseph, author of a clever little history of Trinidad, by an old half-caste Indian, Señor Trinidada by name, who was said then to be nigh one hundred years of age. Surely the people among whom such a myth could spring up, were worthy of a nobler fate.

At Last (London and New York, 1871).

THE LACHINE RAPIDS

DOUGLAS SLADEN

FROM St. Anne's to Lachine is not such a very far cry, and it was at Lachine that the great La Salle had his first seigniory. This Norman founder of Illinois, who reared on the precipices of Fort St. Louis the white flag and his great white cross nearly a couple of centuries before the beginnings of the Metropolis of the West, made his beginnings at his little seigniory round Fort Remy, on the Island of Montreal.

The son of a wealthy and powerful burgher of Rouen, he had been brought up to become a Jesuit. La Salle was well fitted for an ecclesiastic, a prince of the Church, a Richelieu, but not for a Jesuit, whose effacement of self is the keystone of the order. To be one step, one stone in the mighty pyramid of the Order of Jesus was not for him, a man of mighty individuality like Columbus or Cromwell, and accordingly his piety, asceticism, vast ambition, and superhuman courage were lost to the Church and gained to the State. So says Parkman. . . .

His seigniory and fort—probably the Fort Remy of which a contemporary plan has come down to us—were just where the St. Lawrence begins to widen into Lake St. Louis, abreast of the famous Rapids of Lachine, shot by so

THE LACHINE RAPIDS.

many tourists with blanched cheeks every summer. I say tourists, for, as I have said before, there is nothing your true Canadian loves so much as the off-chance of being drowned in a cataract or "splifficated" on a toboggan slide. It is part of the national education, like the Bora Bora, or teeth-drawing, of the Australian aborigines. The very name Lachine breathes a memory of La Salle, for it was so christened in scorn by his detractors—the way by which La Salle thinks he is going to get to China. A palisade containing, at any rate, the house of La Salle, a stone mill still standing, and a stone barrack and ammunition house, now falling into most picturesque and pitfallish decay—such is Fort Remy, founded nearly two centuries and a quarter ago, when England was just beginning to feel the invigorating effects of a return to the blessings of Stuart rule. This was in 1667, but La Salle was not destined to remain here long. In two years' time he had learned seven or eight Indian languages, and felt himself ready for the ambition of his life: to find his way to the Vermilion Sea—the Gulf of California—for a short cut to the wealth of China and Japan,—an ambition which resolved itself into founding a province or Colonial Empire for France at the mouth of the Mississippi, when he discovered later on that the Mississippi flowed into the Gulf of Mexico and not into the Gulf of California.

We cannot follow him in his long connection with the Illinois Indians and Fort St. Louis. We must leave him gazing from the walls of his seigniory across the broad bosom of Lake St. Louis at the forests of Beauharnais and

Chateauguay (destined afterwards to be Canada's Thermopylæ) and the sunset, behind which must be a new passage to the South Seas and the treasures of Cathay and Cipango—the dream which had fired the brain of every discoverer from Columbus and Vasco Nuñez downwards.

Nowadays Lachine suggests principally the canal by which the rapids are avoided, the rapids themselves, and the superb Canadian Pacific Railway Bridge, which is a link in the realization of La Salle's vast idea. Hard by, too, the St. Lawrence opens out into the expanse of Lake St. Louis, dear to Montreallers in the glowing Canadian summer. Seen from the bank, the rapids are most disappointing to people who expect them to look like Niagara. Seen from the deck of the steamer which runs in connection with the morning and evening train from Montreal, they make the blood of the novice creep, though the safety of the trip is evinced by the fact that it is no longer considered necessary to take a pilot from the neighbouring Indian village of Caughnawaga. It is said that, if the steamer is abandoned to the current, it is impossible for her to strike, the scour being so strong; certainly, her engines are slowed; she reels about like a drunken man; right and left you see fierce green breakers with hissing white fillets threatening to swamp you at every minute. Every second thud of these waves upon the sides convinces you that the ship is aground and about to be dashed to pieces. There seems absolutely no chance of getting safely out of the boiling waters, which often rush together like a couple of fountains. Yet, after a few trips, you know that the Captain is quite justified in sitting in his easy chair and smoking a cigarette all through it. It is admirably described in brief by Dawson: "As the steamer enters the long and turbulent rapids of the Sault St. Louis, the river is contracted and obstructed by islands; and trap dykes, crossing the softer limestone rocks, make, by their uneven wear, a very broken bottom. The fall of the river is also considerable, and the channel tortuous, all which circumstances combined cause this rapid to be more feared than any of the others.

"As the steamer enters the rapids the engines are slowed, retaining a sufficient speed to give steerage way, and, rushing along with the added speed of the swift current, the boat soon begins to labour among the breakers and eddies. The passengers grow excited at the apparently narrow escapes, as the steamer seems almost to touch rock after rock, and dips her prow into the eddies, while the turbulent waters throw their spray over the deck."

On the Cars and Off (London, New York and Melbourne, 1895).

LAKE ROTORUA

H. R. HAWEIS

THE thermæ, or hot baths, of the near future are without doubt the marvellous volcanic springs of Rotorua and the Lake Taupo district, in the North Island. They can now be reached from London, *via* Francisco, in thirty-three days. They concentrate in a small area all the varied qualities of the European springs, and other curative properties of an extraordinary character, which are not possessed in the same degree by any other known waters. Before Mr. Froude's *Oceana*, and the subsequent destruction of the famous pink terraces, little attention had been called to one of the most romantic and amazing spectacles in the world. The old terraces are indeed gone. The idyllic villages, the blossoming slopes are a waste of volcanic ashes and scoriæ through which the dauntless vegetation is only now beginning to struggle. The blue waters are displaced and muddy, but the disaster of one shock could not rob the land of its extraordinary mystery and beauty. For a distance of three hundred miles, south of Lake Taupo and running north, a volcanic crust, sometimes thin enough to be trodden through, separates the foot from a seething mass of sulphur, gas, and boiling water, which around Rotorua and Waikari finds strange and ample vents, in hot streams, clouds of vapour, warm lakes, geysers, occasionally devel-

LAKE ROTORUA.

oping into appalling volcanic outbursts, which certainly invest this region with a weird terror, but also with an inconceivable charm, as white vapour breaks amidst flowering bushes, in the midst of true valleys of paradise; the streams ripple hot and crystalline over parti-coloured rocks or through emerald-hued mossy dells; the warm lakes sleep embedded in soft, weedy banks, reflecting huge boulders, half clothed in tropical foliage; coral-like deposits here and there of various tints reproduce the famous terraces in miniature; and geysers, in odd moments, spout huge volumes of boiling water with an unearthly roar eighty feet into the air. At Waikari, near Lake Taupo, specimens of all these wonders are concentrated in a few square miles—the bubbling white mud pools, like foaming plaster of Paris, the petrifying springs, into which a boy fell some time ago, and getting a good silicate coat over him was taken out months afterwards "as good as ever," so my guide explained.

"What," I said, "did he not feel even a little poorly?"

"What's that?" said the guide, and the joke dawning on him burst into a tardy roar.

And time would fail me to tell of the dragon's mouth, and open rock vomiting sulphur and steam; the lightning pool, in whose depths for ever flash queer opaline subaqueous flashes; the champagne pool, the Prince of Wales's Feathers, a geyser which can be made to play half an hour after a few clods of mud have blocked up a little hot stream; the steam hammer, the fairy bath, the donkey engine, etc.

At Rotorua we bought blocks of soap and threw them in to make a certain big geyser spout. The Maoris have still the monopoly there; you pay toll, cross a rickety bridge with a Maori girl as guide, and then visit the pools, terraces, and boiling fountains. They are not nearly so picturesque as at Waikari, which is a wilderness of blossoming glens, streams, and wooded vales. But you see the Maori in his native village.

The volcanic crust is warm to the feet; the Maori huts of "toitoi" reeds and boards are all about; outside are warm pools; naked boys and girls are swimming in them; as we approach they emerge half out of the water; we throw them threepenny bits. The girls seem most eager and dive best—one cunning little girl about twelve or thirteen, I believe, caught her coin each time under water long before it sank, but throwing up her legs half out of water dived deep, pretending to fetch it up from the bottom. Sometimes there was a scramble under water for the coin; the girls generally got it; the boys seemed half lazy. We passed on.

"Here is the brain pot," said our Maori belle; a hollowed stone. It was heated naturally—the brains cooked very well there in the old days—not very old days either.

"Here is the bread oven." She drew off the cloth, and sure enough in a hole in the hot ground there were three new loaves getting nicely browned. "Here are potatoes," and she pointed to a little boiling pool, and the potatoes were nearly done; and "here is meat,"—a tin let into the earth, that was all, contained a joint baking; and farther on was a very good stew—at least, it being one o'clock, it smelt well enough. And so there is no fuel and no fire wanted in this and dozens of other Maori pahs or hamlets. In the cold nights the Maoris come out of their tents naked, and sit or even sleep in the hot shallow lakelets and pools hard by. Anything more uncanny than this walk through the Rotorua Geyser village can hardly be conceived. The best springs are rented from the Maoris by the Government, or local hotel-keepers. These are now increasingly fashionable bathing resorts. The finest bath specific for rheumatism is the Rachel bath, investing the body with a soft, satiny texture, and a pearly complexion; the iron, sulphur, and especially the oil bath, from which when you emerge you have but to shake yourself dry. But the Priest's bath, so called from the discoverer, Father Mahoney—who cured himself of obstinate rheumatism—is perhaps of all the most miraculous in its effects, and there are no two opinions about it. Here take place the most incredible cures of sciatica, gout, lumbago, and all sorts of rheumatic affections. It is simply a question of fact.

The Countess of Glasgow herself told me about the cure of a certain colonel relative or aide-de-camp of the Governor, the Earl of Glasgow. The Colonel had for years been a perfect martyr to rheumatism and gout. He went to Rotorua with his swollen legs and feet, and came away wearing tight boots, and "as good as ever," as my guide would have said. But indeed I heard of scores of similar cases. Let all victims who can afford it lay it well to heart. A pleasure trip, of only thirty-two days, changing saloon rail carriage but three times, and steamer cabins but twice, will insure them an almost infallible cure, even when chronically diseased and no longer young. This is no "jeujah" affair. I have seen and spoken to the fortunate *beneficiares*—you meet them all over New Zealand. Of course, the fame of the baths is spreading: the region is only just made accessible by the opening of the railway from Auckland to Rotorua—a ten hours' run. The Waikari and Taupo baths are very similar, and the situation is infinitely more romantic, but the Government, on account of the railway, are pushing the Rotorua baths.

I stole out about half-past ten at night; it was clear and frosty. I made my way to a warm lake at the bottom of the hotel grounds, a little shed and a tallow candle being the only accommodation provided. Anything more weird than that starlight bath I never experienced. I stepped in the deep night from the frosty bank into a temperature of about 80°.

It was a large shallow lake. I peered into the dark, but I could not see its extent by the dim starlight; no, not even the opposite banks. I swam about until I came to the margin—a mossy, soft margin. Dark branches of trees dipped in the water, and I could feel the fallen leaves floating about. I followed the margin round till the light in my wood cabin dwindled to a mere spark in the distance, then I swam out into the middle of the lake. When I was upright the warm water reached my chin; beneath my feet seemed to be fine sand and gravel. Then leaning my head back I looked up at the Milky Way, and all the expanse of the starlit heavens. There was not a sound; the great suns and planets hung like golden balls above me in the clear air. The star dust of planetary systems—whole universes—stretched away bewilderingly into the unutterable void of boundless immensity, mapping out here and there the trackless thoroughfares of God in the midnight skies. "*Dont la poussière*," as Lamartine finely writes in oft-plagiarised words, "*sont les Étoiles qui remontent et tombent devant Lui.*"

How long I remained there absorbed in this supermundane contemplation I cannot say. I felt myself embraced simultaneously by three elements—the warm water, the darkness, and the starlit air. They wove a threefold spell about my senses, whilst my intellect seemed detached, free. Emancipated from earthly trammels, I seemed mounting up and up towards the stars. Suddenly I found myself growing faint, luxuriously faint. My head sank back, my eyes closed, there was a humming as of some distant waterfall in my ears. I seemed falling asleep, pillowed on the warm water, but common sense rescued me just in time. I was alone in an unknown hot lake in New Zealand at night, out of reach of human call. I roused myself with a great effort of will. I had only just time to make for the bank when I grew quite dizzy. The keen frosty air brought me unpleasantly to my senses. My tallow dip was guttering in its socket, and hastily resuming my garments, in a somewhat shivering condition, I retraced the rocky path, then groped my way over the little bridge under which rushed the hot stream that fed the lakelet, and guided only by the dim starlight I regained my hotel.

I had often looked up at the midnight skies before—at Charles's Wain and the Pleiades on the Atlantic, at the Southern Cross on the Pacific, and the resplendent Milky Way in the Tropics, at Mars and his so-called canals, at "the opal widths of the moon" from the snowy top of Mount Cenis, but never, no, never had I studied astronomy under such extraordinary circumstances and with such peculiar and enchanted environments as on this night at the Waikari hot springs.

Travel and Talk (London and New York, 1896).

THE BIG TREES OF CALIFORNIA

C. F. GORDON-CUMMING

AT last we entered the true forest-belt, and anything more beautiful you cannot conceive. We forgot our bumps and bruises in sheer delight. Oh the loveliness of those pines and cedars, living or dead! For the dead trees are draped with the most exquisite golden-green lichen, which hangs in festoons many yards in length, and is unlike any other moss or lichen I ever saw. I can compare it to nothing but gleams of sunshine in the dark forest. Then, too, how beautiful are the long arcades of stately columns, red, yellow, or brown, 200 feet in height, and straight as an arrow, losing themselves in their own crown of misty green foliage; and some standing solitary, dead and sunbleached, telling of careless fires, which burnt away their hearts, but could not make them fall!

There are so many different pines and firs, and cedars, that as yet I can scarcely tell one from another. The whole air is scented with the breath of the forests—the aromatic fragrance of resin and of dried cones and pine-needles baked by the hot sun (how it reminds me of Scotch firs!); and the atmosphere is clear and crystalline —a medium which softens nothing, and reveals the farthest distance in sharpest detail. Here and there we crossed deep gulches, where streams (swollen to torrents by the melting snow on the upper hills) rushed down over great boulders and prostrate trees and the victims of the winter gales.

Then we came to quiet glades in the forest, where the soft lawn-like turf was all jewelled with flowers; and the sunlight trickled through the dripping boughs of the feathery Douglas pines, and the jolly little chip-munks played hide-and-seek among the great cedars, and chased one another to the very tops of the tall pitch-pines, which stand like clusters of dark spires, more than 200 feet in height. It was altogether lovely; but I think no one was sorry when we reached a turn in the road, where we descended from the high forest-belt, and crossing a picturesque stream—"Big Creek"—by name—we found ourselves in this comfortable ranch, which takes its name from one of the pioneers of the valley.

We have spent a long day of delight in the most magnificent forest that it is possible to imagine; and I have realized an altogether new sensation, for I have seen the Big Trees of California, and have walked round about them, and inside their cavernous hollows, and have done homage as beseems a most reverent tree-worshipper. They are wonderful—they are stupendous! But as to beauty—no. They shall never tempt me to swerve from my allegiance to my true tree-love—the glorious Deodara forest of the Himalayas.

If size alone were to be considered, undoubtedly the Sequoia stands preëminent, for to-day we have seen several trees at least three times as large as the biggest Deodara in

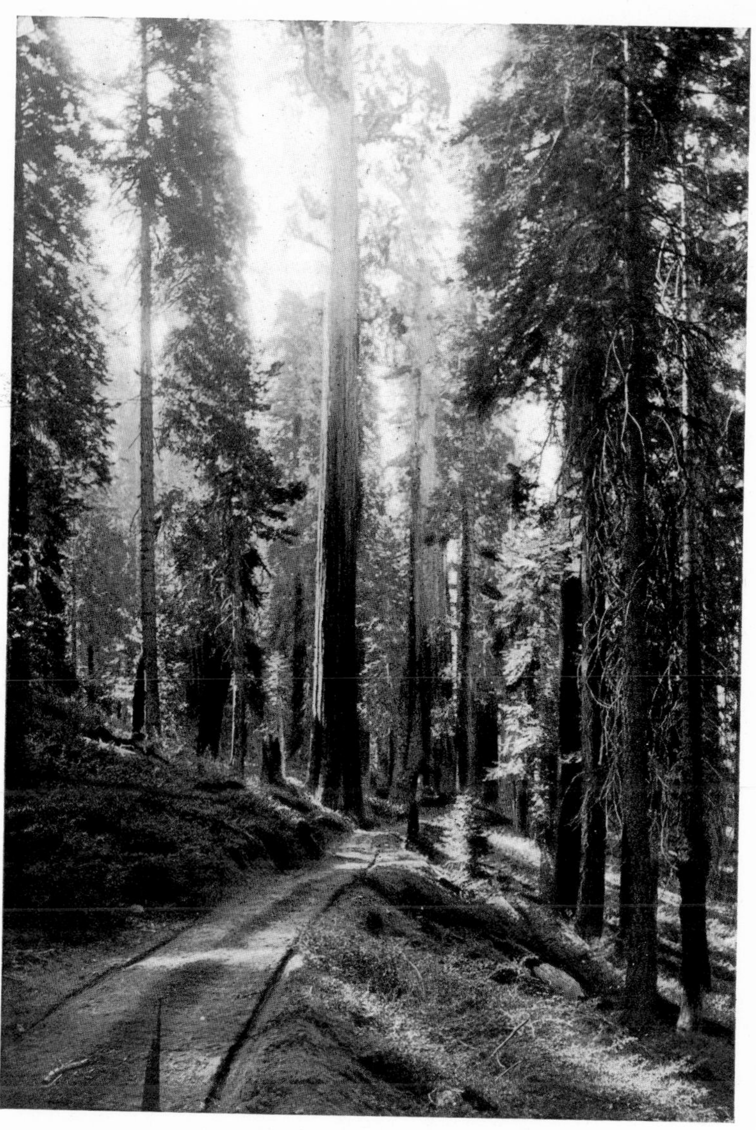

THE BIG TREES OF CALIFORNIA.

the cedar shades of Kunai; but for symmetry, and grace, and exquisitely harmonious lines, the "God-given" cedar of Himala stands alone, with its wide spreading, twisted arms, and velvety layers of foliage studded with pale-green cones,—its great red stem supporting a pyramid of green, far more majestic than the diminutive crown of the Big Trees. So at first it was hard to realize that the California cedars are altogether justified in concentrating all their growing power in one steady upward direction, so intent on reaching heaven that they could not afford to throw out one kindly bough to right or left. They remind me of certain rigidly good Pharisees, devoid of all loving sympathies with their fellows, with no outstretched arms of kindly charity—only intent on regulating their own lives by strictest unvarying rule.

Great Towers of Babel they seem to me, straining upward towards the heaven which they will never reach.

There is nothing lovable about a Sequoia. It is so gigantic that I feel overawed by it, but all the time I am conscious that I am comparing it with the odd Dutch trees in a Noah's Ark, with a small tuft of foliage on the top of a large red stem, all out of proportion. And another unpleasant simile forces itself on my mind—namely, a tall penguin, or one of the wingless birds of New Zealand, with feeble little flaps in place of wings, altogether disproportioned to their bodies.

But this is merely an aside—lest you should suppose that each new land I visit wins my affections from earlier loves. The Deodara forests must ever keep their place in my innermost heart: no sunlight can ever be so lovely as that which plays among their boughs—no sky so blue—no ice-peaks so glittering as those which there cleave the heaven; and I am sure that these poor wretched-looking Digger Indians can never have the same interest for me as the wild Himalayan highlanders—the Paharis—who assemble at the little temples of carved cedar-wood in the Great Forest Sanctuary, to offer their strange sacrifices, and dance in mystic sunwise procession.

Having said this much, I may now sing the praises of a newly found delight, for in truth these forests of the Sierras have a charm of their own, which cannot be surpassed, in the amazing variety of beautiful pines, firs, and cedars of which they are composed. The white fir, the Douglas spruce, sugar-pine, and pitch-pine are the most abundant, and are scattered singly or in singularly picturesque groups over all the mountains hereabouts.

But the Big Trees are only found in certain favoured spots—sheltered places watered by snow-fed streams, at an average of from 5,000 to 7,000 feet above the sea. Eight distinct groves have been discovered, all growing in rich, deep, vegetable mould, on a foundation of powdered granite. Broad gaps lie between the principal groves, and it is observed that these invariably lie in the track of the great ice-rivers, where the accumulation of powdered rock and gravel formed the earliest commencement of the soil, which by slow degrees became rich, and deep, and fertile. There is even reason to believe that these groves are pre-Adamite. A very average tree (only twenty-three feet in diameter) having been felled, its annual rings were counted by three different persons, whose calculations varied from 2,125 to 2,137; and this tree was by no means very aged-looking—probably not half the age of some of its big relations, one of which (on King's river) is forty-four feet in diameter.

Then, again, some of the largest of these trees are lying prostrate on the ground; and in the ditches formed by their crash, trees have grown up of such a size, and in such a position, as to prove that the fallen giants have lain there for centuries—a thousand years or more; and although partially embedded in the earth, and surrounded by damp forest, their almost imperishable timber is as sound as if newly felled. So it appears that a Sequoia may lie on damp earth for untold ages without showing any symptom of decay. Yet in the southern groves huge prostrate trees are found quite rotten, apparently proving that they must have lain there for an incalculable period.

Of the eight groves aforesaid, the most northerly is Calaveras, and the most southerly is on the south fork of the Tule river. The others are the Stanislaus, the Merced and Crane Flat, the Mariposa, the Fresno, the King's and Kaweah rivers, and the north fork of the Tule river. It is worthy of note that the more northerly groves are found at the lowest level, Calaveras being only 4,759 feet above the sea, while the Tule and Kaweah belts range over the Sierras at about 7,000 feet.

The number of Sequoias in the northern groves is reckoned to be as follows: Calaveras, ninety trees upwards of fifteen feet in diameter; Stanislaus, or South Calaveras grove, distant six miles from North Calaveras, contains 1,380 trees over one foot in diameter (many of them being over thirty feet in diameter). Mariposa has its 600 Sequoias; and the beautiful Fresno grove, some miles from Mariposa, has 1,200. Merced has fifty, and Tuolumne thirty. The southern belts have not yet been fully explored, but are apparently the most extensive.

The Mariposa grove, where we have been to-day, is the only one which has been reserved by Government as a park for the nation. It lies five miles from here. I should rather say there are two groves. The lower grove lies in a sheltered valley between two mountain-spurs; the upper grove, as its name implies, occupies a higher level, 6,500 feet above the sea.

We breakfasted very early, and by 6 A. M. were in the saddle. Capital, sure-footed ponies were provided for all who chose to ride. Some of the gentlemen preferred walking. From this house we had to ascend about 2,500 feet.

As we gradually worked uphill through the coniferous belts, the trees seemed gradually to increase in size, so that the eye got accustomed by degrees; and when at length we actually reached the Big-Tree grove we scarcely realized that we were in the presence of the race of giants. Only when we occasionally halted at the base of a colossal pillar, somewhere about eighty feet in circumference, and about 250 in height, and compared it with its neighbours, and, above all, with ourselves—poor, insignificant pigmies—could we bring home to our minds a sense of its gigantic proportions.

With all the reverence due to antiquity, we gazed on these Methuselahs of the forest, to whom a few centuries more or less in the record of their long lives are a trifle scarcely worth mentioning. But our admiration was more freely bestowed on the rising generation, the beautiful young trees, only about five or six hundred years of age, and averaging thirty feet in circumference; while still younger trees, the mere children of about a hundred years old, still retain the graceful habits of early youth, and are very elegant in their growth—though, of course, none but mere babies bear the slightest resemblance to the tree as we know it on English lawns.

It really is heartbreaking to see the havoc that has been done by careless fires. Very few of the older trees have escaped scathless. Most of this damage has been done by Indians, who burn the scrub to scare the game, and the fire spreads to the trees, and there smoulders unheeded for weeks, till happily some chance extinguishes it. Many lords of the forest have thus been burnt out, and have at last fallen, and lie on the ground partly embedded, forming great tunnels, hollow from end to end, so that in several cases two horsemen can ride abreast inside the tree from (what was once) its base to its summit.

We halted at the base of the Grizzly Giant, which well deserves its name; for it measures ninety-three feet in circumference, and looks so battered and weather-worn that it probably is about the most venerable tree in the forest. It is one of the most picturesque Sequoias I have seen, just because it has broken through all the rules of symmetry, so rigidly observed by its well conditioned, well-grown brethren; and instead of being a vast cinnamon-coloured column, with small boughs near the summit, it has taken a line of its own, and thrown out several great branches, each about six feet in diameter—in other words, about as large as a fine old English beech-tree!

This poor old tree has a great hollow burnt in it (I think the Indians must have used it as a kitchen), and our half dozen ponies and mules were stabled in the hollow—a most picturesque group. It seems strange to see trees thus scorched and charred, with their insides clean burnt out, yet, on looking far, far overhead, to perceive them crowned with fresh blue-green, as if nothing ailed them, so great is their vitality. Benjamin Taylor says of such a one, "It did not know that it ought to be dead. The tides of life flowed so mightily up that majestic column!"

The Indians say that all other trees grow, but that the Big Trees are the special creation of the Great Spirit. So here too, you see, we have, not tree-worship, but something of the reverence accorded to the cedar in all lands. The Hebrew poet sang of "the trees of the Lord, even the cedars of Lebanon which He hath planted." And the Hill tribes of Northern India build a rudely carved temple beneath each specially magnificent clump of Deodar, to mark that they are "God's trees"; while in the sacred Sanskrit poems they are called Deva dara or Deva daru, meaning the gift, the spouse, the word of God, but in any case, denoting the sanctity of the tree.

Whether these Californian Indians had any similar title

for their Big Trees, I have failed to learn; but the name by which they are known to the civilized world is that of Sequoyah, a half-caste Cherokee Indian, who distinguished himself by inventing an alphabet and a written language for his tribe. It was a most ingenious alphabet, consisting of eighty-six characters, each representing a syllable, and was so well adapted to its purpose that it was extensively used by the Indians before the white man had ever heard of it. Afterwards it was adopted by the missionaries, who started a printing-press, with types of this character, and issued a newspaper for the Cherokee tribe, by whom this singular alphabet is still used.

When the learned botanist, Endlicher, had to find a suitable name for the lovely redwood cedars, he did honour to Sequoyah, by linking his memory forever with that of the evergreen forests of the Coast Range. And when afterwards these Big Trees of the same race were discovered on the Sierras, they of course were included under the same family name.

Granite Crags (Edinburgh and London, 1884).

GERSOPPA FALLS

W. M. YOOL

THESE, the most famous falls in India, are situated on the Siruvatti (or *Sharavati*) river, which at that part of its course forms the boundary between the north-west corner of the native state of Mysore and the Bombay Presidency. The source of the river is in Mysore, half-way up Koda Chadri, a hill about five thousand feet high, near the famous old town of Nuggur, once the seat of the Rajahs of Mysore, where are still to be seen the ruins of an old fort and palace, and the walls of the town, eight miles in circumference.

The natives have a legend that the god Rama shot an arrow from his bow on to Koda Chadri, and that the river sprang from the spot where the arrow fell, and hence the name Siruvatti or "arrow-born." From its source the river flows north for nearly thirty miles through the heart of the Western Ghauts, and then turns west and flows down through the jungles of North Canara to the Indian Ocean —another thirty miles. Shortly after taking the bend west-wards there comes the fall, which, on account of its height, is worthy of being reckoned amongst the great waterfalls of the world. Here, at one leap, the river falls eight hundred and thirty feet; and as, at the brink, it is about four hundred

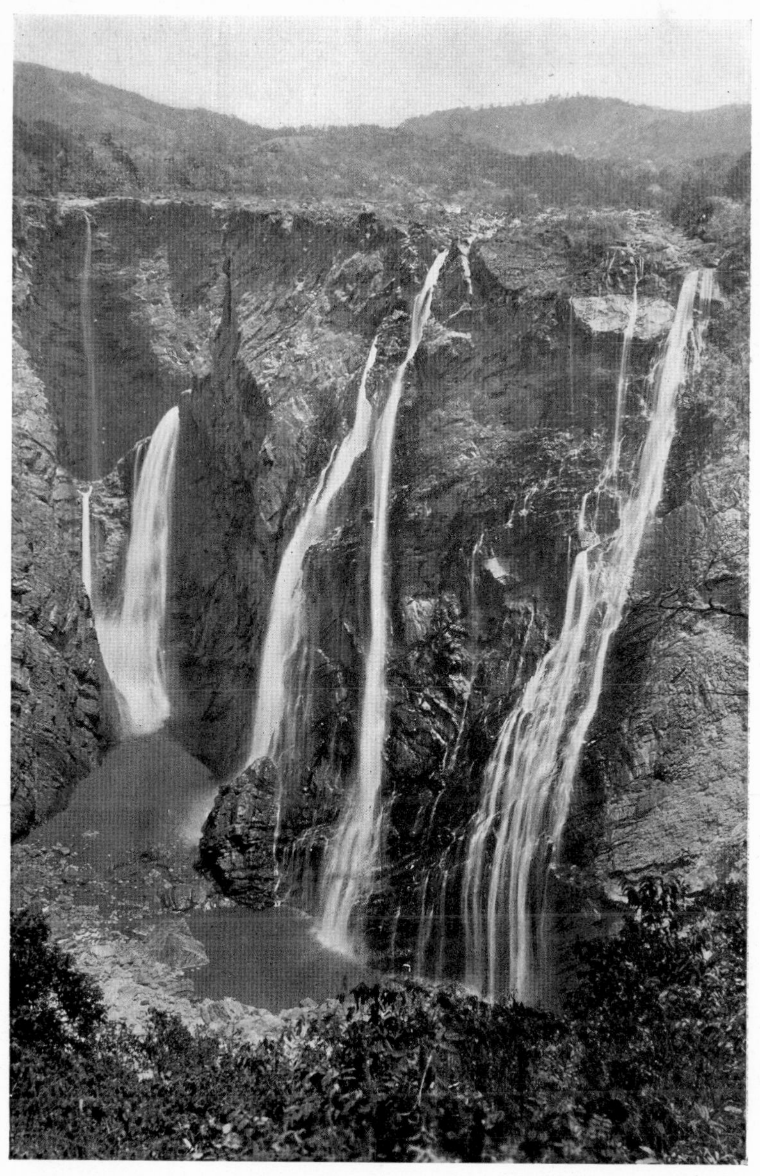

GERSOPPA FALLS.

yards wide, there are few, if any, falls in the world to match it.

During the dry weather the river comes over in four separate falls, but in the height of the monsoon these become one, and as at that time the water is nearly thirty feet deep, the sight must be truly one of the world's wonders. It has been calculated that in flood-time more horse-power is developed by the Gersoppa Falls than by Niagara. This of course is from the much greater height of Gersoppa, eight hundred and thirty feet against about one hundred and sixty feet of Niagara, although the Niagara Falls are much wider and vaster in volume. The Kaieteur Falls of the Essequibo in British Guiana are seven hundred and forty-one feet sheer and eighty-eight more of sloping cataract, but the river there is only one hundred yards wide. At the Victoria Falls, the Zambesi, one thousand yards wide, falls into an abyss four hundred feet deep.

My friend and I visited the falls in the end of September, about a month after the close of the monsoon, when there were four falls with plenty of water in them. The dry weather is the best for the sight-seer, as, during the monsoon, the rain is so heavy and continuous that there would not be much pleasure in going there, although doubtless the sight would be grander and more awe-inspiring. The drainage area above the falls is seven hundred and fifty square miles, and the average yearly rainfall over this tract is two hundred and twenty inches, nearly the whole of which falls in the three monsoon months, June, July, August; so it can be imagined what an enormous body of water comes down the river in these months. There is a bungalow for the use of visitors on the Bombay side of the river, about a hundred yards away from the falls, built on the very brink of the precipice overhanging the gorge through which the river flows after taking the leap. So close to the edge is it that one could jump from the veranda sheer into the bed of the river nearly a thousand feet below.

The four falls are called *The Rajah*, *The Roarer*, *The Rocket*, and *La Dame Blanche*. The *Rajah* and *Roarer* fall into a horseshoe-shaped cavern, while the *Rocket* and *La Dame Blanche* come over where the precipice is at right angles to the flow of the river, and are very beautiful falls. The *Rajah* comes over with a rush, shoots clear out from the rock, and falls one unbroken column of water the whole eight hundred and thirty feet. The *Roarer* comes rushing at an angle of sixty degrees down a huge furrow in the rock for one hundred and fifty feet, making a tremendous noise, then shoots right out into the middle of the horseshoe, and mingles its waters with those of the *Rajah* about half-way down. The *Rocket* falls about two hundred feet in sheer descent on to a huge knob of rock, where it is dashed into spray, which falls in beautiful smoky rings, supposed to resemble the rings formed by the bursting of rockets. *La Dame Blanche*, which my friend and I thought the most beautiful, resembles a snow-white muslin veil falling in graceful folds, and clothing the black precipice from head to foot.

From the bungalow a fine view is got of the *Rocket* and *La Dame Blanche*, and when the setting sun lights up these falls and forms numerous rainbows in the spray, it makes an indescribably beautiful scene. Here one is alone with Nature, not a house or patch of cultivation anywhere. In front is the river, and all around are mountains and primeval forests, while the ceaseless roar of the waterfall adds a grandeur and a solemnity not easily described.

Near where the *Rajah* goes over is a projecting rock called the *Rajah's Rock*, so named because one of the Rajahs of Nuggur tried to build a small pagoda on it, but before being finished, it was washed away. The cutting in the rock for the foundation is still visible. To any one who has a good head, a fine view of the horseshoe cavern can be had from this rock. The plan is to lie down on your stomach, crawl to the edge, and look over, when you can see straight down into the pool where the waters are boiling and seething nearly a thousand feet below. I took a few large stones to the edge and dropped them over, but they were lost to view long before they reached the bottom. It was quite an appreciable time after my losing sight of them before I observed the faint splash they made near the edge of the pool.

In order to get to the foot of the falls it is necessary to cross the river to the Mysore side, as there is no possibility of getting down to the Bombay side. About half a mile above the falls there is a canoe, dug out of the trunk of a tree, which belongs to the native who looks after the bungalow, and ferries people across. A path has been made to enable visitors to get to the foot of the falls, and many fine views of all four are got while descending. The first half of the way down is fairly easy, but after that the track is a succession of steps down great boulders and across slabs of rock, rendered as slippery as ice by the constant spray. Ere my friend and I reached the bottom we were soaking wet, and realized when too late that we should have left the greater part of our clothes behind us. By going to the bottom a much better idea of the immense height of the falls is got, and the climb up again helps still more to make one realize it. From the bungalow the largest rocks in the bed of the river looked like sheep; but we found them to be huge boulders, ten and twelve feet high and about twenty feet across.

The falls seem to have become known to Europeans about 1840, but were very seldom visited in those days. Even now the number of visitors is small, as the nearest railway is eighty miles off, and there is no way of procuring supplies with the exception of a little milk and a chicken to be had from the above-mentioned native.

For a good many years there was great uncertainty about the height of the falls, but the question was finally set at rest by two naval lieutenants who plumbed them in 1857. The *modus operandi* was as follows: Their ship being off the coast near the mouth of the river, they got a cable transported to the falls, and stretched it across the horseshoe—a distance of seventy-four yards. Having seen that the cable was properly secured at both ends, they got a cage fixed on, and one of them got into it and was hauled out until he was in the centre. From the cage he let down a sounding line with a buoy attached to the end of it, and found the depth to the surface of the water to be eight hundred and thirty feet. After satisfactorily accomplishing this feat, they proceeded to the foot of the falls, and constructed a raft so as to plumb the pools, which they did, and found the greatest depth to be one hundred and thirty-two feet. This was done near the end of the dry weather, when there was very little water in the river, and they were able to temporarily divert the *Rajah* and *Roarer* into the *Rocket*, without doing which it would have been impossible to plumb the horseshoe pool—the deepest one—satisfactorily.

About a mile from the bungalow is a hill called Nishani Goodda or Cairn Hill, from the top of which a magnificent view of the surrounding country is got. To the east lie the table-lands of the Deccan and Mysore, the flat expanse broken here and there by an occasional hill. North and south stretches the chain of the Ghauts, rising peak after peak as far as the eye can see (Koda Chadri, where the Siruvatti rises, being very conspicuous); while to the west one looks down on the lowlands of jungle-covered Canara, with glimpses of the river here and there, and beyond them gleams the Indian Ocean.

The bungalow book in which visitors inscribe their names is very interesting reading. The records go back to 1840, and many travellers have written a record of what they did when there; while a few, inspired by the scene, have expressed their feelings in poetry, some of it well worth copying and preserving by any one who has seen the falls.

Chambers' Journal (London, 1896).

ETNA

ALEXANDRE DUMAS

THE word Etna, according to the *savants*, is a Phœnician word meaning the *mouth of the furnace*. The Phœnician language, as you see, was of the order of that one spoken of by Covielle to the *Bourgeois Gentilhomme*, which expressed many things in a few words. Many poets of antiquity pretend that it was the spot where Deucalion and Pyrrha took refuge during the flood. Upon this score, Signor Gemellaro, who was born at Nicolosì, may certainly claim the honour of having descended in a direct line from one of the first stones which they threw behind them. That would leave, as you see, the Montmorencys, the Rohans, and the Noailles, far behind.

Homer speaks of Etna, but he does not designate it a volcano. Pindar calls it one of the pillars of the sky. Thucydides mentions three great explosions, from the epoch of the arrival of the Grecian colonies up to his own lifetime. Finally, there were two eruptions in the time of Denys; then they followed so rapidly that only the most violent ones have been counted.[1]

[1] The principal eruptions of Etna took place in the year 662, B. C., and in A. D. 225, 420, 812, 1169, 1285, 1329, 1333, 1408, 1444, 1446, 1447, 1536, 1603, 1607, 1610, 1614, 1619, 1634, 1669, 1682, 1688, 1689, 1702, 1766, and 1781.

ETNA.

Since the eruption of 1781, Etna has had some little desire to overthrow Sicily; but, as these caprices have not had serious results, Etna may be is permitted to stand upon what it has accomplished—it is unique in its self-respect—and to maintain its eminence as a volcano.

Of all these eruptions, one of the most terrible was that of 1669. As the eruption of 1669 started from Monte Rosso, and as Monte Rosso is only half a mile to the left of Nicolosì, we took our way, Jadin and I, to visit the crater, after having promised Signor Gemellaro to come to dinner with him.

It must be understood beforehand that Etna regards itself too far above ordinary volcanos to proceed in their fashion: Vesuvius, Stromboli, and even Hekla pour the lava over their craters, just as wine spills over a too-full glass; Etna does not give itself this trouble. Its crater is only a crater for show, which is content to play cup and ball with incandescent rocks large as ordinary houses, which one follows in their aërial ascension as one would follow a bomb issuing from a mortar; but, during this time the force of the eruption is really felt elsewhere. In reality, when Etna is at work, it throws up very simply upon its shoulders, at one place or another, a kind of boil about the size of Montmartre; then this boil breaks, and out of it streams a river of lava which follows the slope, descends, burning, or overturning everything that it finds before it, and ends by extinguishing itself in the sea. This method of procedure is the cause of Etna's being covered with a number of little craters which are formed like immense hay-mows; each of these secondary volcanos has its date and its own name, and all have occasioned in their time, more or less noise and more or less ravage.

We got astride of our mounts and started on our way upon a night that seemed to us of terrible darkness as we issued from a well-lighted room; but, by degrees, we began to distinguish the landscape, thanks to the light of the myriads of stars that sprinkled the sky. It seemed from the way in which our mules sank beneath us that we were crossing sand. Soon we entered the second region, or the forest region, that is if the few scattered, poor, and crooked trees merit the name of forest. We marched about two hours, confidently following the road our guide took us, or rather our mules, a road which, moreover, to judge by the eternal declivities and ascents, seemed terribly uneven. Already, we realized the wisdom of Signor Gemellaro's provisions against the cold, and we wrapped ourselves in our hooded great-coats a full hour before we arrived at a kind of roofless hovel where our mules stopped of themselves. We were at the *Casa del Bosco* or *della Neve*, that is to say, the *Forest* or the *Snow*, names which it merits in either summer or winter. Our guide told us this was our halting-place. Upon his invitation, we alighted and entered. We were half-way on the road to the *Casa Inglese*.

During our halt the sky was enriched by a crescent, which, although slender, gave us a little light. We continued to march a quarter of an hour longer between trees which became scarcer every twenty feet and finally disappeared altogether. We were about to enter the third region of Etna, and we knew from the steps of the mules when they were passing over lava, crossing ashes, or when they trampled a kind of moss, the only vegetation that creeps up to this point. As for our eyes, they were of very little use, the sheen appearing to us more or less coloured, and that was all, for we could not distinguish a single detail in the midst of this darkness.

However, in proportion as we ascended, the cold became more intense, and, notwithstanding our cloaks, we were freezing. This change of temperature had checked conversation, and each of us, occupied in trying to keep himself warm, advanced in silence. I led the way, and if I could not see the ground on which we advanced, I could distinguish perfectly on our right the gigantic escarpments and the immense peaks, that reared themselves like giants, and whose black silhouettes stood out boldly upon the deep blue of the sky. The further we advanced, the stranger and more fantastic shapes did these apparitions assume; we well understood that Nature had not originally made these mountains as they are and that it was a long contest that had ravaged them. We were upon the battlefield of the Titans; we clambered over Pelion piled upon Ossa.

All this was terrible, sombre, and majestic; I saw and I felt thoroughly the poetry of this nocturnal trip, and meanwhile I was so cold that I had not the courage to exchange a word with Jadin to ask him if all these visions were not the result of the weakness that I experienced, and if I were not dreaming. From time to time strange and unfamiliar noises, that did not resemble in the slightest degree any noises that one is accustomed to hear, started from the bowels of the earth, and seemed to moan and wail like a living being. These noises had something so unexpectedly lugubrious and solemn about them that they made your blood run cold. . . . We walked about three-quarters of an hour upon the steep and rough road, then we found ourselves upon a slightly inclined slope where every now and then we crossed large patches of snow and in which I was plunged up to my knees, and these finally became continuous. At length the dark vault of the sky began to pale and a feeble twilight illumined the ground upon which we walked, bringing with it air even more icy than we had heretofore breathed. In this wan and uncertain light we perceived before us something resembling a house; we approached it, Jadin trotting upon his mule, and I coming as fast as possible. The guide pushed open the door and we found ourselves in the *Casa Inglese*, built at the foot of the cone, for the great relief of travellers.

It was half-past three o'clock in the morning; our guide reminded us that we had still three-quarters of an hour's climb at least, and, if we wished to reach the top of the cone before sunrise, we had not a moment to lose.

We left the *Casa Inglese*. We began to distinguish objects: all around us extended a vast field of snow, in the centre of which, making an angle of about forty-five degrees, the cone of Etna rose. Above us all was in darkness; towards the east only a light tint of opal coloured the sky on which the mountains of Calabria were vigorously outlined.

At a hundred feet from the *Casa Inglese* we encountered the first waves of the lava plateau whose black hue did not accord with the snow, in the midst of which it rose like a sombre island. We had to mount these solid waves, jumping from one to another, as I had done at Chamouni and the Mer de Glace, with this difference, that the sharp edges tore the leather of our shoes and cut our feet. This passage, which lasted a quarter of an hour, was one of the most trying of the route.

We were now about a third of the way up, and we had only taken about half an hour to ascend four hundred feet; the east brightened more and more; the fear of not arriving at the summit of the cone in time to see the sunrise lent us courage, and we started again with new enthusiasm, without pausing to look at the immense horizon which widened beneath our feet at each step; but the further we advanced, the more the difficulties increased; at each step the slope became more abrupt, the earth more friable, and the air rarer. Soon, on our right, we began to hear subterranean roarings that attracted our attention; our guide walked in front of us and led us to a fissure from which came a great noise and a thick sulphurous smoke blown out by an interior current of air. Approaching the edges of this cleft, we saw at an unfathomable depth a bottom of incandescent and red liquid; and when we stamped our feet, the ground resounded in the distance like a drum. Happily it was perfectly calm, for if the wind had blown this smoke over to our side, we should have been asphyxiated, for it is charged with a terrible fumes of sulphur.

We found ourselves opposite the crater,—an immense well, eight miles in circumference and 900 feet deep; the walls of this excavation were covered with scarified matter of sulphur and alum from top to bottom; in the bottom as far as we could see at the distance from where we stood, there was some matter in eruption, and from the abyss there ascended a tenuous and tortuous smoke, resembling a gigantic serpent standing on his tail. The edges of the crater were cut out irregularly at a greater or less height. We were at one of the highest points.

Our guide permitted us to look at this sight for a moment, holding us back, however, every now and then by our clothing when we approached too near the precipice, for the rock is so friable that it could easily give way beneath our feet, and we should repeat the joke of Empedocles; then he asked us to remove ourselves about twenty feet from the crater to avoid all accidents, and to look around us.

The east, whose opal tints we had noticed when leaving the *Casa Inglese*, had changed to tender rose, and was now inundated with the flames of the sun whose disc we began to perceive above the mountains of Calabria. Upon the sides of these mountains of a dark and uniform blue, the towns and villages stood out like little white points. The strait of Messina seemed a simple river, while to the right and left we saw the sea like an immense mirror. To the left, this mirror was spotted with several black dots: these black dots were the islands of the Lipariote archipelago. From time to time one of these islands glimmered like an intermittent light-house; this was Stromboli, throwing out flames. In the west, everything was in darkness. The shadow of Etna cast itself over all Sicily.

For three-quarters of an hour the spectacle did nothing but gain in magnificence. I have seen the sun rise on Rigi and the Faulhorn, those two Titans of Switzerland: nothing is comparable to the view on Etna's summit; Calabria from Pizzo to Cape dell Armi, the pass from Scylla to Reggio, the Tyrrhenian Sea, the Ionian Sea and the Æolian Islands that seem within reach of your hand; to the right, Malta floating on the horizon like a light mist; around us the whole of Sicily, seen from a bird's-eye view with its shores denticulated with capes, promontories, harbours, creeks and roads; its fifteen cities and three hundred villages; its mountains which seem like hills; its valleys which we know are furrowed with ploughs; its rivers which seem threads of silver, as in autumn they fall from the sky to the grasses of the meadows; and, finally, the immense roaring crater, full of flames and smoke, overhead Heaven and at its feet Hell: such a spectacle, made us forget fatigue, danger, and suffering. I admired it all without reservation, with my eyes and my soul. Never had God seemed so near and, consequently, so great.

We remained there an hour, dominating all the old world of Homer, Virgil, Ovid, and Theocritus, without the idea of touching a pencil occurring to Jadin or myself, until it seemed to us that this picture had entered deeply into our hearts and remained graven there without the aid of ink or sketch. Then we threw a last glance over this horizon of three hundred leagues, a sight seen once in a lifetime, and we began our descent.

Le Speronare : Impressions de Voyage (Paris, 1836.)

PIKE'S PEAK AND THE GARDEN OF THE GODS

IZA DUFFUS HARDY

COLORADO SPRINGS—so called because the springs are at Manitou, five miles off, is a prairie town on a plateau six thousand feet high, above which Pike's Peak stands sentinel, lifting his snow-capped head fourteen thousand feet into the clear depths of azure light, in which no fleck of cloud floats from morn to night and night to morn again. It is April, and not a drop of rain has fallen since the previous August. Mid-April, and not a leaf upon a tree. Not a flower or a bird seems to flourish here. No spring-blossom scents the keen fresh life-giving air; no warbler soars high up into the stainless sapphire sky. The leafless cottonwood trees stand out white in the flood of sunlight like trees of silver, their delicate bare branches forming a shining tangle of silvery network against that intense blue background.

The place all looks bleak and barren to us; the wild grandeur of the mountains is unrelieved by the rich shadows of the pine forests or the sunny green glints of meadows that soften Alpine scenery. No flower gardens, no smiling valleys, no velvet turf, no fragrant orchards, no luxuriant hedge rows; only the lonely mountain range, the crowning height of Pike's Peak stern and solitary in his icy exaltation, and the dead level of the prairie, stretching away eastward for hundreds and hundreds of miles, declining always at a gradual and imperceptible angle till it slopes down to the very banks of the great Mississippi, over a thousand miles away.

But, although the spot does not seem altogether a Paradise to us, it is a veritable Eden for consumptive invalids. Here they come to find again the lost angel of Health, and seldom seek again, unless they come too late. People live here who can live nowhere else. They long to return to their far-off homes; but home to them means death. They must live in this Colorado air, or die. There is a snake in the grass of this Eden, where they have drunk the elixir of a new life, and its name is Nostalgia. They long—some of them—for the snowy winters and flowery summers of their eastern homes. Others settle happily and contentedly in the endless sunshine of winterless, summerless Colorado.

We rattled along cheerily in our light spring-waggon over the smooth, fine roads, viewing the landscape from beneath the parasols which only partially shielded us from the blazing sun. Although the gentleman from Tennessee preserved a truly western taciturnity, our driver beguiled the way with instructive and amusing converse. He pointed out to us, flourishing by the wayside, the soap-weed, whose root is a perfect substitute for soap, and taught us to distinguish between the blue joint-grass—yellow as hay in winter, but now taking on its hue of summer green—and the greyish neutral-tinted buffalo-grass, which is most succulent and

THE GARDEN OF THE GODS.

nutritious, although its looks belie it, for a less tempting-looking herb I never had the pleasure of seeing. He also pointed out the dead body of a cow lying on a desolate plain, and informed us it would dry up to a mummy in no time; it was the effect of the air; dead cattle speedily mummified, and were no nuisance. Another dried-up bovine skeleton bore witness to the truth of his assertion.

We observed that the soil looked barren as desert sand; but he replied that it only required irrigation to be extremely fertile, showed us the irrigating ditches cut across the meadows, and described to us some of the marvellous productions of Colorado—a single cabbage-head weighing forty pounds, etc. He told us of the wondrous glories of the Arkansas cañon and the Mount of the Holy Cross—which, alas! we were not to see, the roads thither being as yet rough travelling for ladies. He sang the praises of the matchless climate, and the joys of the free, healthful life, far from the enervating and deteriorating influences of great cities. Indeed, it appeared from his conversation that nowhere on the face of the habitable globe could there be found any spot even remotely emulating the charms of Colorado—an opinion shared by every Coloradian with whom we held any intercourse.

Our way then led up the Ute Pass, once, in days not so far back frequented by the Ute Indians. Now, not an Indian is to be seen for miles; they have all been swept back on to a reservation, and the story of the Ute outbreak there of the past autumn is yet fresh in the minds of all. The Ute Pass is a winding, uphill road along the side of a deep cañon, the rocks here and there overhanging it threateningly, and affording a welcome shade from the piercing sun-rays, which follow us even here. The steep walls of the cañon are partly clothed and crowned with pine-trees, and along its depths a rapid, sparkling stream bubbles and leaps over the rocks and boulders.

Up the pass a waggon-train is toiling on its way to the great new mining centre—the giant baby city—Leadville, the youngest and most wonderful child of the prolific west! In this train we get entangled, and move slowly along with it—waggons and cattle before us, waggons and cattle behind us—tourists, teamsters, miners, drivers, drovers, dogs, all huddled together in seemingly inextricable confusion.

At the top of the pass, we tourists turn: and, while the waggon-train plods on its slow way, we make the best of our way back down the hill, and take the road to the Garden of the Gods.

Why the *Garden* of the Gods? I do not myself perceive the appropriateness of the appellation. There is not a flower in sight; only a few stunted shrubs, and forlorn-looking, thin trees. It is a natural enclosure, of fifty or more acres, such as in Colorado is called a "park," scattered with rocks of a rich red hue, and the wildest and most grotesque shapes imaginable.

The giants might have made it their playground, and left their playthings around them. Here, tossed and flung about as if by a careless hand, lie the huge round boulders with which they played at ball. Here they amused themselves by balancing an immense mass of stone on a point so cunningly that it has stood there for centuries looking as if a touch would overturn it. There they have hewn a high rock into the rough semblance of a veiled woman—here they have sculptured a man in a hat—there piled up a rude fortress, and there built a church.

But the giants have deserted their playground ages ago, and trees have grown up between the fantastic formations they left. It is a strange weird scene, and suggested to us forcibly that if we would "view it aright" we should

"Go view it by the pale moonlight!'

How spectral those strange shapes would look in the gloom! What ghostly life would seem to breathe in them when the white moonbeams bathed their eerie outlines in her light! There is a something lost in the Garden of the Gods to us who only saw it with a flood of sunshine glowing on its ruddy rocks. Most of these have been christened according to their form—the Nun, the Scotchman, the Camel, and so on.

Two huge walls of red and white stone, rising perpendicularly a sheer three hundred feet, form the gate of the Garden. Through this colossal and for-ever-open gate we looked back with a sigh of farewell—our glimpse of the scene seemed so brief!—and we half-fancied that the veiled Nun bowed her dark head in the sunshine in parting salute as we were whirled out of sight.

Between Two Oceans, or Sketches of American Travel (London, 1884).

THE GREAT GEYSIR OF ICELAND

SIR RICHARD F. BURTON

ON the eastern slope of the Frachytic pile and extending round the north of the rock-wall are the Hvers and Geysirs. Nothing can be meaner than their appearance, especially to the tourist who travels as usual from Reykjavik; nothing more ridiculous than the contrast of this pin's point, this atom of pyritic formation, with the gigantic theory which it was held to prove, earth's central fire, the now obsolete dream of classical philosophers and "celebrated academicians"; nothing more curious than the contrast between Nature and Art, between what we see in life and what we find in travellers' illustrations. Sir John Stanley, perpetuated by Henderson, first gave consistence to the popular idea of "that most wonderful fountain, the Great Geysir;" such is the character given to it by the late Sir Henry Holland, a traveller who belonged to the "wunderbar" epoch of English travel, still prevalent in Germany. From them we derive the vast background of black mountain, the single white shaft of fifty feet high, domed like the popular pine-tree of Vesuvian smoke, the bouquet of water, the Prince of Wales feathers, double-plumed and triple-plumed, charged with stones; and the minor jets and side squirts of the foreground, where pigmies stand and extend the arm of illustration and the hand of marvel.

On this little patch, however, we may still study the seven forms of Geysir life. First, is the baby still sleeping in the bosom of Mother Earth, the airy wreath escaping from the hot clay ground; then comes the infant breathing strongly, and at times puking in the nurse's lap; third, is the child simmering with impatience; and fourth, is the youth whose occupation is to boil over. The full-grown man is represented by the "Great Gusher" in the plenitude of its lusty power; old age, by the tranquil, sleepy "laug"; and second childhood and death, mostly from diphtheria or quinsy, in the empty red pits strewed about the dwarf plain. "Patheticum est!" as the old scholiast exclaimed.

It is hardly fair to enter deeply in the history of the Great Geysir, but a few words may be found useful. The silence of Ari Fródi (A. D., 1075), and of the Landnáma-bók, so copious in its details, suggests that it did not exist in the Eleventh Century; and the notice of Saxo Grammaticus in the preface to his History of Denmark proves that it had become known before the end of the Thirteenth. Hence it is generally assumed that the volcanic movements of A. D., 1294, which caused the disappearance of many hot springs, produced those now existing. Forbes clearly proved the growth of the tube by deposition of silex on the lips; a process which will end by scaling the spring: he placed its birth about 1060 years ago, which seems to be thoroughly reasonable; and thus for its manhood we have a period of about six centuries.

In 1770 the Geyser spouted eleven times a day; in 1814 it erupted every six hours; and in 1872 once between two and a week. Shepherd vainly wasted six days; a French party seven; and there are legends of a wasted fortnight.

Remains now only to walk over the ground, which divides itself into four separate patches: the extinct, to the north-west, below and extending round the north of the Laugarfjall buttress; the Great Geysir; the Strokkr and the Thikkuhverar to the south.

In the first tract earth is uniformly red, oxidized by air, not as in poetical Syria by the blood of Adonis. The hot, coarse bolus, or trachytic clay, soft and unctuous, astringent, and adhering to the tongue is deposited in horizontal layers, snowy-white, yellow-white, ruddy, light-blue, blue-grey, mauve, purple, violet, and pale-green are the Protean tints; often mixed and mottled, the effect of alum, sulphuric acid, and the decomposition of bisulphide of iron. The saucer of the Great Geysir is lined with Geysirite (silica hydraté), beads or tubercles of grey-white silica; all the others want these fungi or coral-like ornaments. The dead and dying springs show only age-rusty moulds and broken-down piles, once chimneys and ovens, resembling those of Reykir, now degraded and deformed to countless heaps of light and dark grey. Like most of the modern features, they drained to the cold rivulet on the east, and eventually to the south. The most interesting feature is the Blesi (pronounced *Blese*), which lies 160 feet north of the Great Geysir. This hot-water pond, a Grotto Azurra, where cooking is mostly done, lies on a mound, and runs in various directions. To the north it forms a dwarf river-valley flowing west of the Great Geysir; eastward it feeds a hole of bubbling water which trickles in a streak of white sinter to the eastern rivulet and a drip-hole, apparently communicating underground with an ugly little boiler of grey-brown, scum-streaked, bubbling mud, foul-looking as a drain. The "beautiful quiescent spring" measures forty feet by fifteen,[1] and is of reniform or insect shape, the waist being represented by a natural arch of stone spanning the hot blue depths below the stony ledges which edge them with scallops and corrugations. Hence the name; this bridge is the "blaze" streaking a pony's face. Blesi was not sealed by deposition of silex; it suddenly ceased to erupt in A. D., 1784, the year after the Skaptár convulsion, a fact which suggests the origin of the Geysirs. It is Mackenzie's "cave of blue water"; and travellers who have not enjoyed the *lapis lazuli* of the Capri grotto, indulge in raptures about its colouration. North-west of the Blesi, and distant 200 feet, is another ruin, situated on a much higher plane and showing the remains of a large silicious mould: it steams, but the breath of life comes feebly and irregularly. This is probably the "Roaring Geysir" or the "Old Geysir," which maps and plans place eighty yards from the Great Geysir.

[1] More exactly the two divisions are each about twenty feet long; the smaller is twelve and the greater is eighteen feet broad; the extreme depth is thirty feet.

The Great Geysir was unpropitious to us, yet we worked hard to see one of its expiring efforts. An Englishman had set up a pyramid at the edge of the saucer, and we threw in several hundredweights, hoping that the silex, acted upon by the excessive heat, might take the effect of turf; the only effects were a borborygmus which sounded somewhat like B'rr'rr't, and a shiver as if the Foul Fiend had stirred the depths. The last eruption was described to us as only a large segment of the tube, not exceeding six feet in diameter. About midnight the veteran suffered slightly from singultus. On Monday the experts mispredicted that he would exhibit between 8 and 9 A. M., and at 1 A. M. on Tuesday there was a trace of second-childhood life. After the usual eructation, a general bubble, half veiled in white vapour, rose like a gigantic glass-shade from the still surface, and the troubled water trickled down the basin sides in miniature boiling cascades. There it flowed eastwards by a single waste-channel which presently forms a delta of two arms, the base being the cold, rapid, and brawling rivulet; the northern fork has a dwarf "force," used as a *douche*, and the southern exceeds it in length, measuring some 350 paces.

We were more fortunate with the irascible Strokkr, whose name has been generally misinterpreted. Dillon calls it the piston, or "churning-staff"; and Barrow the "shaker": it is simply the "hand-churn" whose upright shaft is worked up and down—the churn-like column of water suggested the resemblance. This feature, perhaps the "New Geysir" of Sir John Stanley and Henderson, formerly erupted naturally, and had all the amiable eccentricity of youth: now it must be teased or coaxed. Stanley gave it 130 feet of jet, or 36 higher than the Great Geysir; Henderson 50 to 80; Symington, 100 to 150 feet; Bryson, "upwards of a hundred"; and Baring-Gould, "rather higher than the Geysir." We found it lying 275 feet (Mackenzie 131 yards) south of the big brother, of which it is a mean replica. The outer diameter of the saucer is only seven feet, the inner about eighteen; and it is too well drained by its silex-floored channel ever to remain full.

The most interesting part to us was the fourth or southern tract. It is known as the Thikku-hverar, thick caldrous (hot springs), perhaps in the sense opposed to thin or clear water. Amongst its "eruptiones flatuum," the traveller feels that he is walking

> "*Per ignes*
> *Suppositos cineri doloso.*"

There are at least fifty items in operation over this big lime-kiln; some without drains, others shedding either by sinter-crusted channels eastward or westward through turf and humus to the swampy stream. It shows an immense variety, from the infantine puff to the cold turf-puddle; from Jack-in-the-box to the cave of blue-green water; surrounded by ledges of silex and opaline sinter (hydrate of silica), more or less broad: the infernal concert of flip-flopping, spluttering, welling, fizzing, grunting, rumbling, and growling never ceases. The prevalent tints are green and white, but livelier hues are not wanting. One "gusherling" discharges red water; and there is a spring which spouts, like an escape pipe, brown, high and strong. The "Little Geysir," which Mackenzie places 106 yards south of the Strokkr, and which has been very churlish of late years, was once seen to throw up ten to twelve feet of clean water, like the jet of a fire-play. The "Little Strokkr of older travellers, a wonderfully amusing formation, which darts its waters in numerous diagonal columns every quarter of an hour," is a stufa or steam-jet in the centre of the group, but it has long ceased its "funning."

Ultima Thule; or, a Summer in Iceland (London and Edinburgh, 1875).

THE RAPIDS OF THE DANUBE

WILLIAM BEATTIE

A SHORT way below Grein commences the rapid called "Greiner-schwall," where the river, suddenly contracting its channel, and walled in by rugged precipices, assumes a new aspect of foam and agitation; while the roar of its downward course breaks deeper and harsher on the ear. This rugged defile is the immediate inlet to the Strudel and Wirbel—the Scylla and Charybdis of the Danube. This is by far the most interesting and remarkable region of the Danube. It is the fertile theme of many legends and traditions; and in pages of history and romance affords ample scope for marvellous incidents and striking details. Not a villager but can relate a hundred instances of disasters incurred, and dangers overcome, in this perilous navigation—of lives sacrificed and cargoes sunk while endeavouring to weather the three grand enemies of the passage—whirlpools, rocks, and robbers. But, independently of these local traditions, and the difficulties and dangers of the strait—the natural scenery which here arrests the eye is highly picturesque, and even sublime. It is the admiration of all voyagers on the Upper Danube, and keeps a firm hold of the memory long after other scenes and impressions have worn off. Between

Ulm and the confines of the Ottoman Empire, there is only one other scene calculated to make anything like so forcible an impression on the tourist; and that is near the cataracts of the Iron Gate—a name familiar to every German reader.

After descending the Greiner-schwall, or rapids of the Grein above mentioned, the river rolls on for a considerable space, in a deep and almost tranquil volume, which, by contrast with the approaching turmoil, gives increased effect to its wild, stormy, and romantic features. At first, a hollow, subdued roar, like that of distant thunder strikes the ear and rouses the traveller's attention. This increases every second, and the stir and activity which now prevail among the hands on board shows that additional force, vigilance, and caution are to be employed in the use of helm and oars. The water is now changed in its colour—chafed into foam, and agitated like a seething cauldron. In front, and in the centre of the channel, rises an abrupt, isolated, and colossal rock, fringed with wood, and crested with a mouldering tower, on the summit of which is planted a lofty cross, to which, in the moment of danger, the ancient boatmen were wont to address their prayers for deliverance. The first sight of this used to create no little excitement and apprehension on board; the master ordered strict silence to be observed—the steersman grasped the helm with a firm hand,—the passengers moved aside—so as to leave free space for the boatmen, while the women and children were hurried into the cabin, there to await, with feelings of no little anxiety, the result of the enter-

THE IRON GATES OF THE DANUBE.

prise. Every boatman, with his head uncovered, muttered a prayer to his favourite saint; and away dashed the barge through the tumbling breakers, that seemed as if hurrying it on to inevitable destruction. All these preparations, joined by the wildness of the adjacent scenery, the terrific aspect of the rocks, and the tempestuous state of the water, were sufficient to produce a powerful sensation on the minds even of those who had been all their lives familiar with dangers; while the shadowy phantoms with which superstition had peopled it, threw a deeper gloom over the whole scene.

Now, however, these ceremonies are only cold and formal; for the danger being removed, the invocation of guardian saints has become less fervent, and the cross on the Wörther Isle, we fear, is often passed with little more than the common sign of obeisance.

Within the last fifty years the rocks in the bed of the river have been blasted, and the former obstruction so greatly diminished, that in the present day, the Strudel and Wirbel present no other dangers than what may be caused by the ignorance or negligence of boatmen; so that the tourist may contemplate the scene without alarm, and enjoy, in all its native grandeur, the picture here offered to his eye and imagination —

> Frowning o'er the weltering flood,
> Castled rock and waving wood,
> Monkish cell and robbers' hold —
> Rugged as in days of old,
> From precipices, stern and grey,
> Guard the dark and dreaded way.

The tourist who has happily escaped the perils of the

Strudel rapids, has still to encounter, in his descent, the whirlpool of the Wirbel, which is distant from the former little more than five hundred fathoms. Between the two perils of this passage in the Danube there is a remarkable similarity—*magna componere parvis*—with that of the Faro of Messina; where the hereditary terrors of Scylla and Charybdis still intimidate the pilot, as he struggles to maintain a clear course through the strait:

> "There, in foaming whirls Charybdis curls,
> Loud Scylla roars to larboard;
> In that howling gulf, with the dog and wolf,
> Deep moored to-night, with her living freight,
> That goodly ship is harboured!"

The cause of the whirlpool is evident at first sight. In the centre of the stream is an island called the Hansstein, about a hundred and fifty yards long, by fifty in breadth, consisting of primitive rock, and dividing the river—which at this point descends with tremendous force—into the two separate channels of the Hössgang and the Strudel already mentioned. In its progress to this point, it meets with that portion of the river which runs smoothly along the northern shore, and breaking it into a thousand eddies, forms the Wirbel. This has the appearance of a series of foaming circles, each deepening as it approaches the centre, and caused by the two opposite streams rushing violently against each other. That such is the real cause of the Wirbel is sufficiently proved by the fact, that, in the great autumnal inundation of 1787, when the flood ran so high as to cover the Hansstein, the Wirbel, to the astonishment of the oldest boatmen and natives of the country, had entirely disappeared. For the obstacle being thus counteracted by the depth of the flood, and the stream being now unbroken by the rock, rushed down in one continuous volume, without exhibiting any of those gyratory motions which characterize the Wirbel.

The sombre and mysterious aspects of the place, its wild scenery, and the frequent accidents which occurred in the passage, invested it with awe and terror; but above all, the superstitions of the time, a belief in the marvellous, and the credulity of the boatmen, made the navigation of the Strudel and the Wirbel a theme of the wildest romance. At night, sounds that were heard far above the roar of the Danube, issued from every ruin. Magical lights flashed through their loop-holes and casements—festivals were held in the long-deserted halls—maskers glided from room to room—the waltzers maddened to the strains of an infernal orchestra—armed sentinels paraded the battlements, while at intervals the clash of arms, the neighing of steeds, and the shrieks of unearthly combatants smote fitfully on the boatman's ear. But the tower in which these scenes were most fearfully enacted was that on the Longstone, commonly called the "Devil's Tower," as it well deserved to be—for here, in close communion with his master, resided the "Black Monk," whose office it was to exhibit false lights and landmarks along the gulf, so as to decoy the vessels into the whirlpool, or dash them against the rocks.

Returning to Orsova, we re-embarked in boats provided by the Navigation Company, and proceeded to encounter the perils of the Eisen Thor—the Iron Gate of the Danube—which is so apt to be associated in the stranger's imagination with something of real personal risk and adventure. The "Iron Gate" we conjecture, is some narrow, dark and gloomy defile, through which the water, hemmed in by stupendous cliffs, and "iron-bound," as we say, foams and bellows, and dashes over a channel of rocks, every one of which, when it cannot drag you into its own whirlpool, is sure to drive you upon some of its neighbours, which, with another rude shove, that makes your bark stagger and reel, sends you smack upon a third! "But the 'gate'?" "Why the gate is nothing more or less than other gates, the 'outlet'; and I dare say we shall be very glad when we are 'let out quietly.'" "Very narrow at that point, s'pose?" "Very. You have seen an iron gate?" "To be sure I have." "Well, I'm glad of that, because you can more readily imagine what the Iron Gate of the Danube is." "Yes, and I am all impatience to see it; but what if it should be locked when we arrive?" "Why, in that case, we should feel a little awkward." "Should we have to wait long?" "Only till we got the key, although we might have to send to Constantinople for it." "Constantinople! well, here's a pretty situation! I wish I had gone by the 'cart.'" "You certainly had your choice, and might have done so—the Company provide both waggon and water conveyance to Gladova; but I dare say we shall find the gate open." "I hope we shall; and as for the rocks and all that, why we got over the Wirbel and Strudel and Izlay and twenty others, and s'pose we get over this too. It's only the gate that puzzles me—the Handbook says not a word about that—quite unpardonable such an omission! Write to the publisher."

By this time we were ready to shoot the rapids; and certainly, at first appearance, the enterprise was by no means inviting. The water, however, was in good volume at the time; and although chafed and fretted by a thousand cross, curling eddies, which tossed their crests angrily against our bark, we kept our course with tolerable steadiness to the left, and without apparent danger, unless it might have arisen from sheer ignorance or want of precaution. More towards the centre of the channel there would certainly have been some risk; for there the river is tortured and split into numberless small threads of foam, by the rocky spikes which line the channel, and literally tear the water into shreds, as it sweeps rapidly over them—and these, more than the declivity itself, are what present a more formidable appearance in the descent. But when the river is full, they are not much observed, although well-known by their effects in the cross-eddies, through which, from the channel for boats being always intricate and irregular, it demands more caution and experience to steer. The entire length of these rapids is rather more than seventeen hundred yards, with a perpendicular fall of nearly one yard in every three hundred, and a velocity of from three to five yards in every second. Boats, nevertheless, are seen from time to time, slowly ascending, close under the left bank of the river, dragged by teams of oxen. "But the Iron Gate?" said an anxious voice, again addressing his fellow-tourist. "I see nothing like a gate—but of course we have to pass the gorge first?" "We have passed both," said his friend, "and here is Gladova." "Passed both! 'Tell that to the marines!' I know a gorge when I see it, and a gate when I see it; but as yet we've passed neither." "Why, *there* they are," reiterated the other, pointing to the stern; "those white, frothing eddies you see dancing in the distance—those *are* the 'Iron-Gate!' and very luckily we found the 'key.'"[1] The inquirer now joined heartily in the laugh, and taking another view of the "Gate" we glided smoothly down to the little straggling, thatch-clad village of Gladova.

The Danube (London, 1844).

[1] At the Iron Gate the Danube quits the Austrian Dominions and enters those of Turkey. The country on the south continues for some time mountainous, then hilly, and by degrees sinks into a plain: on the north is the great level of Wallachia. In its course towards the Black Sea, the Danube divides, frequently forming numerous islands, especially below Silistria. Its width where undivided now averages from fifteen hundred to two thousand yards, its depth above twenty feet. Before reaching its mouth, several large rivers flow into it, as the Alt, Sereth, and Pruth. On its junction with the last-mentioned river it divides into several branches, which do not again unite, and it at last terminates its long course by issuing through seven several mouths into the Black Sea.

THE MAMMOTH CAVE

BAYARD TAYLOR

THERE was no outbreathing from the regions below as we stood at the entrance to the cave, the upper atmosphere having precisely the same temperature. We advanced in single file down the Main Avenue, which, from the increased number of lamps, showed with greater distinctness than on our first trip. Without pausing at any of the objects of interest on the road, we marched to the Giant's Coffin, crawled through the hole behind it, passed the Deserted Chambers, and reached the Bottomless Pit, the limit of our journey in this direction the previous day.

Beyond the Pit we entered upon new ground. After passing from under its Moorish dome the ceiling became low and the path sinuous and rough. I could only walk by stooping considerably, and it is necessary to keep a sharp look-out to avoid striking your head against the transverse jambs of rock. This passage is aptly called the Valley of Humiliation. It branches off to the right into another passage called Pensico Avenue, which contains some curious stalactitic formations, similar to the Gothic Gallery. We did not explore it, but turned to the left and entered an extremely narrow, winding passage, which meanders through the solid rock. It is called Fat Man's Misery, and any one whose body is more than eighteen inches in breadth will have trouble to get through. The largest man who ever passed it weighed two hundred and sixty pounds, and any gentleman weighing more than that must leave the best part of the cave unexplored. None of us came within the scope of prohibition (Nature, it seems, is opposed to corpulence), and after five minutes' twisting we emerged into a spacious hall called the Great Relief. Its continuation forms an avenue which leads to Bandits' Hall—a wild, rugged vault, the bottom of which is heaped with huge rocks that have fallen from above. All this part of the cave is rich in striking and picturesque effects, and presents a more rude and irregular character than anything we had yet seen.

At the end of Bandits' Hall is the Meat-Room, where a fine collection of limestone hams and shoulders are suspended from the ceiling, as in a smoke-house, the resemblance, which is really curious, is entirely owing to the action of the water. The air now grew perceptibly damp, and a few more steps brought us to the entrance of River Hall. Here the ceiling not only becomes loftier, but the floor gradually slopes away before you, and you look down into the vast depths and uncertain darkness, and question yourself if the Grecian fable be not indeed true. While I paused on the brink of these fresh mysteries the others of the party had gone ahead under the charge of Mat; Stephen, who remained with me, proposed that we should descend to the banks of the Styx and see them crossing the river upon the Natural Bridge. We stood on the brink of the black, silent water; the arch of the portal was scarcely visible in the obscurity far above us. Now, as far below, I saw the twinkle of a distant lamp, then another and another. "Is it possible," I asked, "that they have descended so much further?" "You forget," said Stephen, "that you are looking into the river and see their reflected images. Stoop a little and you will find that they are high above the water." I stooped and looked under an arch, and saw the slow procession of golden points of light passing over the gulf under the eaves of a great cliff; but another procession quite as distinct passed on below until the last lamp disappeared and all was darkness again.

Five minutes more and the roughest and most slippery scrambling brought us to the banks of the Lethe River, where we found the rest of the party.

The river had risen since the previous day, and was at the most inconvenient stage possible. A part of the River Walk was overflowed, yet not deep enough to float the boats. Mat waded out and turned the craft, which was moored to a projecting rock, as near to us as the water would allow, after which he and Stephen carried us one by one upon their shoulders and deposited us in it. It was a rude, square scow, well plastered with river mud. Boards were laid across for the ladies, the rest of us took our seats on the muddy gunwales, the guides plied their paddles, and we were afloat on Lethe.

After a ferriage of about one hundred yards, we landed on a bank of soft mud besides a small arm of the river, which had overflowed the usual path. We sank to our ankles in the moist, tenacious soil, floundering laboriously along until we were brought to a halt by Echo River, the third and last stream. This again is divided into three or four arms, which, meandering away under low arches, finally unite.

As we stood on the wet rocks, peering down into the black translucence of the silent, mysterious water, sounds—first distant, then near, then distant again—stole to us from under the groined vaults of rock. First, the dip of many oars; then a dull, muffled peal, rumbling away like the echoes of thunder; then a voice marvellously sweet, but presently joined by others sweeter still, taking up the dying notes ere they faded into silence, and prolonging them through remoter chambers. The full, mellow strains rose until they seemed sung at our very ears, then relapsed like ebbing waves, to wander off into solitary halls, then approached again, and receded, like lost spirits seeking here and there for an outlet from the world of darkness. Or was it a chorus of angels come on some errand of pity and mercy to visit the Stygian shores? As the heavenly harmonies thickened, we saw a gleam on the water, and presently a clear light, floating above its mirrored counterfeit, swept into sight. It was no angel, but Stephen, whose single voice had been multiplied into that enchanting chorus.

The whole party embarked in two small boats, and after a last voyage of about two hundred yards, were landed beyond the waters, and free to explore the wonderful avenues of that new world of which Stephen is the Columbus. The River Hall here terminates, and the passages are broken and irregular for a short distance. A few minutes of rough travel brought us to a large circular hall with a vaulted ceiling, from the centre of which poured a cascade of crystal water, striking upon the slant side of a large reclining boulder, and finally disappearing through a funnel-shaped pit in the floor. It sparkled like a shower of pearls in the light of our lamps, as we clustered around the brink of the pit to drink from the stores gathered in those natural bowls which seem to have been hollowed out for the uses of the invisible gnomes.

Beyond Cascade Hall commences Silliman's Avenue, a passage about twenty feet wide, forty or fifty in height, and a mile and a half in length.

Our lamps were replenished and we entered El Ghor, which is by far the most picturesque avenue in the cave. It is a narrow, lofty passage meandering through the heart of a mass of horizontal strata of limestone, the broken edges of which assume the most remarkable forms. Now there are rows of broad, flat shelves overhanging your head; now you sweep around the stern of some mighty vessel with its rudder set hard to starboard; now you enter a little vestibule with friezes and mouldings of almost Doric symmetry and simplicity; and now you wind away into a Cretan labyrinth most uncouth and fantastic, whereof the Minotaur would be a proper inhabitant. It is a continual succession of surprises, and, to the appreciative visitor, of raptures. The pass is somewhat more than *a mile and a half* in length, and terminates in a curious knot or entanglement of passages leading to two or more tiers of avenues.

We were now, according to Stephen's promises, on the threshold of wonders. Before proceeding further we stopped to drink from a fine sulphur spring which fills a natural basin in the bottom of a niche made on purpose to contain it. We then climbed a perpendicular ladder, passing through a hole in the ceiling barely large enough to admit our bodies, and found ourselves at the entrance of a narrow, lofty passage leading upwards. When all had made the ascent the guides exultingly lifted their lamps and directed our eyes to the rocks overhanging the aperture; there was the first wonder, truly! Clusters of grapes gleaming with blue and violet tints through the water which trickled over them, hung from the cliffs, while a stout vine, springing from the base and climbing nearly to the top, seemed to support them. Hundreds on hundreds of bunches clustering so thickly as to conceal the leaves, hang forever ripe and forever unplucked in that marvellous vintage of the subterranean world. For whose hand shall squeeze the black, infernal wine from grapes that grow beyond Lethe?

Mounting for a short distance, this new avenue suddenly turned to the left, widened, and became level; the ceiling is low, but beautifully vaulted, and Washington's Hall, which we soon reached, is circular, and upwards of a hundred feet in diameter. This is the usual dining-room of parties who go beyond the rivers. Nearly five hours had now elapsed since we entered the cave, and five hours spent in that bracing, stimulating atmosphere might well justify the longing glances which we cast upon the baskets carried by the guides. Mr. Miller had foreseen our appetites, and there were stores of venison, biscuit, ham, and pastry, more than sufficient for all. We made our midday, or rather midnight meal sitting, like the nymph who wrought Excalibur

"Upon the hidden bases of the hills,"

buried far below the green Kentucky forests, far below the forgotten sunshine. For in the cave you forget that there is an outer world somewhere above you. The hours have no meaning: Time ceases to be; no thought of labour, no sense of responsibility, no twinge of conscience intrudes to suggest the existence you have left. You walk in some limbo beyond the confines of actual life, yet no nearer the world of spirits. For my part, I could not shake off the impression that I was wandering on the *outside* of Uranus or Neptune, or some planet still more deeply buried in the frontier darkness of our solar system.

Washington Hall marks the commencement of Elindo Avenue, a straight hall about sixty feet wide, twenty in height, and *two miles* long. It is completely encrusted from end to end with crystallizations of gypsum, white as snow. This is the crowning marvel of the cave, the pride and the boast of the guides. Their satisfaction is no less than yours, as they lead you through the diamond grottoes, the gardens of sparry efflorescence, and the gleaming vaults of this magical avenue. We first entered the "Snow-ball Room," where the gnome-children in their sports have peppered the grey walls and ceiling with thousands of snow-white projecting discs, so perfect in their fragile beauty, that they seem ready to melt away under the blaze of your lamp. Then commences Cleveland's Cabinet, a gallery of crystals, the richness and variety of which bewilder you. It is a subterranean conservatory, filled with the flowers of all the zones; for there are few blossoms expanding on the upper earth but are mimicked in these gardens of Darkness. I cannot lead you from niche to niche, and from room to room, examining in detail the enchanted growths; they are all so rich and so wonderful that the memory does not attempt to retain them. Sometimes the hard limestone rock is changed into a pasture of white roses; sometimes it is starred with opening daisies; the sunflowers spread their flat discs and rayed leaves; the feathery chalices of the cactus hang from the clefts; the night-blooming cereus opens securely her snowy cup, for the morning never comes to close it; the tulip is here a virgin, and knows not that her sisters above are clothed in the scarlet of shame.

In many places the ceiling is covered with a mammary crystallization, as if a myriad bubbles were rising beneath its glittering surface. Even on this jewelled soil which sparkles all around you, grow the lilies and roses, singly overhead, but clustering together towards the base of the vault, where they give place to long, snowy, pendulous cactus-flowers, which droop like a fringe around diamonded niches. Here you see the passion-flower, with its curiously curved pistils; there an iris with its lanceolate leaves; and again, bunches of celery with stalks white and tender enough for a fairy's dinner. There are occasional patches of gypsum, tinged of a deep amber colour by the presence of iron. Through the whole length of the avenue there is no cessation of the wondrous work. The pale rock-blooms burst forth everywhere, crowding on each other until the brittle sprays cannot bear their weight, and they fall to the floor. The slow, silent efflorescence still goes on, as it has done for ages in that buried tropic.

What mostly struck me in my underground travels was the evidence of *design* which I found everywhere. Why should the forms of the earth's outer crust, her flowers and fruits, the very heaven itself which spans her, be so wonderfully reproduced? What laws shape the blossoms and the foliage of that vast crystalline garden? There seemed to be something more than the accidental combinations of a blind chance in what I saw—some evidence of an informing and directing Will. In the secret caverns, the agencies which produced their wonders have been at work for thousands of years, perhaps thousands of ages, fashioning the sparry splendours in the womb of darkness with as exquisite a grace, as true an instinct of beauty as in the palm or the lily, which are moulded by the hands of the sun. What power is it which lies behind the mere chemistry of Nature, impregnating her atoms with such subtle laws of symmetry? What but Divine Will, which first gave her being, and which is never weary of multiplying for man the lessons of His infinite wisdom?

At the end of Elindo Avenue the floor sinks, then ascends, and is at last blocked up by a huge pile of large, loose rocks. When we had reached the foot, the roof of the avenue suddenly lifted and expanded, and the summit of the Rocky Mountains, as they are called, leaned against a void waste of darkness. We climbed to the summit, about a hundred feet above, whence we looked down into an awful gulf, spanned far above our heads by a hollow dome of rock. The form of this gigantic hall was nearly elliptical. It was probably 150 feet in height, by 500 in length, the ends terminating near the roof in the cavernous mouths of other avenues. The guides partly descended the hill and there kindled a brilliant Bengal light, which disclosed more clearly the form of the hall, but I thought it more impressive as its stupendous proportions were first dimly revealed by the light of our lamps. Stephen, who discovered this place, gave it the name of the Dismal Hollow.

Scrambling along the ridge of the Rocky Mountains, we gained the entrance to the cavern opening on the left, which we followed for about two hundred yards, when it terminated in a lofty circular dome, called Crogan's Hall. The floor on one side dropped suddenly into a deep pit, around which were several cushions of stalagmite, answering to short stalactites, hanging from the ceiling far above. At the extremity of the hall was a sort of recess, formed by stalactitic pillars. The wall behind it was a mass of veined alabaster. "Here," said Stephen, "is your Ultima Thule. This is the end of the Mammoth Cave, nine miles from daylight." But I doubt whether there is really an end of the cave any more than an end of the earth. Notwithstanding the ground we had traversed, we had left many vast avenues unexplored, and a careful search would no doubt lead to further discoveries.

We retraced our steps slowly along Elindo Avenue, stopping every few minutes to take a last look at the bowers of fairy blossoms. After reaching Washington's Hall we noticed that the air was no longer still, but was flowing fresh and cool in our faces. Stephen observed it also, and said: "There has been a heavy rain outside." Entering the pass of El Ghor again at Martha's Vineyard, we walked rapidly forward, without making a halt, to its termination at Silliman's Avenue. The distance is reckoned by the guides at a little more than a mile and a half, and we were just forty minutes in walking it. We several times felt fatigue, especially when passing the rougher parts of the cave, but the sensation always passed away in some unaccountable manner, leaving us fresh and buoyant. The crossing of the rivers was accomplished with some labour, but without accident. I accompanied Stephen on his return through the second arch of Echo River. As I sat alone in the silent, transparent darkness of the mysterious stream, I could hear the tones of my boatman's voice gliding down the caverns like a wave, flowing more and more faintly until its vibrations were too weak to move the ear. Thus, as he sang, there were frequently three or four notes, each distinctly audible, floating away at different degrees of remoteness. At the last arch there was only a space of eighteen inches between the water and the rock. We lay down on our backs in the muddy bottom of the boat, and squeezed through to the middle branch of Echo River, where we found the rest of the party, who had gone round through Purgatory.

After again threading Fat Man's Misery, passing the Bottomless Pit and the Deserted Chambers, we at last emerged into the Main Avenue at the Giant's Coffin. It was six o'clock, and we had been ten hours in the cave.

When we heard the tinkling drops of the little cascade over the entrance, I looked up and saw a patch of deep, tender blue set in the darkness. In the midst of it twinkled a white star—whiter and more dazzling than any star I ever saw before. I paused and drank at the trough under the waterfall, for, like the Fountain of Trevi at Rome, it may be that those who drink there shall return again. When we ascended to the level of the upper world we found that a fierce tornado had passed along during the day; trees had been torn up by the roots and hurled down in all directions; stunning thunders had jarred the air, and the wet earth was fairly paved with leaves cut off by the heavy hail—yet we, buried in the heart of the hills, had heard no sound, nor felt the slightest tremour in the air.

The stars were all in their places as I walked back to the hotel. I had been twelve hours under ground, in which I had walked about twenty-four miles. I had lost a day—a day with its joyous morning, its fervid noon, its tempest, and its angry sunset of crimson and gold; but I had gained an age in a strange and hitherto unknown world —an age of wonderful experience, and an exhaustless store of sublime and lovely memories.

At Home and Abroad (New York, 1864).

STROMBOLI

ALEXANDRE DUMAS

AS we advanced, Stromboli became more and more distinct every moment, and through the clear evening air we could perceive every detail; this mountain is formed exactly like a hay-mow, its summit being surmounted by a peak; it is from this summit that the smoke escapes, and, at intervals of a quarter of an hour, a flame; during the daytime this flame does not apparently exist, being lost in the light of the sun; but when evening comes, and the Orient begins to darken, this flame becomes visible and you can see it dart forth from the midst of the smoke which it colours, and fall again in jets of lava.

Towards seven o'clock we reached Stromboli; unfortunately the port is in the east, and we came from the west; so that we had to coast along the whole length of the island where the lava descended down a sharp slope into the sea. For a breadth of twenty paces at its summit and a hundred and fifty at its base, the mountain at this point is covered with cinders and all vegetation is burned.

The captain was correct in his predictions: we arrived half an hour after the port had been closed; all we could say to make them open to us was lost eloquence.

However, the entire population of Stromboli had run to the shore. Our *Speronare* was a frequent visitor to this harbour and our sailors were well known in the island. . . . It was in Stromboli that Æolus held bound the *luctantes ventos tempestatesque sonoras*. Without doubt, at the time of the song of Æneas, and when Stromboli was called Strongyle, the island was not known for what it really is, and hid within its depths the boiling masses and periodical ejaculations which make this volcano the most obliging one in the world. In sooth, you know what to expect from Stromboli: it is not like Vesuvius or Etna, which make the traveller wait sometimes three, five or even ten years for a poor little eruption. I have been told that this is doubtless owing to the position they hold in the hierarchy of fire-vomiting mountains, a hierarchy that permits them to be aristocratic at their own pleasure: this is true enough; and we must not take it amiss if Stromboli allows her social position to be assailed an instant, and to have understood that it is only a little toy volcano to which one would not pay the slightest attention if it made itself so ridiculous as to put on airs.

Moreover, it did not keep us waiting. After scarcely five minutes' expectation, a heavy rumbling was heard, a detonation resembling twenty cannon fired in succession, and a long jet of flame leaped into the air and fell again in a shower of lava; a part of this shower fell again into the crater of the volcano, while the other, rolling down the slope hurried like a brooklet of flame to extinguish itself, hissing, into the sea. Ten minutes later the same phenomenon was repeated, and at every succeeding ten minutes throughout the night.

I admit that this was one of the most curious nights I ever spent in my life; neither Jadin nor I could tear ourselves away from this terrible and magnificent spectacle. There were such detonations that the very atmosphere seemed excited, and you imagined the whole island trembling like a frightened child; it was only Milord that these fire-works put into a state of exaltation impossible to describe; he wanted to jump into the water every moment to devour the burning lava which sometimes fell ten feet from us, like a meteor precipitating itself into the sea.

As for our boatswain, he was so accustomed to this spectacle, that, after asking if we needed anything and upon our reply in the negative, he retired between decks and neither the lightnings that illuminated the air nor the thunders that shook it had power to disturb his slumbers.

We stayed here until two o'clock; finally, overcome with fatigue and sleep, we decided to retire to our cabin. As for Milord, nothing would persuade him to do as we did and he stayed all night on deck, growling and barking at the volcano.

We woke in the morning at the first movement of the *Speronare*. With the return of daylight the mountain lost all its fantastic appearance.

We constantly heard the detonations; but the flame had become invisible; and that burning lava stream of the night was confused in the day with the reddish ashes over which it rolls.

Ten minutes more and we were again in port. This time we had no difficulty in entering. Pietro and Giovanni got off with us; they wished to accompany us on our ascent.

We entered, not an inn (there are none in Stromboli), but a house whose proprietors were related to our captain. As it would not have been prudent to have started on our way fasting, Giovanni asked permission of our hosts to make breakfast for us while Pietro went to hunt for guides, —a permission not only accorded to us with much grace but our host also went out and came back in a few moments with the most beautiful grapes and figs that he could find.

After we had finished our breakfast, Pietro arrived with two Stromboliotes who consented, in consideration of half a piastre each, to serve as guides. It was already nearly eight o'clock: to avoid a climb in the greatest heat of the day, we started off immediately.

The top of Stromboli is only twelve or fifteen hundred feet above the level of the sea; but its slope is so sharp that you cannot climb in a direct manner, but must zigzag eternally. At first, on leaving the village, the road was easy enough; it rose in the midst of those vines laden with grapes that make the commerce of the island and from which the fruit hangs in such great quantity that any one may help himself to all he wants without asking the permission of the owner; however, upon leaving the region of the vineyards, we found no more roads, and we had to walk at random, looking for the best ground and the easiest slopes. Despite all these precautions, there came a moment when we were obliged to scramble on all fours: there was nothing to do but climb up; but this place once passed, I vow that on turning around and seeing it, jutting almost perpendicularly over the sea, I asked in terror how we could ever descend; our guides then said that we would come down by another road: that pacified me a little. Those who like myself are unhappy enough to have vertigo when they see a chasm below their feet will understand my question and still more the importance I attached to it.

This break-neck spot passed, the ascent became easier for a quarter of an hour; but soon we came to a place which at the first glance seemed impassable; it was a perfectly sharp-pointed angle that formed the opening of the first volcano, and part of which was cut out perpendicularly upon the crater while the other fell with so sharp a slope to the sea that it seemed to me if I should fall perpendicularly on the other side I could not help rolling from top to bottom. Even Jadin, who ordinarily climbs like a chamois without ever troubling about the difficulties of the ground, stopped short when we came to this passage, asking if there was not some way to avoid it. As you may imagine, this was impossible.

The crater of Stromboli is formed like a vast funnel, from the bottom and the centre of which is an opening through which a man can enter a little way, and which communicates with the internal furnace of the mountain; it is through this opening, resembling the mouth of a canon, that the shower of projectiles darts forth, which, falling again into the crater, sweeps with it down the inclined slope of stones the cinders and lava that, rolling to the bottom, block up that funnel. Then the volcano seems to gather its forces together for several minutes, compressed as it is by the stoppage of its valve; but after a moment its smoke trembles like a breath; you hear a deep roaring run through the hollow sides of the mountain; then the cannonade bursts forth again, throwing up two hundred feet above the summit new stones and new lava, which, falling back and closing the orifice of the passage anew, prepare for a new outburst.

Seen from where we were, that is from top to bottom, this spectacle was superb and terrifying; at each internal convulsion that the mountain essayed, you felt it tremble beneath you, and it seemed as if it would burst asunder; then came the explosion, similar to a gigantic tree of flame and smoke that shook its leaves of lava.

Finally, we reached the extremity of this new lake of Sodom, and we found ourselves in an oasis of vines, pomegranates and olives. We had not the courage to go any farther. We lay down in the grass, and our guides brought us an armful of grapes and a hatful of figs.

It was marvellous to us; but there was not the smallest drop of water for our poor Milord to drink, and we perceived him devouring the skin of the figs and grapes. We gave him part of our repast, and for the first, and probably for the last, time in his life he dined off figs and grapes.

I have often a desire to put myself in the place of Milord and write his memoirs as Hoffmann wrote those of his cat,

Murr. I am convinced that he must have had, seen from the canine point of view, (I beg the Académie's pardon for the expression) extremely new impressions of the people and countries that he has visited.

A quarter of an hour after this halt we were in the village, writing upon our tablets this judicious observation—that the volcanoes follow but do not resemble each other: we were nearly frozen when ascending Etna, and we were nearly roasted when descending Stromboli.

Jadin and I each extended a hand towards the mountain and swore that notwithstanding Vesuvius, Stromboli was the last volcano whose acquaintance we would make.

Le Capitaine Aréna: Impressions de Voyage (Paris, 1836).

THE HIGH WOODS

CHARLES KINGSLEY

IN the primeval forest, looking upon that which my teachers and masters, Humboldt, Spix, Martius, Schomburgk, Waterton, Bates, Wallace, Gosse, and the rest, had looked already, with far wiser eyes than mine, comprehending somewhat at least of its wonders, while I could only stare in ignorance. There was actually, then, such a sight to be seen on earth; and it was not less, but far more wonderful than they had said.

My first feeling on entering the high woods was helplessness, confusion, awe, all but terror. One is afraid at first to venture in fifty yards. Without a compass or the landmark of some opening to or from which he can look, a man must be lost in the first ten minutes, such a sameness is there in the infinite variety. That sameness and variety make it impossible to give any general sketch of a forest. Once inside, "you cannot see the woods for the trees." You can only wander on as far as you dare, letting each object impress itself on your mind as it may, and carrying away a confused recollection of innumerable perpendicular lines, all straining upwards, in fierce competition, towards the light-food far above; and next on a green cloud, or rather mist, which hovers round your head, and rises, thick-

THE HIGH WOODS.

ening and thickening to an unknown height. The upward lines are of every possible thickness, and of almost every possible hue; what leaves they bear, being for most part on the tips of the twigs, give a scattered, mist-like appearance to the under-foliage. For the first moment, therefore, the forest seems more open than an English wood. But try to walk through it, and ten steps undeceive you. Around your knees are probably Mamures, with creeping stems and fan-shaped leaves, something like those of a young cocoa-nut palm. You try to brush among them, and are caught up instantly by a string or wire belonging to some other plant. You look up and round: and then you find that the air is full of wires—that you are hung up in a network of fine branches belonging to half-a-dozen different sorts of young trees, and intertwined with as many different species of slender creepers. You thought at your first glance among the tree-stems that you were looking through open air; you find that you are looking through a labyrinth of wire-rigging, and must use the cutlass right and left at every five steps. You push on into a bed of strong sedge-like Sclerias, with cutting edges to their leaves. It is well for you if they are only three, and not six feet high. In the midst of them you run against a horizontal stick, triangular, rounded, smooth, green. You take a glance along it right and left, and see no end to it either way, but gradually discover that it is the leaf-stalk of a young Cocorite palm. The leaf is five-and-twenty feet long, and springs from a huge ostrich plume, which is sprawling out of the ground and up above your head a few yards off. You cut the leaf-stalk through right and left, and walk on, to be stopped suddenly (for you get so confused by the multitude of objects that you never see anything till you run against it) by a grey lichen-covered bar, as thick as your ankle. You follow it up with your eye, and find it entwine itself with three or four other bars, and roll over with them in great knots and festoons and loops twenty feet high, and then go up with them into the green cloud over your head, and vanish, as if a giant had thrown a ship's cable into the tree-tops. One of them, so grand that its form strikes even the Negro and the Indian, is a Liantasse. You see that at once by the form of its cable—six or eight inches across in one direction, and three or four in another, furbelowed all down the middle into regular knots, and looking like a chain cable between two flexible iron bars. At another of the loops, about as thick as your arm, your companion, if you have a forester with you, will spring joyfully. With a few blows of his cutlass he will sever it as high up as he can reach, and again below, some three feet down; and, while you are wondering at this seemingly wanton destruction, he lifts the bar on high, throws his head back, and pours down his thirsty throat a pint or more of pure cold water. This hidden treasure is, strange as it may seem, the ascending sap, or rather the ascending pure rain-water which has been taken up by the roots, and is hurrying aloft, to be elaborated into sap, and leaf, and flower, and fruit, and fresh tissue for the very stem up which it originally climbed; and therefore it is that the woodman cuts the Watervine through first at the top of the piece which he wants, and not at the bottom; for so rapid is the ascent of the sap that if he cut the stem below, the water would have all fled upwards before he could cut it off above. Meanwhile, the old story of Jack and the Bean-stalk comes into your mind. In such a forest was the old dame's hut; and up such a bean-stalk Jack climbed, to find a giant and a castle high above. Why not? What may not be up there? You look up into the green cloud, and long for a moment to be a monkey. There may be monkeys up there over your head, burly red Howler, or tiny peevish Sapajou, peering down at you; but you cannot peer up at them. The monkeys, and the parrots, and the humming-birds, and the flowers, and all the beauty, are upstairs—up above the green cloud. You are in "the empty nave of the cathedral," and "the service is being celebrated aloft in the blazing roof."

We will hope that as you look up, you have not been careless enough to walk on; for if you have you will be tripped up at once: nor to put your hand out incautiously to rest it against a tree, or what not, for fear of sharp thorns, ants, and wasps' nests. If you are all safe, your next steps, probably, as you struggle through the bush between the tree-trunks of every possible size, will bring you face to face with huge upright walls of seeming boards, whose rounded edges slope upward till, as your eye follows them, you will find them enter an enormous stem, perhaps round, like one of the Norman pillars of Durham nave, and just as huge; perhaps fluted, like one of William of Wykeham's columns at Winchester. There is the stem: but where is the tree? Above the green cloud. You struggle up to it, between two of the broad walls, but find it not so easy to reach. Between you and it, are a half-a-dozen tough strings which you had not noticed at first—the eye cannot focus itself rapidly enough in this confusion of distances—which have to be cut through ere you can pass. Some of them are rooted in the ground, straight and tense; some of them dangle and wave in the wind at every height. What are they? Air-roots of wild Pines, or of Matapalos, or of Figs, or of Seguines, or of some other parasite? Probably: but you cannot see. All you can see is, as you put your chin close against the trunk of the tree and look up, as if you were looking up against the side of a great ship set on end, that some sixty or eighty feet up in the green cloud, arms as big as English forest trees branch off; and that out of their forks a whole green garden of vegetation has tumbled down twenty or thirty feet, and half climbed up again. You scramble round the tree to find whence this aërial garden has sprung: you cannot tell. The tree-trunk is smooth and free from climbers; and that mass of verdure may belong possibly to the very cables which you meet ascending into the green cloud twenty or thirty yards back, or to that impenetrable tangle, a dozen yards on, which has climbed a small tree, and then a taller one again, and then a taller still, till it has climbed out of sight and possibly into the lower branches of the big tree. And what are their species? What are their families? Who knows? Not even the most experienced woodman or botanist can tell you the names of plants of which he only sees the stems. The leaves, the flowers, the fruit, can only be examined by felling the tree; and not even always then, for sometimes the tree when cut refuses to fall, linked as it is by chains of liane to all the trees around. Even that wonderful water-vine which we cut through just now may be one of three or even four different plants.

Soon, you will be struck by the variety of the vegetation; and will recollect what you have often heard, that social plants are rare in the tropic forests. Certainly they are in the Trinidad; where the only instances of social trees are the Moras (which I have never seen growing wild) and the Moriche palms. In Europe, a forest is usually made up of one dominant plant of firs or of pines, of oaks or of beeches, of birch or of heather. Here no two plants seem alike. There are more species on an acre here than in all the New Forest, Savernake, or Sherwood. Stems rough, smooth, prickly, round, fluted, stilted, upright, sloping, branched, arched, jointed, opposite-leaved, alternate-leaved, leafless, or covered with leaves of every conceivable pattern, are jumbled together, till the eye and brain are tired of continually asking "What next?" The stems are of every colour—copper, pink, grey, green, brown, black as if burnt, marbled with lichens, many of them silvery white, gleaming afar in the bush, furred with mosses and delicate creeping film-ferns, or laced with air-roots of some parasite aloft. Up this stem scrambles a climbing Seguine with entire leaves; up the next another quite different, with deeply-cut leaves; up the next the Ceriman spreads its huge leaves, latticed and forked again and again. So fast do they grow, that they have not time to fill up the spaces between their nerves, and are consequently full of oval holes; and so fast does its spadix of flowers expand, that (as do some other Aroids) an actual genial heat, and fire of passion, which may be tested by the thermometer, or even by the hand, is given off during fructification. Beware of breaking it, or the Seguines. They will probably give off an evil smell, and as probably a blistering milk. Look on at the next stem. Up it, and down again, a climbing fern which is often seen in hot-houses has tangled its finely-cut fronds. Up the next, a quite different fern is crawling, by pressing tightly to the rough bark its creeping root-stalks, furred like a hare's leg. Up the next, the prim little Griffe-chatte plant has walked, by numberless clusters of small cats'-claws, which lay hold of the bark. And what is this delicious scent about the air? Vanille? Of course it is; and up that stem zigzags the green fleshy chain of the Vanille Orchis. The scented pod is far above, out of your reach; but not out of the reach of the next parrot, or monkey, or Negro hunter, who winds the treasure. And the stems themselves: to what trees do they belong? It would be absurd for one to try to tell you who cannot tell one-twentieth of them himself. Suffice it to say, that over your head are perhaps a dozen kinds of admirable timber, which might be turned to a hundred uses in Europe, were it possible to get them thither: your guide (who here will be a second hospitable and cultivated Scot) will point with pride to one column after another, straight as those of a cathedral, and sixty to eighty feet without branch or knob. That, he will say, is Fiddlewood; that a Carapo, that a Cedar, that a Roble (oak); that, larger than all you have seen yet, a Locust; that, a Poui; that, a Guatecare; that an Olivier, woods which, he will tell you, are all but incorruptible, defying weather and insects. He will show you, as curiosities, the smaller but intensely hard Letter wood, Lignum vitæ, and Purple heart. He will pass by as useless weeds, Ceibas and Sandbox-trees, whose bulk appalls you. He will look up, with something like a malediction, at the Matapalos, which, every fifty yards, have seized on mighty trees, and are enjoying, I presume, every different stage of the strangling art, from the baby Matapalo, who, like one which you saw in the Botanic Garden, has let down his first air-root along his victim's stem, to the old sinner whose dark crown of leaves is supported, eighty feet in air, on innumerable branching columns of every size, cross-clasped to each other by transverse bars. The giant tree on which his seed first fell has rotted away utterly, and he stands in its place, prospering in his wickedness, like certain folk whom David knew too well. Your guide walks on with a sneer. But he stops with a smile of satisfaction as he sees lying on the ground dark green glossy leaves, which are fading into a bright crimson; for overhead somewhere there must be a Balata, the king of the forest; and there, close by, is his stem—a madder-brown column, whose head may be a hundred and fifty feet or more aloft. The forester pats the side of his favourite tree, as a breeder might that of his favourite race-horse. He goes on to evince his affection, in the fashion of West Indians, by giving it a chop with his cutlass; but not in wantonness. He wishes to show you the hidden virtues, of this (in his eyes) noblest of trees—how there issues out swiftly from the wound a flow of thick white milk, which will congeal, in an hour's time, into a gum intermediate in its properties between caoutchouc and gutta-percha. He talks of a time when the English gutta-percha market shall be supplied from the Balatas of the northern hills, which cannot be shipped away as timber. He tells you how the tree is a tree of a generous, virtuous and elaborate race—"a tree of God, which is full of sap," as one said of old of such—and what could he say better, less or more? For it is a Sapota, cousin to the Sapodilla, and other excellent fruit-trees, itself most excellent even in its fruit-bearing power; for every five years it is covered with such a crop of delicious plums, that the lazy Negro thinks it worth his while to spend days of hard work, besides incurring the penalty of the law (for the trees are Government property), in cutting it down for the sake of its fruit. But this tree your guide will cut himself. There is no gully between it and the Government station; and he can carry it away; and it is worth his while to do so; for it will square, he thinks, into a log more than three feet in diameter, and eighty, ninety—he hopes almost a hundred—feet in length of hard, heavy wood, incorruptible, save in salt water; better than oak, as good as teak, and only surpassed in this island by the Poui. He will make a stage round it, some eight feet high, and cut it above the spurs. It will take his convict gang (for convicts are turned to some real use in Trinidad) several days to get it down, and many more days to square it with the axe. A trace must be made to it through the wood, clearing away vegetation for which a European millionaire, could he keep it in his park, would gladly pay a hundred pounds a yard. The cleared stems, especially those of the palms, must be cut into rollers; and the dragging of the huge log over them will be a work of weeks, especially in the wet season. But it can be done, and it shall be; so he leaves a significant mark on his new-found treasure, and leads you on through the bush, hewing his way with light strokes right and left, so carelessly that you are inclined to beg him to hold his hand, and not destroy in a moment things so beautiful, so curious, things which would be invaluable in an English hothouse.

And where are the famous Orchids? They perch on every bough and stem; but they are not, with three or four exceptions, in flower in the winter; and if they were, I know nothing about them—at least, I know enough to know how little I know. Whosoever has read Darwin's *Fertilization of Orchids*, and finds in his own reason that the book is true, had best say nothing about the beautiful monsters till he has seen with his own eyes more than his master.

And yet even the three or four that are in flower are worth going many a mile to see. In the hothouse, they seem almost artificial from their strangeness: but to see them "natural," on natural boughs, gives a sense of their reality, which no unnatural situation can give. Even to look up at them perched on bough and stem, as one rides by; and to guess what exquisite and fantastic form may issue, in a few months or weeks, out of those fleshy, often unsightly leaves, is a strange pleasure; a spur to the fancy which is surely wholesome, if we will but believe that all these things were invented by A Fancy, which desires to call out in us, by contemplating them, such small fancy as we possess; and to make us poets, each according to this power, by showing a world in which, if rightly looked at, all is poetry.

Another fact will soon force itself on your attention, unless you wish to tumble down and get wet up to your knees. The soil is furrowed everywhere by holes; by graves, some two or three feet wide and deep, and of uncertain length and shape, often wandering about for thirty or forty feet, and running confusedly into each other. They are not the work of man, nor of an animal; for no earth seems to have been thrown out of them. In the bottom of the dry graves you sometimes see a decaying root: but most of them just now are full of water, and of tiny fish also, who burrow in the mud and sleep during the dry season, to come out and swim during the wet. These graves are some of them, plainly quite new. Some, again, are very old; for trees of all sizes are growing in them and over them.

What makes them? A question not easily answered. But the shrewdest foresters say that they have the roots of trees now dead. Either the tree has fallen and torn its roots out of the ground, or the roots and stumps have rotted in their place, and the soil above them has fallen in.

But they must decay very quickly, these roots, to leave their quite fresh graves thus empty; and—now one thinks of it—how few fallen trees, or even dead sticks, there are about. An English wood, if left to itself, would be cumbered with fallen timber; and one has heard of forests in North America, through which it is all but impossible to make way, so high are piled up, among the still-growing trees, dead logs in every stage of decay. Such a sight may be seen in Europe, among the high Silver-fir forests of the Pyrenees. How is it not so here? How indeed? And how comes it—if you will, look again—that there are few or no fallen trees, and actually no leaf-mould? In an English wood there would be a foot—perhaps two feet—of black soil, renewed every autumn leaf fall. Two feet? One has heard often enough of bison-hunting in Himalayan forests among Deodaras one hundred and fifty feet high, and scarlet Rhododendrons thirty feet high, growing in fifteen or twenty feet of leaf-and-timber mould. And here in a forest equally ancient, every plant is growing out of the bare yellow loam, as it might in a well-hoed garden bed. Is it not strange?

Most strange; till you remember where you are—in one of nature's hottest and dampest laboratories. Nearly eighty inches of yearly rain and more than eighty degrees of perpetual heat make swift work with vegetable fibre, which, in our cold and sluggard clime, would curdle into leaf-mould, perhaps into peat. Far to the north, in poor old Ireland, and far to the south, in Patagonia, begin the zones of peat, where dead vegetable fibre, its treasures of light and heat locked up, lies all but useless age after age. But this is the zone of illimitable sun-force, which destroys as swiftly as it generates, and generates again as swiftly as it destroys. Here, when the forest giant falls, as some tell me that they have heard him fall, on silent nights, when the cracking of the roots below the lianes aloft rattles like musketry through the woods, till the great trunk comes down, with a boom as of a heavy gun, re-echoing on from mountain-side to mountain-side; then—

> "Nothing in him that doth fade
> But doth suffer an *air!* change
> Into something rich and strange."

Under the genial rain and genial heat the timber tree itself, all its tangled ruin of lianes and parasites, and the boughs and leaves snapped off not only by the blow, but by the very wind, of the falling tree—all melt away swiftly and peacefully in a few months—say almost a few days—into the water, and carbonic acid, and sunlight, out of which they were created at first, to be absorbed instantly by the green leaves around, and, transmuted into fresh forms of beauty, leave not a wrack behind. Explained thus—and this I believe to be the true explanation—the absence of leaf-mould is one of the grandest, as it is one of the most startling, phenomena, of the forest.

Look here at a fresh wonder. Away in front of us a smooth grey pillar glistens on high. You can see neither the top nor the bottom of it. But its colour, and its perfectly cylindrical shape, tell you what it is—a glorious

Palmiste ; one of those queens of the forest which you saw standing in the fields; with its capital buried in the green cloud and its base buried in that bank of green velvet plumes, which you must skirt carefully round, for they are prickly dwarf palm, called Black Roseau. Close to it rises another pillar, as straight and smooth, but one-fourth of the diameter—a giant's walking cane. Its head, too, is in the green cloud. But near are two or three younger ones only forty or fifty feet high, and you see their delicate feather heads, and are told that they are Manacques; the slender nymphs which attend upon the forest queen, as beautiful, though not as grand, as she.

The land slopes down fast now. You are tramping through stiff mud, and those Roseaux are a sign of water. There is a stream or gulley near: and now for the first time you can see clear sunshine through the stems; and see, too, something of the bank of foliage on the other side of the brook. You can catch sight, it may be, of the head of a tree aloft, blazing with golden trumpet flowers, which is a Poui; and of another low-one covered with hoar-frost, perhaps a Croton; and of another, a giant covered with purple tassels. That is an Angelim. Another giant overtops even him. His dark glossy leaves toss off sheets of silver light as they flicker in the breeze; for it blows hard aloft outside while you are in the stifling calm. That is a Balata. And what is that on high? Twenty or thirty square yards of rich crimson a hundred feet above the ground. The flowers may belong to the tree itself. It may be Mountain-mangrove, which I have never seen in flower: but take the glasses and decide. No. The flowers belong to a liane. The "wonderful" Prince of Wales' feather has taken possession of the head of a huge Mombin, and tiled it all over with crimson combs which crawl out to the ends of the branches, and dangle twenty or thirty feet down, waving and leaping in the breeze. And all over blazes the cloudless blue.

You gaze astounded. Ten steps downward, and the vision is gone. The green cloud has closed again over your head, and you are stumbling in the darkness of the bush, half blinded by the sudden change from the blaze to the shade. Beware. "Take care of the Croc-chien!" shouts your companion: and you are aware of, not a foot from your face, a long, green, curved whip, armed with pairs of barbs some four inches apart; and you are aware also, at the same moment, that another has seized you by the arm, another by the knees, and that you must back out, unless you are willing to part with your clothes, and your flesh afterwards. You back out, and find that you have walked into the tips—luckily only into the tips—of the fern-like fronds of a trailing and climbing palm such as you see in the Botanic Gardens. That came from the East, and furnishes the rattan-canes. This furnishes the gri-gri-canes, and is rather worse to meet, if possible, than the rattan. Your companion, while he helps you to pick the barbs out, calls the palm laughingly by another name, "Suelta-mi-Ingles"; and tells you the old story of the Spanish soldier at San Josef. You are near the water now; for here is a thicket of Balisiers. Push through, under their great plantain-like leaves. Slip down the muddy bank to that patch of gravel. See first, though, that it is not tenanted already by a deadly Mapepire, or rattlesnake, which has not the grace, as his cousin in North America has, to use his rattle.

The brooklet, muddy with last night's rain, is dammed and bridged by winding roots, in the shape like the jointed wooden snakes which we used to play with as children. They belong probably to a fig, whose trunk is somewhere up in the green cloud. Sit down on one, and look, around and aloft. From the soil to the sky, which peeps through here and there, the air is packed with green leaves of every imaginable hue and shape. Round our feet are Arums, with snow-white spadixes and hoods, one instance among many here of brilliant colour developing itself in deep shade. But is the darkness of the forest actually as great as it seems? Or are our eyes, accustomed to the blaze outside, unable to expand rapidly enough, and so liable to mistake for darkness air really full of light reflected downwards, again and again, at every angle, from the glossy surfaces of a million of leaves? At least we may be excused; for a bat has made the same mistake, and flits past us at noonday. And there is another—No; as it turns, a blaze of metallic azure off the upper side of the wings proves this one to be no bat, but a Morpho—a moth as big as a bat. And what was that second larger flash of golden green, which dashed at the moth, and back to yonder branch not ten feet off? A Jacamar—kingfisher, as they miscall her here, sitting fearless of man, with the moth in her long beak. Her throat is snowy white, her underparts rich red brown. Her breast, and all her upper plumage and long tail, glitter with golden green. There is light enough in this darkness, it seems. But now look again at the plants. Among the white-flowered Arums are other Arums, stalked and spotted, of which beware; for they are the poisonous Seguine-diable, the dumb-cane, of which evil tales were told in the days of slavery. A few drops of its milk, put into the mouth of a refractory slave, or again into the food of a cruel master, could cause swelling, choking, and burning agony for many hours.

Over our heads bend the great arrow leaves and purple leaf-stalks of the Tanias; and mingled with them, leaves often larger still: oval, glossy, bright, ribbed, reflecting from their underside a silver light. They belong to Arumas; and from their ribs are woven the Indian baskets and packs. Above these, again, the Balisiers bend their long leaves, eight or ten feet long apiece; and under the shade of the leaves their gay flower-spikes, like double rows of orange and black-birds' beaks upside down. Above them, and among them, rise stiff upright shrubs, with pairs of pointed leaves, a foot long some of them, pale green above, and yellow or fawn-coloured beneath. You may see, by the three longitudinal nerves in each leaf, that they are Melastomas of different kinds—a sure token that you are in the Tropics—a probable token that you are in Tropical America.

And over them, and among them, what a strange variety of foliage. Look at the contrast between the Balisiers and that branch which has thrust itself among them, which you take for a dark copper-coloured fern, so finely divided are its glossy leaves. It is really a Mimosa-Bois Mulâtre as they call it here. What a contrast again, the huge feathery fronds of the Cocorite palms which stretch right away hither over our heads, twenty and thirty feet in length. And what is that spot of crimson flame hanging in the darkest spot of all from an under-bough of that low weeping tree? A flower-head of the Rosa del Monte. And what that bright straw-coloured fox's brush above it, with a brown hood like that of an Arum, brush and hood nigh three feet long each? Look—for you require to look more than once, sometimes more than twice—here, up the stem of that Cocorite, or as much of it as you can see in the thicket. It is all jagged with the brown butts of its old fallen leaves; and among the butts perch broad-leaved ferns, and fleshy Orchids, and above them, just below the plume of mighty fronds, the yellow fox's brush, which is its spathe of flower.

What next? Above the Cocorites dangle, amid a dozen different kinds of leaves, festoons of a liane, or of two, for one has purple flowers, the other yellow—Bignonias, Bauhinias—what not? And through them a Carat palm has thrust its thin bending stem, and spread out its flat head of fan-shaped leaves twenty feet long each: while over it, I verily believe, hangs eighty feet aloft the head of the very tree upon whose roots we are sitting. For amid the green cloud you may see sprigs of leaf somewhat like that of a weeping willow; and there, probably, is the trunk to which they belong, or rather what will be a trunk at last. At present it is like a number of round edged boards of every size, set on end, and slowly coalescing at their edges. There is a slit down the middle of the trunk, twenty or thirty feet long. You may see the green light of the forest shining through it. Yes, that is probably the fig; or, if not, then something else. For who am I, that I should know the hundredth part of the forms on which we look?

And above all you catch a glimpse of that crimson mass of Norantea which we admired just now; and, black as yew against the blue sky and white cloud, the plumes of one Palmiste, who has climbed towards the light, it may be for centuries, through the green cloud; and now, weary and yet triumphant, rests her dark head among the bright foliage of a Ceiba, and feeds unhindered on the sun.

There, take your tired eyes down again; and turn them right, or left, or where you will, to see the same scene, and yet never the same. New forms, new combinations; wealth of creative Genius—let us use the wise old word in its true sense—incomprehensible by the human intellect or the human eye, even as He is who makes it all, Whose garment, or rather Whose speech, it is. The eye is not filled with seeing, or the ear with hearing; and never would be, did you roam these forests for a hundred years. How many years would you need merely to examine and discriminate the different species? And when you had done that, how many more to learn their action and reaction on each other? How many more to learn their virtues, properties, uses? How many more to answer that perhaps ever unanswerable question—How they exist and grow at all? By what miracle they are compacted out of light, air, and water, each after its kind. How, again, those kinds began to be, and what they were like at first? Whether those crowded, struggling, competing shapes are stable or variable? Whether or not they are varying still? Whether even now, as we sit here, the great God may not be creating, slowly but surely, new forms of beauty round us. Why not? If He chose to do it, could He not do it? And even had you answered that question, which would require whole centuries of observation as patient and accurate as that which Mr. Darwin employed on Orchids and climbing plants, how much nearer would you be to the deepest question of all—Do these things exist, or only appear? Are they solid realities, or a mere phantasmagoria, orderly indeed, and law-ruled, but a phantasmagoria still; a picture-book by which God speaks to rational essences, created in His own likeness? And even had you solved that old problem, and decided for Berkeley or against him, you would still have to learn from these forests a knowledge which enters into man not through the head, but through the heart; which (let some modern philosophers say what they will) defies all analysis, and can be no more defined or explained by words than a mother's love. I mean, the causes and effects of their beauty; that "Æsthetic of plants," of which Schleiden has spoken so well in that charming book of his *The Plant*, which all should read who wish to know somewhat of "The Open Secret."

But when they read it, let them read with open hearts. For that same "Open Secret" is, I suspect, one of those which God may hide from the wise and prudent, and yet reveal to babes.

At least, so it seemed to me, the first day that I went, awe-struck, into the High Woods; and so it seemed to me, the last day that I came, even more awe-struck, out of them.

At Last: a Christmas in the West Indies (London and New York, 1871).

THE YO-SEMITÉ VALLEY

C. F. GORDON-CUMMING

THE valley can be approached from several different points. That by which we entered is, I think, known as Inspiration Point. When we started from Clarke's Ranch, we were then at about the same level as we are at this moment—namely, 4,000 feet above the sea. The road gradually wound upwards through beautiful forest and by upland valleys, where the snow still lay pure and white: and here and there, where it had melted and exposed patches of dry earth, the red flame-like blossoms of the snow-plant gleamed vividly.

It was slow work toiling up those steep ascents, and it must have taken us much longer than our landlord had expected, for he had despatched us without a morsel of luncheon; and ere we reached the half-way house, where we were to change horses, we were all ravenous. A dozen hungry people, with appetites sharpened by the keen, exhilarating mountain air! No provisions of any sort were to be had; but the compassionate horse-keeper, hearing our pitiful complaints, produced a loaf and a pot of blackberry jelly, and we all sat down on a bank, and ate our "piece" (as the bairns in Scotland would say) with infinite relish, and drank from a clear stream close by. So we were satisfied with bread here in the wilderness. I confess to many qualms as to how that good fellow fared himself, as loaves cannot grow abundantly in those parts.

Once more we started on our toilsome way across mountain meadows and forest ridges, till at last we had gained a height of about 7,000 feet above the sea. Then suddenly we caught sight of the valley lying about 3,000 feet below us, an abrupt chasm in the great rolling expanse of billowy granite ridges—or I should rather describe it as a vast sunken pit, with perpendicular walls, and carpeted with a level meadow, through which flows a river gleaming like quicksilver.

Here and there a vertical cloud of spray on the face of the huge crags told where some snow-fed stream from the upper levels had found its way to the brink of the chasm—a perpendicular fall of from 2,000 to 3,000 feet.

The fall nearest to where we stood, yet a distance of seven miles, was pointed out as the Bridal Veil. It seemed a floating film of finest mist, on which played the loveliest rainbow lights. For the sun was already lowering behind us, though the light shown clear and bright on the cold white granite crags, and on the glittering snow-peaks of the high Sierras.

Each mighty precipice, and rock-needle, and strange granite dome was pointed out to us by name as we halted on the summit of the pass ere commencing the steep descent. The Bridal Veil falls over a granite crag near the entrance of the valley, which, on the opposite side, is guarded by a stupendous square-cut granite mass, projecting

THE YOSEMITÉ VALLEY.

so far as seemingly to block the way. These form the gateway of this wonderful granite prison. Perhaps the great massive cliff rather suggests the idea of a huge keep wherein the genii of the valley braved the siege of the Ice-giants.

The Indians revere it as the great chief of the valley, but white men only know it as El Capitan. If it must have a new title, I think it should at least rank as a field-marshal in the rock-world, for assuredly no other crag exists that can compare with it. Just try to realize its dimensions: a massive face of smooth cream-coloured granite, half a mile long, half a mile wide, three-fifths of a mile high. Its actual height is 3,300 feet—(I think that 5,280 feet go to a mile). Think of our beautiful Castle Rock in Edinburgh, with its 434 feet; or Dover Castle, 469 feet; or even Arthur's Seat, 822 feet,—what pigmies they would seem could some wizard transport them to the base of this grand crag, on whose surface not a blade of grass, not a fern or a lichen, finds holding ground, or presumes to tinge the bare, clean-cut precipice, which, strange to tell, is clearly visible from the great San Joaquin Valley, a distance of sixty miles!

Imagine a crag just the height of Snowdon, with a lovely snow-stream falling perpendicularly from its summit to its base, and a second and larger fall in the deep gorge where it meets the rock-wall of the valley. The first is nameless, and will vanish with the snows; but the second never dries up, even in summer. It is known to the Indians as Lung-oo-too-koo-ya, which describes its graceful length; but white men call it The Virgin's Tears or The Ribbon Fall—a blending of millinery and romance doubtless devised by the same genius who changed the Indian name of Pohono to The Bridal Veil.

We passed close to the latter as we entered the valley—in fact, forded the stream just below the fall—and agreed that if Pohono be in truth, as the Indian legend tells, the spirit of an evil wind, it surely must be repentant glorified spirit, for nothing so beautiful could be evil. It is a sight to gladden the angels—a most ethereal fall, light as steam, swaying with every breath.

It falls from an overhanging rock, and often the current produced by its own rushing seems to pass beneath the rock, and so checks the whole column, and carries it upward in a wreath of whitest vapour, blending with the true clouds.

When the rainbow plays on it, it too seems to be wafted up, and floats in a jewelled spray, wherein sapphires and diamonds and opals, topaz and emeralds, all mingle their dazzling tints. At other times it rushes down in a shower of fairy-like rockets in what appears to be a perpendicular column 1,000 feet high, and loses itself in a cloud of mist among the tall dark pines which clothe the base of the crag.

A very accurate gentleman has just assured me that it is not literally perpendicular, as, after a leap of 630 feet, it strikes the rock, and then makes a fresh start in a series of almost vertical cascades, which form a dozen streamlets ere they reach the meadows. He adds that the fall is about fifty feet wide at the summit.

The rock-mass over which it falls forms the other great granite portal of the valley, not quite so imposing as its massive neighbour, but far more shapely. In fact, it bears so strong a resemblance to a Gothic building that it is called the Cathedral Rock. It is a cathedral for the giants, being 2,660 feet in height; and two graceful rock-pinnacles attached to the main rock, and known as the Cathedral Spires, are each 500 feet in height.

Beyond these, towers a truly imposing rock-needle, which has been well named The Sentinel. It is an obelisk 1,000 feet in height, rising from the great rock-wall, which forms a pedestal of 2,000 more.

As if to balance these three rock-needles on the right-hand side, there are, on the left, three rounded mountains which the Indians call Pompompasus—that is, the Leaping-Frog Rocks. They rise in steps, forming a triple mountain 3,630 feet high. Tall frogs these, even for California. Imaginative people say the resemblance is unmistakable, and that all the frogs are poised as if in readiness for a spring, with their heads all turned the same way. For my own part, I have a happy knack of not seeing these accidental likenesses, and especially those faces and pictures (generally grotesque) which some most aggravating people are always discovering among the lines and weather-stains on the solemn crags, and which they insist on pointing out to their unfortunate companions. Our coachman seemed to consider this a necessary part of his office, so I assume there must be some people who like it.

Farther up the valley, two gigantic Domes of white

granite are built upon the foundation of the great encompassing wall. One stands on each side of the valley. The North Dome is perfect, like the roof of some vast mosque; but the South, or Half Dome, is an extraordinary freak of nature, very puzzling to geologists, as literally half of a stupendous mass of granite has disappeared, leaving no trace of its existence, save a sheer precipitous rock-face, considerably over 4,000 feet in height, from which the corresponding half has evidently broken off, and slipped down into some fearful chasm, which apparently it has been the means of filling up.

Above the Domes, and closing in the upper end of the valley, is a beautiful snow mountain, called Cloud's Rest, which, seen from afar, is the most attractive point of all, and one which I must certainly visit some day. But meanwhile there are nearer points of infinite interest, the foremost being the waterfall from which the valley takes its name, and which burst suddenly upon our amazed vision when we reached the base of the Sentinel Rock.

It is so indescribably lovely that I altogether despair of conveying any notion of it in words, so shall not try to do so yet a while.

But from what I have told you, you must perceive that each step in this strange valley affords a study for weeks, whether to an artist, a geologist, or any other lover of beautiful and wonderful scenes; and more than ever, I congratulate myself on having arrived here while all the oaks, alders, willows, and other deciduous trees, are bare and leafless, so that no curtain of dense foliage conceals the countless beauties of the valley. Already I have seen innumerable most beautiful views, scarcely veiled by the filmy network of twigs, but which evidently will be altogether concealed a month hence, when these have donned their summer dress. To me these leafless trees rank with fires and snows. I have not seen one since I left England, so I look at them with renewed interest, and delight in the beauty of their anatomy, as you and I have done many a time in the larch woods and the "birken braes" of the Findhorn (where the yellow twigs of the larch, and the grey aspen, and claret-coloured sprays of birch, blend with russet oak and green Scotch firs, and produce a winter colouring well-nigh as varied as that of summer).

Here there is an enchanting reminder of home in the tall poplar-trees—the Balm of Gilead—which are just bursting into leaf, and fill the air with heavenly perfume. They grow in clumps all along the course of the Merced, the beautiful "river of Mercy," which flows through this green level valley so peacefully, as if it was thankful for this quiet interval in the course of its restless life.

There is no snow in the valley, but it still lies thickly on the hills all round. Very soon it will melt, and then the falls will all be in their glory, and the meadows will be flooded and the streams impassable. I am glad we have arrived in time to wander about dry-footed, and to learn the geography of the country in its normal state.

The valley is an almost dead level, about eight miles long, and varies in width from half a mile to two miles. It is like a beautiful park of greenest sward, through which winds the clear, calm river—a capital trout-stream, of about eighty feet in width. In every direction are scattered picturesque groups of magnificent trees, noble old oaks, and pines of 250 feet in height! The river is spanned by two wooden bridges; and three neat hotels are well placed about the middle of the valley, half a mile apart—happily not fine, incongruous buildings, but wooden bungalows, well suited to the requirements of such pilgrims as ourselves. . . .

May-day, 1877.

May-day! What a vision of langsyne! Of the May-dew we used to gather from off the cowslips by the sweet burnside, in those dear old days

> "When we all were young together,
> And the earth was new to me."

I dare say you forgot all about May-day this morning, in the prosaic details of town life. But here we ran no such risk, for we had determined to watch the Beltane sunrise, reflected in the glassiest of mountain-tarns, known as the Mirror Lake; and as it lies about three miles from here, in one of the upper forks of the valley, we had to astir betimes.

So, when the stars began to pale in the eastern sky, we were astir, and with the earliest ray of dawn set off like true pilgrims bound to drink of some holy spring on May morning. For the first two miles our path lay across quiet meadows, which as yet are only sprinkled with blossom. We found no cowslips, but washed our faces in Californian May-dew, which we brushed from the fresh young grass and ferns. Soon, they tell me, there will be violets, cowslips, and primroses. We passed by the orchard of the first settler in the valley; his peach and cherry trees were laden with pink and white blossoms, his strawberry-beds likewise promising an abundant crop.

It was a morning of calm beauty, and the massive grey crags all around the valley lay "like sleeping kings" robed in purple gloom, while the pale yellow light crept behind them, the tall pines forming a belt of deeper hue round their base.

About two miles above the Great Yo-semité Falls, the valley divides into three branches—canyons, I should say, or, more correctly cañons. The central one is the main branch, through which the Merced itself descends from the high Sierras, passing through the Little Yo-semité Valley, and thence rushing down deep gorges, and leaping two precipices of 700 and 400 feet (which form the Nevada and the Vernal Falls), and so entering the Great Valley, where for eight miles it finds rest.

The canyon which diverges to the right is that down which rushes the South Fork of the Merced, which bears the musical though modern name of Illillouette. It rises at the base of Mount Starr King, and enters the valley by the graceful falls which bear this pretty name.

At the point where we left the main valley to turn into the Tenaya Fork, the rock-wall forms a sharp angle, ending in a huge columnar mass of very white granite 2,400 feet in height. The Indians call it Hunto, which means one who keeps watch; but the white men call it Washington Column.

Beside it, the rock-wall has taken the form of gigantic arches. The lower rock seems to have weakened and crumbled or split off in huge flakes, while the upper portions remain, overhanging considerably, and forming regularly arched cliffs 2,000 feet in height. I cannot think how it has happened that in so republican a community these mighty rocks should be known as the Royal Arches, unless from some covert belief that they are undermined, and liable to topple over. Their original name is To-coy-œ, which describes the arched hood of an Indian baby's cradle—a famous nursery for giants.

The perpendicular rock-face beneath the arches is a sheer, smooth surface, yet seamed with deep cracks as though it would fall, were it not for the mighty buttresses of solid rock which project for some distance, casting deep shadows across the cliff. As a test of size, I noticed a tiny pine growing from a crevice in the rock-face, and on comparing it with another in a more accessible position, I found that it was really a very large, well-grown tree.

Just at this season, when the snows on the Sierras are beginning to melt, a thousand crystal streams find temporary channels along the high levels till they reach the smooth verge of the crags, and thence leap in white foam, forming temporary falls of exceeding beauty. Three such graceful falls at present overleap the mighty arches, and, in their turn, produce pools and exquisitely clear streams, which thread their devious way through woods and meadows, seeking the river of Mercy.

So the air is musical with the lullaby of hidden waters, and the murmur of the unseen river rippling over its pebbly bed.

Turning to the right, we next ascended Tenaya valley, which is beautifully wooded, chiefly with pine and oak, and strewn with the loveliest mossy boulders. Unfortunately, the number of rattlesnakes is rather a drawback to perfect enjoyment here. I have so long been accustomed to our perfect immunity from all manner of noxious creatures in the blessed South Sea Isles, that I find it difficult at first to recall my wonted caution, and to "gang warily." However, to-day we saw no evil creatures—only a multitude of the jolliest little chip-munks, which are small grey squirrels of extreme activity. They are very tame, and dance about the trees close to us, jerking their brush, and giving the funniest little skips, and sometimes fairly chattering to us!

Beyond this wood we found the Mirror Lake. It is a small pool, but exquisitely cradled in the very midst of stern granite giants, which stand all around as sentinels, guarding its placid sleep. Willows, already covered with downy tufts, and now just bursting into slender leaflets, fringe its shores, and tall cedars and pines overshadow its waters, and are therein reflected in the stillness of early dawn, when even the granite crags far overhead also find themselves mirrored in the calm lakelet. But with the dawn comes a whispering breeze; and just as the sun's first gleam kisses the waters, the illusion vanishes, and there remains only a somewhat muddy and troubled pool.

It lies just at the base of that extraordinary Half-Dome of which I told you yesterday—a gigantic crest of granite, which rises above the lake almost precipitously to a height of 4,737 feet. Only think of it!—nearly a mile! Of this the upper 2,000 feet is a sheer face of granite crag, absolutely vertical, except that the extreme summit actually projects somewhat; otherwise it is as clean cut as if the mighty Dome had been cloven with a sword. A few dark streaks near the summit (due, I believe, to a microscopic fungus or lichen) alone relieve the unbroken expanse of glistening, creamy white.

The lower half slopes at a very slight incline, and is likewise a solid mass of granite—not made up of broken fragments, of which there are a wonderfully small proportion anywhere in the valley. So the inference is, that in the tremendous convulsion this mighty chasm was created, the great South Dome was split from the base to the summit, and that half of it slid down into the yawning gulf: thus the gently rounded base, between the precipice and the lake, was doubtless originally the summit of the missing half mountain.

I believe that geologists are now satisfied that this strange valley, with its clean-cut, vertical walls, was produced by what is called in geology "a fault,"—namely, that some of the earth's ribs having given away internally, a portion of the outer crust has subsided, leaving an unoccupied space. That such was the case in Yo-semité, is proved by much scientific reasoning. It is shown that the two sides of the valley in no way correspond, so the idea of a mere gigantic fissure cannot be entertained. Besides, as the valley is as wide at the base as at the summit, the vertical walls must have moved apart bodily,—a theory which would involve a movement of the whole chain of the Sierras for a distance of a half a mile.

There is not trace of any glacier having passed through the valley, so that the Ice-giants have had no share in making it. Neither can it have been excavated by the long-continued action of rushing torrents, such as have carved great canyons in many parts of the Sierra Nevada. These never have vertical walls; and besides, the smoothest faces of granite in Yo-semité are turned towards the lower end of the valley, proving at once that they were never produced by forces moving downward.

So it is simply supposed that a strip of the Sierras caved in, and that in time the melting snows and streams formed a great deep lake, which filled up the whole space now occupied by the valley. In the course of ages the *débris* of the hills continually falling into the lake, must have filled up the chasm to a level with the canyon, which is the present outlet from the valley; and as the glaciers on the upper Sierras disappeared, and the water-supply grew less, the lake must have gradually dried up (and that in comparatively recent times), and its bed of white granite sand, mingled with vegetable mould, was transformed into a green meadow, through which the quiet river now glides peacefully.

This evening the sun set in a flood of crimson and gold—such a glorious glow as would have dazzled an eagle. It paled to a soft primrose, then ethereal green. Later, the pearly-grey clouds were rose-flushed by an afterglow more vivid than the sunset itself—a rich full carmine, which quickly faded away to the cold, intense blue of a Californian night. It was inexpressibly lovely.

Then the fitful wind rose in gusts—a melancholy, moaning wail, vibrating among rocks, forests, and waters, with a low, surging sound—a wild mountain melody.

No wonder the Indians reverence the beautiful Yo-semité Falls. Even the white settlers in the valley cannot resist their influence, but speak of them with an admiration that amounts to love. Some of them have spent the winter here, and seem almost to have enjoyed it.

They say that if I could see the falls in their winter robes, all fringed with icicles, I should gain a glimpse of fairyland. At the base of the great fall the fairies build a real ice-palace, something more than a hundred feet high. It is formed by the ever falling, freezing spray; and the bright sun gleams on this glittering palace of crystal, and the falling water, striking upon it, shoots off in showers like myriad opals and diamonds.

Now scarcely an icicle remains, and the falls are in their glory. I had never dreamt of anything so lovely. . . . . Here we stand in the glorious sunlight, among pine-trees a couple of hundred feet in height; and they are pigmies like ourselves in presence of even the lowest step of the stately fall, which leaps and dashes from so vast a height that it loses all semblance of water. It is a splendid bouquet of glistening rockets, which, instead of rushing heavenward, shoot down as if from the blue canopy, which seems to touch the brink nearly 2,700 feet above us.

Like myriad falling stars they flash, each keeping its separate course for several hundred feet, till at length it blends with ten thousand more, in the grand avalanche of frothy, fleecy foam, which for ever and for ever falls, boiling and raging like a whirlpool, among the huge black boulders in the deep cauldron below, and throwing back clouds of mist and vapour.

The most exquisite moment occurs when you reach some spot where the sun's rays, streaming past you, transform the light vapour into brilliant rainbow-prisms, which gird the falls with vivid iris-bars. As the water-rockets flash through these radiant belts, they seem to carry the colour onwards as they fall; and sometimes it wavers and trembles in the breeze, so that the rainbow knows not where to rest, but forms a moving column of radiant tri-colour.

So large a body of water rushing through the air, naturally produces a strong current, which, passing between the face of the rock and the fall, carries the latter well forward, so that it becomes the sport of every breeze that dances through the valley; hence this great column is forever vibrating from side to side, and often it forms a semi-circular curve.

The width of the stream at the summit is about twenty to thirty feet, but at the base of the upper fall it has expanded to a width of fully 300 feet; and, as the wind carries it to one side or the other, it plays over a space of fully

1,000 feet in width, of a precipitous rock-face 1,600 feet in depth. That is the height of the upper fall.

As seen from below the Yo-semité, though divided into three distinct falls, is apparently all on one plane. It is only when you reach some point from which you see it sideways, that you realize that the great upper fall lies fully a quarter of a mile farther back than the middle and lower falls, and that it rushes down this space in boiling cascades, till it reaches a perpendicular rock, over which it leaps about 600 feet, and then gives a third and final plunge of about 500, making up a total of little under 2,700 feet.

When we came to the head of the valley, whence diverge the three rocky canyons, we bade adieu to the green meadows, and passing up a most exquisite gorge, crossed the Illillouette by a wooden bridge, and followed the main fork of the Merced, up the central canyon. I do not anywhere know a lovelier mile of river scenery than on this tumultuous rushing stream, leaping from rock to rock, sweeping around mossy boulders and falling in crystalline cascades—the whole fringed with glittering icicles, and overshadowed by tall pine-trees, whose feathery branches fringe the steep cliffs and wave in the breeze.

Presently a louder roar of falling water told us that we were nearing the Vernal Falls, and through a frame of dark pines we caught a glimpse of the white spirit-like spray-cloud. Tying up my pony, we crept to the foot of the falls, whence a steep flight of wooden steps has been constructed, by which a pedestrian can ascend about 400 feet to the summit, and thence resume his way, thus saving a very long round. But of course four-footed creatures must be content to go by the mountain; and so the pony settled our route, greatly to our advantage, for the view thence, looking down the canyon and across to Glacier Point, proved to be about the finest thing we had seen, as an effect of mountain gloom.

Just above the Vernal Falls comes a reach of the river known as The Diamond Race,—a stream so rapid and so glittering, that it seems like a shower of sparkling crystals, each drop a separate gem. I have never seen a race which, for speed and dazzling light, could compare with these musical, glancing waters.

For half a mile above it, the river is a tumultuous raging flood, rushing at headlong speed down a boulder-strewn channel. At the most beautiful point it is crossed by a light wooden bridge; and on the green mountain-meadow just beyond, stands the wooden house, to which a kindly landlord gave us a cheery, hearty welcome.

Here the lullaby for the weary is the ceaseless roar of the mighty Nevada Falls, which come thundering down the cliffs in a sheer leap of 700 feet, losing themselves in a deep rock-pool, fringed with tall pines, which loom ghostly and solemn through the ever-floating tremulous mists of fine spray.

It is a fall so beautiful as fairly to divide one's allegiance to Yo-semité, especially as we first beheld it at about three in the afternoon, when the western rays of the lowering sun lighted up the dark firs with a golden glow, and dim rainbows played on the spray-clouds. It was as if fairy weavers had woven borders of purple and blue, green and gold, orange and delicate rose-colour, on a tissue of silvery gauze; and each dewy drop that rested on the fir-needles caught the glorious light, and became a separate prism, as though the trees were sprinkled with liquid radiant gems.

Anything more wonderful than the beauty of the Diamond Race in the evening light, I never dreamt of. It is like a river in a fairy tale, all turned to spray—jewelled, glittering spray—rubies, diamonds, and emeralds, all dancing and glancing in the sunlight.

Just below this comes a little reach of the smoothest, clearest water, which seems to calm and collect itself ere gliding over the edge of a great square-hewn mass of granite 400 feet deep, forming the Vernal Falls. Along the summit of this rock there runs a very remarkable natural ledge about four feet in height, so exactly like the stone parapet of a cyclopean rampart that it is scarcely possible to believe it is not artificial. Here you can lean safely within a few feet of the fall, looking straight down the perpendicular crag. But for this ledge, it would be dangerous even to set foot on that smooth, polished rock, which is as slippery as ice.

Early rising here is really no exertion, and it brings its own reward, for there is an indescribable charm in the early gloaming as it steals over the Sierras—a freshness and an exquisite purity of atmosphere which thrills through one's being like a breath of the life celestial.

If you would enjoy it to perfection, you must steal out alone ere the glory of the starlight has paled,—as I did this morning, following a devious pathway between thickets of azalea, whose heavenly fragrance perfumed the valley. Then, ascending a steep track through the pine-forest, I reached a bald grey crag, commanding a glorious view of the valley, and of some of the high peaks beyond. And thence I watched the coming of the dawn.

A pale daffodil light crept upward, and the stars faded from heaven. Then the great ghostly granite domes changed from deep purple to a cold dead white, and the far-distant snow-capped peaks stood out in a glittering light, while silvery-grey mists floated upward from the canyons, as if awakening from their sleep. Here, just as in our own Highlands, a faint chill breath of some cold current invariably heralds the daybreak, and the tremulous leaves quiver, and whisper a greeting to the dawn.

Suddenly a faint flush of rosy light just tinged the highest snow-peaks, and, gradually stealing downward, overspread range beyond range; another moment, and the granite domes and the great Rock Sentinel alike blazed in the fiery glow, which deepened in colour till all the higher crags seemed aflame, while the valley still lay shrouded in purple gloom, and a great and solemn stillness brooded over all.

Granite Crags (Edinburgh and London, 1884).

THE GOLDEN HORN

ALPHONSE DE LAMARTINE

THE land breeze begins to rise, and we make use of it to approach nearer and nearer to the Dardanelles. Already several large ships, which like us are trying to make this difficult entrance, come near us; their large grey sails, like the wings of night-birds, glide silently between our brig and Tenedos; I go down below and fall asleep.

Break of day: I hear the rapid sailing of vessels and the little morning waves that sound around the sides of the brig like the song of birds; I open the port-hole, and I see on a chain of low and rounded hills the castles of the Dardanelles with their white walls, their towers, and their immense mouths for the cannon; the canal is scarcely more than a league in width at this place; it winds, like a beautiful river, between the exactly similar coasts of Asia and Europe. The castles shut in this sea just like the two wings of a door; but in the present condition of Turkey and Europe, it would be easy to force a passage by sea, or to make a landing and take the forts from the rear; the passage of the Dardanelles is not impregnable unless guarded by the Russians.

The rapid current carries us on like an arrow before Gallipoli and the villages bordering the canal; we see the

THE GOLDEN HORN.

isles in the Sea of Marmora frowning before us; we follow the coast of Europe for two days and two nights, thwarted by the north winds. In the morning we perceive perfectly the isles of the princes, in the Sea of Marmora, and the Gulf of Nicæa, and on our left the castle of the Seven Towers, and the aërial tops of the innumerable minarets of Stamboul, in front of the seven hills of Constantinople. At each tack, we discover something new. At the first view of Constantinople, I experienced a painful emotion of surprise and disillusion. "What! is this," I asked myself, "the sea, the shore, and the marvellous city for which the masters of the world abandoned Rome and the coast of Naples? Is this that capital of the universe, seated upon Europe and Asia; for which all the conquering nations disputed by turns as the sign of the supremacy of the world? Is this the city that painters and poets imagine queen of cities seated upon her hills and her twin seas; enclosed by her gulfs, her towers, her mountains, and containing all the treasures of nature and the luxury of the Orient?" It is here that one makes comparison with the Bay of Naples bearing its white city upon its hollowed bosom like a vast amphitheatre; with Vesuvius losing its golden brow in the clouds of smoke and purple lights, the forest of Castellamare plunging its black foliage into the blue sea, and the islands of Procida and Ischia with their volcanic peaks yellow with vine-branches and white with villas, shutting in the immense bay like gigantic moles thrown up by God himself at the entrance of this port? I see nothing here to compare to that spectacle with which my eyes are always enchanted; I am sailing, it is true, upon a beautiful and lovely sea, but from the low coasts, rounded and monotonous hills rear themselves; it is true that the snows of Olympus of Thrace whiten the horizon, but they are only a white cloud in the sky and do not make the landscape solemn enough. At the back of the gulf I see nothing but the same rounded hills of the same height without rocks, without coves, without indentations, and Constantinople, which the pilot points out with his finger, is nothing but a white and circumscribed city upon a large knoll on the European coast. Is it worth while having come so far to be disenchanted? I did not wish to look at it any longer; however, the ceaseless tackings of the ship brought us sensibly nearer; we coasted along the castle of the Seven Towers, an immense mediæval grey block, severe in construction, which faces the sea at the angle of the Greek walls of the ancient Byzantium, and we came to anchor beneath the houses of Stamboul in the Sea of Marmora, in the midst of a host of ships and boats delayed like ourselves from port by the violence of the north winds. It was five o'clock, the sky was serene and the sun brilliant; I began to recover from my disdain of Constantinople; the walls that enclosed this portion of the city picturesquely built of the *débris* of ancient walls and surmounted by gardens, kiosks and little houses of wood painted red, formed the foreground of the picture; above, the terraces of numerous houses rose in pyramid-like tiers, story upon story, cut across with the tops of orange-trees and the sharp, black spires of cypress; higher still, seven or eight large mosques crowned the hill, and, flanked by their open-work minarets and their mauresque colonnades, lifted into the sky their gilded domes, flaming with the palpitating sunlight; the walls, painted with tender blue, the leaden covers of the cupolas that encircled them, gave them the appearance and the transparent glaze of monuments of porcelain. The immemorial cypresses lend to these domes their motionless and sombre peaks; and the various tints of the painted houses of the city make the vast hill gay with all the colours of a flower-garden. No noise issues from the streets; no lattice of the innumerable windows opens; no movement disturbs the habitation of such a great multitude of men: everything seems to be sleeping under the broiling sunlight; the gulf, furrowed in every direction with sails of all forms and sizes, alone gives signs of life. Every moment we see vessels in full sail clear the Golden Horn (the opening of the Bosphorus), the true harbour of Constantinople, passing by us flying towards the Dardanelles; but we can not perceive the entrance of the Bosphorus, nor even understand its position. We dine on the deck opposite this magical spectacle; Turkish *caïques* come to question us and to bring us provisions and food; the boatmen tell us that there is no longer any plague; I send my letters to the city; at seven o'clock, M. Truqui, the consul-general of Sardaigne, accompanied by officers of his legation, comes to pay us a visit and offer us the hospitality of his house in Pera; there is not the slightest hope of finding a lodging in the recently burned city; the obliging cordiality, and the attraction that M. Truqui inspires at the first moment, induces us to accept. The contrary wind still blows, and the brigs cannot raise anchor this evening: we sleep on board.

At five o'clock I am standing on the deck; the captain lowers a boat; I descend with him, and we set sail towards the mouth of the Bosphorus, coasting along the walls of Constantinople, which the sea washes. After half an hour's navigation through a multitude of ships at anchor, we reach the walls of the Seraglio, which stand next to those of the city, and form, at the extremity of the hill that bears Stamboul, the angle that separates the Sea of Marmora from the canal of the Bosphorus and the Golden Horn, or the grand inner roadstead of Constantinople. It is here that God and man, nature and art, have placed, or created, in concert the most marvellous view that human eyes may contemplate upon the earth. I gave an involuntary cry, and I forgot for ever the Bay of Naples and all its enchantments; to compare anything to this magnificent and gracious combination would be to insult creation.

The walls supporting the circular terraces of the immense gardens of the great Seraglio were a few feet from us to our left, separated from the sea by a narrow sidewalk of stone flags washed by the ceaseless billows, where the perpetual current of the Bosphorus formed little murmuring waves, as blue as those of the Rhône at Geneva; these terraces that rise in gentle inclines up to the Sultan's palace, where you perceive the gilded domes across the gigantic tops of the plantain-trees and the cypresses, are themselves planted with enormous cypresses and plantains whose trunks dominate the walls and whose boughs, spreading beyond the garden, hang over the sea in cascades of foliage shadowing the *caïques;* the rowers stop from time to time beneath their shade; every now and then these groups of trees are interrupted by palaces, pavilions, kiosks, doors sculptured and gilded opening upon the sea, or batteries of cannon of copper and bronze in ancient and peculiar shapes.

Several pulls of the oar brought us to the precise point of the Golden Horn where you enjoy at once a view of the Bosphorus, the Sea of Marmora, and, finally, of the entire harbour, or, rather, the inland sea of Constantinople; there we forgot Marmora, the coast of Asia, and the Bosphorus, taking in with one glance the basin of the Golden Horn and the seven cities seated upon the seven hills of Constantinople, all converging towards the arm of the sea that forms the unique and incomparable city, that is at the same time city, country, sea, harbour, bank of flowers, gardens, wooded mountains, deep valleys, an ocean of houses, a swarm of ships and streets, tranquil lakes, and enchanted solitudes,—a view that no brush can render except by details, and where each stroke of the oar gives the eye and soul contradictory aspects and impressions.

We set sail towards the hills of Galata and Pera; the Seraglio receded from us and grew larger in receding in proportion as the eye embraced more and more the vast outlines of its walls and the multitude of its roofs, its trees, its kiosks and its palaces. Of itself it is sufficient to constitute a large city. The harbour hollows itself out more and more before us; it winds like a canal between the flanks of the curved mountains, and increases as we advance. The harbour does not resemble a harbour in the least; it is rather a large river like the Thames, enclosing the two coasts of the hills laden with towns, and covered from one bank to the other with an interminable flotilla of ships variously grouped the entire length of the houses. We pass by this innumerable multitude of boats, some riding at anchor and some about to set sail, sailing before the wind towards the Bosphorus, towards the Black Sea, or towards the Sea of Marmora; boats of all shapes and sizes and flags, from the Arabian barque, whose prow springs and rises like the beak of antique galleys, to the vessel of three decks with its glittering walls of bronze. Some flocks of Turkish *caïques*, managed by one or two rowers in silken sleeves, little boats that serve as carriages in the maritime streets of this amphibious town, circulate between the large masses, cross and knock against each other without overturning, and jostle one another like a crowd in public places; and clouds of gulls, like beautiful white pigeons, rise from the sea at their approach, to travel further away and be rocked upon the waves. I did not try to count the vessels, the ships, the brigs, the boats of all kinds and the barks that slept or travelled in the harbour of Constantinople, from the mouth of the Bosphorus and the point of the Seraglio to Eyoub and the delicious valleys of sweet waters. The Thames at London offers nothing in comparison. It will suffice to say that independently of the Turkish flotilla and the European men-of-war at anchor in the centre of the canal, the two sides of the Golden Horn are covered two or three vessels deep for about a mile in length. We could only see the ocean by looking between the file of prows and our glance lost itself at the back of the gulf which contracted and ran into the shore amid a veritable forest of masts.

I have just been strolling along the Asian shore on my return this evening to Constantinople, and I find it a thousand times more beautiful than the European shore. The Asian shore owes almost nothing to man; everything here has been accomplished by nature. Here there is no Buyukdere, no Therapia, no palace of ambassadors, and no town of Armenians or Franks; there are only mountains, gorges that separate them, little valleys carpeted with meadows that seem to dig themselves out of the rocks, rivulets that wind about them, cascades that whiten them with their foam, forests that hang to their flanks, glide into their ravines, and descend to the very edges of the innumerable coast gulfs; a variety of forms and tints, and of leafy verdure, which the brush of a landscape-painter could not even hope to suggest. Some isolated houses of sailors or Turkish gardeners are scattered at great distances on the shore, or thrown on the foreground of a wooded hill, or grouped upon the point of rocks where the current carries you, and breaks into waves as blue as the night sky; some white sails of fishermen, who creep along the deep coves, which you see glide from one plane-tree to another, like linen that the washerwomen fold; innumerable flights of white birds that dry themselves on the edge of the meadows; eagles that hover among the heights of the mountains near the sea; mysterious creeks entirely shut in between rocks and trunks of gigantic trees, whose boughs, overcharged with leaves, bend over the waves and form upon the sea cradles wherein the *caïques* creep. One or two villages hidden in the shadow of these creeks with their gardens behind them on those green slopes, and their group of trees at the foot of the rocks, with their barks rocked by the gentle waves before their doors, their clouds of doves on the roofs, their women and children at the windows, their old men seated beneath the plane-trees at the foot of the minaret; labourers returning from the fields in their *caïques;* others who have filled their barks with green faggots, myrtle, or flowering heath to dry it for fuel in the winter; hidden behind these heaps of slanting verdure that border and descend into the water, you perceive neither the bark nor the rower, and you believe that a portion of the bank detached from the earth by the current is floating at haphazard on the sea with its green foliage and its perfumed flowers. The shore presents this same appearance as far as the castle of Mahomet II., which from this coast also seems to shut in the Bosphorus like a Swiss lake; there, it changes its character; the hills, less rugged, sink their flanks and more gently hollow into narrow valleys; the Asiatic villages extend more richly and nearer together; the Sweet Waters of Asia, a charming little plain shadowed by trees and sown with kiosks and Moorish fountains opens out to the vision.

Beyond the palace of Beglierby, the Asian coast again becomes wooded and solitary as far as Scutari, which is as brilliant as a garden of roses, at the extremity of a cape at the entrance of the Sea of Marmora. Opposite, the verdant point of the Seraglio presents itself to the eye; and between the European coast, crowned with its three painted towns, and the coast of Stamboul, all glittering with its cupolas and minarets, opens the immense port of Constantinople, where the ships anchored at the two banks leave only one large water-way for the *caïques*. I glide through this labyrinth of buildings, as in a Venetian gondola under the shadow of palaces, and I land at the *échelle des Morts*, under an avenue of cypresses.

Voyage en Orient (Paris, 1843).

THE YELLOWSTONE[1]

RUDYARD KIPLING

"That desolate land and lone
Where the Big Horn and Yellowstone
Roar down their mountain path."

TWICE have I written this letter from end to end. Twice have I torn it up, fearing lest those across the water should say that I had gone mad on a sudden. Now we will begin for the third time quite solemnly and soberly. I have been through the Yellowstone National Park in a buggy, in the company of an adventurous old lady from Chicago and her husband, who disapproved of scenery as being "ongodly." I fancy it scared them.

We began, as you know, with the Mammoth Hot Springs. They are only a gigantic edition of those pink and white terraces not long ago destroyed by earthquake in New Zealand. At one end of the little valley in which the hotel stands the lime-laden springs that break from the pine-covered hillsides have formed a frozen cataract of white, lemon, and palest pink formations, through and over and in which water of the warmest bubbles and drips and trickles from pale-green lagoon to exquisitely fretted basin.

[1] Published by permission of Rudyard Kipling. Copyright, 1899, by Rudyard Kipling.

COATING SPRINGS, YELLOWSTONE.

The ground rings hollow as a kerosene-tin, and some day the Mammoth Hotel, guests and all, will sink into the caverns below and be turned into a stalactite. When I set foot on the first of the terraces, a tourist—trampled ramp of scabby grey stuff, I met a steam of iron-red hot water, which ducked into a hole like a rabbit. Followed a gentle chuckle of laughter, and then a deep, exhausted sigh from nowhere in particular. Fifty feet above my head a jet of steam rose up and died out in the blue. It was worse than the boiling mountain at Myanoshita. The dirty white deposit gave place to lime whiter than snow; and I found a basin which some learned hotel-keeper has christened Cleopatra's pitcher, or Mark Antony's whisky-jug, or something equally poetical. It was made of frosted silver; it was filled with water as clear as the sky. I do not know the depth of that wonder. The eye looked down beyond grottoes and caves of beryl into an abyss that communicated directly with the central fires of earth. And the pool was in pain, so that it could not refrain from talking about it; muttering and chattering and moaning. From the lips of the lime-ledges, forty feet under water, spurts of silver bubbles would fly up and break the peace of the crystal atop. Then the whole pool would shake and grow dim, and there were noises. I removed myself only to find other pools all equally unhappy, rifts in the ground, full of running red-hot water, slippery sheets of deposit overlaid with greenish grey hot water, and here and there pit-holes dry as a rifled tomb in India, dusty and waterless. Elsewhere the infernal waters had first boiled dead and then embalmed the palms and underwood, or the forest trees had taken heart and smothered up a blind formation with greenery, so that it was only by scraping the earth you could tell what fires had raged beneath. Yet the pines will win the battle in years to come, because Nature, who first forges all her work in her great smithies, has nearly finished this job, and is ready to temper it in the soft brown earth. The fires are dying down; the hotel is built where terraces have overflowed into flat wastes of deposit; the pines have taken possession of the high ground whence the terraces first started. Only the actual curve of the cataract stands clear, and it is guarded by soldiers who patrol it with loaded six-shooters, in order that the tourist may not bring up fence-rails and sink them in a pool, or chip the fretted tracery of the formations with a geological hammer, or, walking where the crust is too thin, foolishly cook himself. . . .

Next dawning, entering a buggy of fragile construction, with the old people from Chicago, I embarked on my perilous career. We ran straight up a mountain till we could see sixty miles away, the white houses of Cook City on another mountain, and the whiplash-like trail leading thereto. The live air made me drunk. If Tom, the driver, had proposed to send the mares in a bee-line to the city, I should have assented, and so would the old lady, who chewed gum and talked about her symptoms. The tub-ended rock-dog, which is but the translated prairie-dog, broke across the road under our horses' feet, the rabbit and the chipmunk danced with fright; we heard the roar of the river, and the road went round a corner. On one side piled rock and shale, that enjoined silence for fear of a general slide-down; on the other a sheer drop, and a fool of a noisy river below. Then, apparently in the middle of the road, lest any should find driving too easy, a post of rock. Nothing beyond that save the flank of a cliff. Then my stomach departed from me, as it does when you swing, for we left the dirt, which was at least some guarantee of safety, and sailed out round the curve, and up a steep incline, on a plank-road built out from the cliff. The planks were nailed at the outer edge, and did not shift or creak very much—but enough, quite enough. That was the Golden Gate. I got my stomach back again when we trotted out on to a vast upland adorned with a lake and hills. Have you ever seen an untouched land—the face of virgin Nature? It is rather a curious sight, because the hills are choked with timber that has never known an axe, and the storm has rent a way through this timber, so that a hundred thousand trees lie matted together in swathes; and since each tree lies where it falls, you may behold trunk and branch returning to the earth whence they sprang—exactly as the body of man returns—each limb making its own little grave, the grass climbing above the bark, till at last there remains only the outline of a tree upon the rank undergrowth.

Then we drove under a cliff of obsidian, which is black glass, some two hundred feet high; and the road at its foot was made of black glass that crackled. This was no great matter, because half an hour before Tom had pulled up in the woods that we might sufficiently admire a mountain who stood all by himself, shaking with laughter or rage. . . .

Then by companies after tiffin we walked chattering to the uplands of Hell. They call it the Norris Geyser Basin on Earth. It was as though the tide of dissolution had gone out, but would presently return, across innumerable acres of dazzling white geyser formation. There were no terraces here, but all other horrors. Not ten yards from the road a blast of steam shot up roaring every few seconds, a mud volcano spat filth to Heaven, streams of hot water rumbled under foot, plunged through the dead pines in steaming cataracts and died on a waste of white where green-grey, black-yellow, and link pools roared, shouted, bubbled, or hissed as their wicked fancies prompted. By the look of the eye the place should have been frozen over. By the feel of the feet it was warm. I ventured out among the pools, carefully following tracks, but one unwary foot began to sink, a squirt of water followed, and having no desire to descend quick into Tophet I returned to the shore where the mud and the sulphur and the nameless fat ooze-vegetation of Lethe lay. But the very road rang as though built over a gulf; and besides how was I to tell when the raving blast of steam would find its vent insufficient and blow the whole affair into Nirvana? There was a potent stench of stale eggs everywhere, and crystals of sulphur crumbled under the foot, and the glare of the sun on the white stuff was blinding. . . .

We curved the hill and entered a forest of spruce, the path serpentining between the tree-boles, the wheels running silent on immemorial mould. There was nothing alive in the forest save ourselves. Only a river was speaking angrily somewhere to the right. For miles we drove till Tom bade us alight and look at certain falls. Wherefore we stepped out of that forest and nearly fell down a cliff which guarded a tumbled river and returned demanding fresh miracles. If the water had run uphill, we should perhaps have taken more notice of it; but 'twas only a waterfall, and I really forget whether the water was warm or cold. There is a stream here called Firehole River. It is fed by the overflow from the various geysers and basins, —a warm and deadly river wherein no fish breed. I think we crossed it a few dozen times in the course of the day.

Then the sun began to sink, and there was a taste of frost about, and we went swiftly from the forest into the open, dashed across a branch of the Firehole River and found a wood shanty, even rougher than the last, at which, after a forty mile drive, we were to dine and sleep. Half a mile from this place stood, on the banks of the Firehole River a "beaver-lodge," and there were rumours of bears and other cheerful monsters in the woods on the hill at the back of the building. . . .

Once upon a time there was a carter who brought his team and a friend into the Yellowstone Park without due thought. Presently they came upon a few of the natural beauties of the place, and that carter turned his friend's team, howling: "Get back o' this, Tim. All Hell's alight under our noses." And they call the place Hell's Half-acre to this day. We, too, the old lady from Chicago, her husband, Tom, and the good little mares came to Hell's Half-acre, which is about sixty acres, and when Tom said: "Would you like to drive over it?" we said: "Certainly no, and if you do, we shall report you to the authorities." There was a plain, blistered and puled and abominable, and it was given over to the sportings and spoutings of devils who threw mud and steam and dirt at each other with whoops and halloos and bellowing curses. The place smelt of the refuse of the Pit, and that odour mixed with the clean, wholesome aroma of the pines in our nostrils throughout the day. Be it known that the Park is laid out, like Ollendorf, in exercises of progressive difficulty. Hell's Half-acre was a preclude to ten or twelve miles of geyser formation. We passed hot streams boiling in the forest; saw whiffs of steam beyond these, and yet other whiffs breaking through the misty green hills in the far distance; we trampled on sulphur, and sniffed things much worse than any sulphur which is known to the upper world; and so came upon a park-like place where Tom suggested we should get out and play with the geysers.

Imagine mighty green fields splattered with lime beds: all the flowers of the summer growing up to the very edge of the lime. That was the first glimpse of the geyser basins. The buggy had pulled up close to a rough, broken, blistered cone of stuff between ten and twenty feet high. There was trouble in that place—moaning, splashing, gurgling, and the clank of machinery. A spurt of boiling water jumped into the air and a wash of water followed. I removed swiftly. The old lady from Chicago shrieked.

"What a wicked waste!" said her husband. I think they call it the Riverside Geyser. Its spout was torn and ragged like the mouth of a gun when a shell has burst there. It grumbled madly for a moment or two and then was still. I crept over the steaming lime—it was the burning marl on which Satan lay—and looked fearfully down its mouth. You should never look a gift geyser in the mouth. I beheld a horrible slippery, slimy funnel with water rising and falling ten feet at a time. Then the water rose to lip level with a rush and an infernal bubbling troubled this Devil's Bethesda before the sullen heave of the crest of a wave lapped over the edge and made me run. Mark the nature of the human soul! I had begun with awe, not to say terror. I stepped back from the flanks of the Riverside Geyser saying: "Pooh! Is that all it can do?" Yet for aught I knew the whole thing might have blown up at a minute's notice; she, he, or it, being an arrangement of uncertain temper.

We drifted on up that miraculous valley. On either side of us were hills from a thousand to fifteen feet high and wooded from heel to crest. As far as the eye could range forward were columns of steam in the air, misshapen lumps of lime, most like preadamite monsters, still pools of turquoise blue, stretches of blue cornflowers, a river that coiled on itself twenty times, boulders of strange colours, and ridges of glaring, staring white.

The old lady from Chicago poked with her parasol at the pools as though they had been alive. On one particularly innocent-looking little puddle she turned her back for a moment, and there rose behind her a twenty-foot column of water and steam. Then she shrieked and protested that "she never thought it would ha' done it," and the old man chewed his tobacco steadily, and mourned for steam power wasted. I embraced the whitened stump of a middle-sized pine that had grown all too close to a hot pool's lip, and the whole thing turned over under my hand as a tree would do in a nightmare. From right and left came the trumpetings of elephants at play. I stepped into a pool of old dried blood rimmed with the nodding cornflowers; the blood changed to ink even as I trod; and ink and blood were washed away in a spurt of boiling sulphurous water spat out from the lee of a bank of flowers. This sounds mad, doesn't it? . . .

We rounded a low spur of hills, and came out upon a field of aching snowy lime, rolled in sheets, twisted into knots, riven with rents and diamonds and stars, stretching for more than half a mile in every direction. In this place of despair lay most of the big geysers who know when there is trouble in Krakatoa, who tell the pines when there is a cyclone on the Atlantic seaboard, and who—are exhibited to visitors under pretty and fanciful names. The first mound that I encountered belonged to a goblin splashing in his tub. I heard him kick, pull a shower-bath on his shoulders, gasp, crack his joints, and rub himself down with a towel; then he let the water out of the bath, as a thoughtful man should, and it all sank down out of sight till another goblin arrived. Yet they called this place the Lioness and the Cubs. It lies not very far from the Lion, which is a sullen, roaring beast, and they say that when it is very active the other geysers presently follow suit. After the Krakatoa eruption all the geysers went mad together, spouting, spurting, and bellowing till men feared that they would rip up the whole field. Mysterious sympathies exist among them, and when the Giantess speaks (of her more anon) they all hold their peace.

I was watching a solitary spring, when, far across the fields, stood up a plume of spun glass, iridescent and superb against the sky. "That," said the trooper, "is Old Faithful. He goes off every sixty-five minutes to the minute, plays for five minutes, and sends up a column of water a hundred and fifty feet high. By the time you have looked at all the other geysers he will be ready to play."

So we looked and we wondered at the Beehive, whose mouth is built up exactly like a hive; at the Turban (which is not in the least like a turban); and at many, many other geysers, hot holes, and springs. Some of them rumbled, some hissed, some went off spasmodically, and others lay still in sheets of sapphire and beryl.

Would you believe that even these terrible creatures have to be guarded by troopers to prevent the irreverent American from chipping the cones to pieces, or worse still, making the geysers sick? If you take of soft-soap a small barrelful and drop it down a geyser's mouth, that geyser will presently be forced to lay all before you and for days afterwards will be of an irritated and inconsistent stomach. When they told me the tale I was filled with sympathy. Now I wish that I had stolen soap and tried the experiment on some lonely little beast of a geyser in the woods. It sounds so probable—and so human.

Yet he would be a bold man who would administer emetics to the Giantess. She is flat-lipped, having no mouth, she looks like a pool, fifty feet long and thirty wide, and there is no ornamentation about her. At irregular intervals she speaks, and sends up a column of water over two hundred feet high to begin with; then she is angry for a day and a half—sometimes for two days. Owing to her peculiarity of going mad in the night not many people have seen the Giantess at her finest; but the clamour of her unrest, men say, shakes the wooden hotel, and echoes like thunder among the hills. When I saw her; trouble was brewing. The pool bubbled seriously, and at five-minute intervals, sank a foot or two, then rose, washed over the rim, and huge steam bubbles broke on the top. Just before an eruption the water entirely disappears from view. Whenever you see the water die down in a geyser-mouth get away as fast as you can. I saw a tiny little geyser suck in its breath in this way, and instinct made me retire while it hooted after me. Leaving the Giantess to swear, and spit, and thresh about, we went over to Old Faithful, who by reason of his faithfulness has benches close to him whence you may comfortably watch. At the appointed hour we heard the water flying up and down the mouth with the sob of waves in a cave. Then came the preliminary gouts, then a roar and a rush, and that glittering column of diamonds rose, quivered, stood still for a minute; then it broke, and the rest was a confused snarl of water not thirty feet high. All the young ladies—not more than twenty—in the tourist band remarked that it was "elegant," and betook themselves to writing their names in the bottoms of shallow pools. Nature fixes the insult indelibly, and the after-years will learn that "Hattie," "Sadie," "Mamie," "Sophie," and so forth, have taken out their hair-pins, and scrawled in the face of Old Faithful. . . .

Next morning Tom drove us on, promising new wonders. He pulled up after a few miles at a clump of brushwood where an army was drowning. I could hear the sick gasps and thumps of the men going under, but when I broke through the brushwood the hosts had fled, and there were only pools of pink, black, and white lime, thick as turbid honey. They shot up a pat of mud every minute or two, choking in the effort. It was an uncanny sight. Do you wonder that in the old days the Indians were careful to avoid the Yellowstone? Geysers are permissible, but mud is terrifying. The old lady from Chicago took a piece of it, and in half an hour it died into lime-dust and blew away between her fingers. All *maya*—illusion,—you see! Then we clinked over sulphur in crystals; there was a waterfall of boiling water; and a road across a level park hotly contested by the beavers. . . .

As we climbed the long path the road grew viler and viler till it became without disguise, the bed of a torrent; and just when things were at their rockiest we emerged into a little sapphire lake—but never sapphire was so blue—called Mary's lake; and that between eight and nine thousand feet above the sea. Then came grass downs, all on a vehement slope, so that the buggy following the new-made road ran on to the two off-wheels mostly, till we dipped head-first into a ford, climbed up a cliff, raced along a down, dipped again and pulled up dishevelled at "Larry's" for lunch and an hour's rest. . . .

The sun was sinking when we heard the roar of falling waters and came to a broad river along whose banks we ran. And then—oh, then! I might at a pinch describe the infernal regions, but not the other place. Be it known to you that the Yellowstone River has occasion to run through a gorge about eight miles long. To get to the bottom of the gorge it makes two leaps, one of about 120 and the other of 300 feet. I investigated the upper or lesser fall, which is close to the hotel. Up to that time nothing particular happens to the Yellowstone, its banks being only rocky, rather steep, and plentifully adorned with pines. At the falls it comes round a corner, green, solid, ribbed with a little foam, and not more than thirty yards wide. Then it goes over still green and rather more solid than before. After a minute or two you, sitting on a rock directly above the drop, begin to understand that something has occurred; that the river has jumped a huge distance between the solid cliff walls and what looks like the gentle froth of ripples lapping the sides of the gorge below is really the outcome of great waves. And the river yells aloud; but the cliffs do not allow the yells to escape.

That inspection began with curiosity and finished in terror, for it seemed that the whole world was sliding in chrysolite from under my feet. I followed with the others round the corner to arrive at the brink of the cañon; we had to climb up a nearly perpendicular ascent to begin with, for the ground rises more than the river drops. Stately pine woods fringe either lip of the gorge, which is—the Gorge of the Yellowstone.

All I can say is that without warning or preparation I looked into a gulf 1,700 feet deep with eagles and fish-hawks circling far below. And the sides of that gulf were one wild welter of colour—crimson, emerald, cobalt, ochre, amber, honey splashed with port-wine, snow-white, vermilion, lemon, and silver-grey, in wide washes. The sides did not fall sheer, but were graven by time and water and air into monstrous heads of kings, dead chiefs, men and women of the old time. So far below that no sound of its strife could reach us, the Yellowstone River ran—a finger-wide strip of jade-green. The sunlight took these wondrous walls and gave fresh hues to those that nature had already laid there. Once I saw the dawn break over a lake in Rajputana and the sun set over Oodey Sagar amid a circle of Holman Hunt hills. This time I was watching both performances going on below me—upside down you understand—and the colours were real! The cañon was burning like Troy town; but it would not burn forever, and, thank goodness, neither pen nor brush could ever portray its splendours adequately. The Academy would reject the picture for a chromo-lithograph. The public would scoff at the letter-press for *Daily Telegraphese*. "I will leave this thing alone," said I; "'tis my peculiar property. Nobody else shall share it with me." Evening crept through the pines that shadowed us, but the full glory of the day flamed in that cañon as we went out very cautiously to a jutting piece of rock—blood-red or pink it was—that overhung the deepest deeps of all. Now I know what it is to sit enthroned amid the clouds of sunset. Giddiness took away all sensation of touch or form; but the sense of blinding colour remained. When I reached the mainland again I had sworn that I had been floating.

From Sea to Sea: Letters of Travel (New York, 1899).